D0171251

About this book

This modern political history of one of Latin America's largest and most important countries offers an exceptionally readable and deeply informed account of the popular opposition of the Mexican people to the official party's monopoly on political power. The authors cover the period from the ruling PRI's lurch to the right in 1940 and betrayal of the 1910 Revolution's radical impulse through to its final ouster from office for the first time in the elections of 2000.

The authors base their account on extensive interview material garnered during more than two decades of close engagement with the country, as well as considerable new documentary sources. Their book is the first to consider the full and diverse panorama of popular resistance to the alliance that was consolidated between the Mexican state bureaucracy, focused on the office of the president, and the business class. This resistance embraced emerging urban labour protest (including struggles for union democracy), new peasant movements, the revolutionary strikes which took place on the railways and amongst teachers, as well as student opposition, and the re-emergence of rural and urban guerrilla struggle which has now culminated in the celebrated resurgence of indigenous peoples' resistance in Chiapas.

Mexico Under Siege contains an analysis of the core parties of the resistance, including the suprisingly central role played by the Mexican Communist Party or militants who received their political formation in it, and an explanation of why the resistance ultimately failed to achieve anything more than its minimum programme of ending the PRI's system of presidential despotism. The authors conclude with some provocative ideas about what social group now constitutes the common people's primary opponent and the prospects currently opened up for genuine struggles in the electoral arena in a context where neo-liberal economic ideology and the Mexican economy's closer integration with the United States dominate the political scene.

About the authors

Donald C. Hodges is Professor of Philosophy and Affiliate Professor of Political Science at Florida State University. The recipient of numerous grants and research awards, including a Soviet Academy of Sciences Research Appointment in 1985, he has lectured widely throughout Eastern Europe and Latin America and taught for two semesters at Mexico's National University.

He is the author of numerous books, the more recent ones including *Intellectual Foundations of the Nicaraguan Revolution*, *Argentina's "Dirty War"*, *America's New Economic Order*, *The Literate Communist: 150 Years of the Communist Manifesto*, and *Class Politics in the Information Age*.

Ross Gandy studied philosophy, history and economics at the Universities of Heidelberg, Mexico and Texas. He was active in the campaign for nuclear disarmament in the United States and helped spread anarcho-marxist viewpoints in Students for a Democratic Society in the sixties. While teaching in California he organised people to end the war against Vietnam. Since 1970 he has lived in Mexico, where he teaches sociology at the National University, and works in social movements such as the progressive Church struggle to defend the poor, anarchist co-operatives, and efforts toward lifting the US blockade of Cuba. His books include *Marx and History* and *Twenty Keys to Mexico*.

Donald Hodges & Ross Gandy

Mexico Under Siege

Popular Resistance to Presidential Despotism

Zed Books

LONDON & NEW YORK

Mexico Under Siege was first published in 2002 by
Zed Books Ltd, 7 Cynthia Street, London N1 9JF, UK and
Room 400, 175 Fifth Avenue, New York, NY 10010, USA.

Distributed in the USA exclusively by Palgrave, a division of
St Martin's Press, LLC,175 Fifth Avenue, New York, NY 10010, USA.

Cover design by Andrew Corbett
Designed and set in 10/13 pt Sabon with Lydian display
by Long House, Cumbria, UK
Printed and bound in the United Kingdom
by Biddles Ltd, Guildford and King's Lynn

A catalogue record for this book
is available from the British Library

ISBN 1 84277 124 8 Hb
ISBN 1 84277 125 6 Pb

Library of Congress Cataloging-in-Publication Data
has been applied for

❋ Contents

What happened at this *finca* now was exactly the same as occurred later throughout the whole Republic: the peons, accustomed for years to masters, tyrants, oppressors, and dictators, were not in truth liberated.... They remained slaves, with the single difference that their masters had changed, that mounted revolutionary leaders were now the wealthy.

B. Traven, *General from the Jungle* (1939)

Never forget that there is a class of men who have gone through the schools of higher learning ... and who fight not with arms but with intelligence, searching for opportunities to lead and to deceive the people.... For that reason, it is imperative that those who take up arms today shall not permit those gentlemen to take advantage of the people's victories, as happened in the last revolution. Pretending to be revolutionaries, these well-prepared political intellectuals pushed aside the genuine revolutionaries, who did not know how to organize a government.

Rubén Jaramillo, undated letter appended to
Renato Ravelo, *Los Jaramillistas* (1978)

✴ Preface

This is a story about violent, repressive, and rebellious Mexico, about the revival of the 1910 insurgencies against the dictator Porfirio Díaz after the Mexican Revolution had given birth to a new regime of presidential despotism that lasted until the end of the century. Known as the *neo-Porfiriato*, it was opposed by successive waves of popular resistance, each of which ended with the intervention of the army, the judicial police, or the government's hired gunmen in a feast of bullets.

Mexican political scientists and sociologists are characteristically interested either in broadly theoretical questions concerning economic dependency, imperialism, and social classes or, at the opposite pole, in narrowly empirical studies of population growth, and so on. Here, theory without history; there, history without theory. In the area of our interest – popular resistance to presidential despotism after 1940 – there are a number of well-documented investigations of the corruption in the official party of the revolution and of opposition movements that arose in response to that corruption. But one searches in vain for an historically based panorama of the resistance.

We began this investigation in 1975 with a specialized study of Rubén Jaramillo. Having discovered that he was the missing link connecting the popular resistance of the 1960s with the revolutionary movements of 1910–1919, we wanted to know: what led him to take the road of armed struggle? How was his movement organized? What were the causes of its failure? What lessons could be learned from Jaramillo's resistance that might be useful to popular movements in the future? But as we advanced in our research we gradually realized that something bigger was at stake. Jaramillo's movement was only the first expression of armed opposition in a wave of popular struggles that began in 1940 and continued to mount after his assassination in 1962.

Our subsequent research focused on this wave of resistance as a whole. The first product of our research was an unpublished *licenciado* thesis in sociology at the National University of Mexico in the name of Juan Sánchez Vargas, but under the formal guidance and with the active collaboration of Donald C. Hodges. Jointly authored, it also benefited from the informal assistance of Ross Gandy in several of the key chapters. Vargas was our guide through Zapatista territory and our principal link to the Jaramillista movement. Beginning with the presidency of Avila Camacho in 1940, the ruling party first lost the confidence and support of broad masses of the Mexican people. Voices rose in favor of transforming the political revolution into a social revolution that would break the ties of dependency on international capitalism and lead the country down the non-capitalist road of development. This was not the path chosen by the leadership of the official party after 1940. Because it insisted on the capitalist road without consulting the people's organizations, the political regime was increasingly denounced for betraying the revolution.

The various movements of resistance that emerged can be classified as broadly populist – a mixture of revolutionary nationalism and democratic socialism dissociated from Marxism. But as our investigation progressed, we discovered beneath this loose popular ideology a hard revolutionary core. The response of the people to the tyranny of the governing party had taken organizational forms that, stripped of their outer layers, revealed a different mechanism underneath. Those socialist ideas compatible with the prevailing ideology of the Mexican Revolution of 1910–1919 were being championed not by the official party but by active militants, expelled cadres, and sympathetic deserters of the Mexican Communist Party (PCM). We were startled to discover that the PCM was both the principal catalyst and the guiding force of the resistance.

This work is a sequel to our book, *Mexico 1910–1982: Reform or Revolution?* (London: Zed Press, 1983), in which we developed the thesis of a bureaucratic political revolution in conjunction with a bourgeois social revolution in Mexico. From 1920 to 1940, the nascent capitalist class was too weak economically to seize the reins of political power; after 1940, the bureaucracy became so corrupted by the spoils of government and the prospect of joining the bourgeoisie that it hesitated to take over the country's economy. The result: a *modus vivendi* or social pact between Mexico's business class and the state bureaucracy ruling through the Institutional Revolutionary Party (PRI).

To round out the picture, this book focuses on popular resistance to the bureaucracy aimed at ending the official party's monopoly of political power. Although the stranglehold on economic life by Mexican and foreign business eroded some of the powers of the bureaucracy after 1940, the regime of presidential despotism remained intact. Repeatedly challenged from both the right and the left, the ruling party did not face the prospect of a major defeat at the polls until the turn of the century.

The unprecedented national defeat of the ruling party at the hands of Vicente Fox in July 2000 was potentially a major transition point in the country's history since the Second World War. Contrary to what the Mexican left expected, the new President broke with Mexico's tradition of a near-monarch at the helm. Fox has yet to run the country like a dictator, so that Mexico's veiled dictatorship may well become a thing of the past.

He also ran afoul of the right-wing National Action Party whose candidate he was. Surprisingly, he began living up to his promises as a populist and not just a conservative. His profession of friendship for the masked guerrilla subcomandante Marcos, leader of the indigenous peoples' insurgency in the State of Chiapas, was nothing short of scandalous. But how long will the democratic opening last? Neoliberal economic policies are taking their toll in the form of increasing unemployment and impoverishment, the guerrillas are still operating in the countryside, the government is in economic straits, the President has gone out on a limb by proposing to tax the poor, and he may be pressured by the leaders of his party to resort to repression as matters become worse.

The term 'presidential despotism' is peculiar to the Mexican political experience. Briefly, it refers to the monopoly of political power by the established party of the revolution, and to the professional bureaucrats or revolutionary family in control of the party that became a millionaire's club headed by *El Presidente*. In this guided democracy, one party ruled; within that party, the revolutionary elite dominated; and within that elite, the president had the final word. The centralization of authority in the person of one man is an outstanding feature of Mexico's political system. Political commentators have gone so far as to compare the President of Mexico with absolute monarchs of the type of Louis XIV and with twentieth century dictators of Mussolini's and Hitler's stripe. Insofar as it is possible to concentrate power in one person, *El Presidente* was the man. The governors and senators of the various states were hand-picked by the president. In Mexico one speaks of presidential designation rather than succession, for each new president was *destapado* (revealed) after having been picked by the old one. In effect, political power was handed down from one presidential protégé to the next.

In Mexico despotism began at the top, but it was reproduced on each rung of the descending ladder of authority. Beneath the throne, a swarm of bureaucrats and petty bureaucrats rivaled each other in an effort to imitate the president. Sycophants in relation to their immediate superiors, they came down hard on their political inferiors. The other side of bureaucratic flunkeyism toward *El Presidente* and the revolutionary family was bureaucratic despotism toward the rest of the country. Despotic rather than democratic centralism lay at the heart of the political system.

Yet official repression in Mexico differed markedly from that of recent military dictatorships in Brazil, Argentina, and Chile. Political kidnappings and assassinations, police torture and brutality were sanctioned by a political party with a populist ideology, with trade-union and peasant support, and with a reputation for winning elections without intervention by the armed forces. The fact remains that for 60 years the minority parties have been mainly satellites of the PRI, out-maneuvered antagonists in the case of the Democratic Revolutionary Party (PRD), or bourgeois 'loyal opposition' in the case of the National Action Party (PAN). These were precluded from governing by the rules of the game, which may be expressed as follows: unless you are a candidate of the PRI, you cannot win an election; if by some fluke you do win, you will be prevented from taking office; if by a miracle you do take office, you cannot govern. Political pluralism in Mexico was an acknowledged farce.

Because this despotic system feathered the nests of a corrupt governmental bureaucracy committed to defending the economic interests of the new bourgeoisie, its popular support was waning. Its crimes against the people had brought forth its own executioner in the form of a swelling movement of popular resistance.

This popular challenge, dating back to the 1940s, is epitomized in a speech by Rubén Jaramillo in the central plaza of the village of Panchimalco, Morelos, on 27 August 1946:

> The government's politics are undemocratic.... They begin from the top down and from Mexico City one man picks the governors for the people to approve and support. This process is called 'guided democracy' and, according to the spongers in the government, it is necessary because the people are incapable of choosing their own representatives and may make mistakes by electing their enemies.... We have to liquidate this old politics on the basis of our own organization and perspectives which we have been giving to the people, especially to the peasants and workers of our state. It is natural for the politicians, who deceive the people, to dislike our politics. They will try to suppress our movement, but we shall know how to resist.

The present work is the first to link up the armed struggles of the 1960s and 1970s, and their resurgence at the century's end, with the Zapatista tradition going back to the revolution of 1910–1919. The connecting link is Rubén Jaramillo – the most important peasant leader since Zapata and the precursor of most of the other significant popular resistance leaders since 1940. A sketch is given of his life and actions – about which so little is known in Mexico and the rest of the world – based on original data and interviews with his close collaborators.

This work explores the political and historical reality masked by the myth of Mexican democracy, the reality of a dictatorship under a president with more power than a constitutional monarch and with as much power as any Latin American dictator. It examines the conditions under which the rule of law was periodically overridden by a political mafia ruling by means of electoral fraud, private armies, police intimidation, military repression, and individual hit-men. Our account also weaves together the different strands of the popular resistance, showing how the workers' struggle for union democracy was tied to the peasants' struggle for redistribution of the big estates, to students' struggle for university autonomy and a share in school administration, and to the armed struggle against and the official party's monopoly of political power. Finally, having set forth the causal sequences, advances and setbacks, popular action and official reaction at different stages, we conclude with a novel explanation of the failure of the resistance despite fulfillment of its minimum program – the end of presidential despotism.

Our coverage of the principal events extends from the close of the Cardenist presidency in December 1940 to that of the Zedillo presidency in December 2000. When the leading parties of the resistance dissolved and merged with the center-left party under Cárdenas' son Cuauhtémoc in 1989, followed by the disappearance of the remaining parties of the left after losing their electoral registration, the era of popular resistance movements led by Marxist-Leninist vanguards came to an end.

Since several of these movements overlapped, we had to choose between following a strict historical chronology and presenting a looser sequence focusing on the integrity of the principal movements. We opted for the latter alternative. Within the range of a single volume, it was impossible without being superficial to cover all of the movements of popular resistance to presidential despotism during the 60-year period leading to its demise. The ones included were the most consequential.

Those omitted did not spread to other popular sectors in their own locality and did not resonate nationally. For example, the mammoth year-long strike at the National University in Mexico City began auspiciously in April 1999 but lost support after the students' original demand for free tuition was conceded. The movement was then taken over by the radical utopian current that wanted a revolution going beyond the art of the possible to the theater of the absurd. Although a referendum was held in January 2000 that voted to end the strike, the poorest students, shabbily dressed and representing an alphabet soup of tiny sects and splinter groups squabbling with one another, held out until the Federal Police invaded the campus in February and hauled some 900 protesters off to jail. Because the strike did not spread to other sectors, it had only marginal significance.

Personal interviews and scarce documents were fundamental to our investigation. During five years of fieldwork we were able to unearth the long-lost Plan of Cerro Prieto, a document that helped launch the resistance – reproduced in translation in the Appendix. We also interviewed at length and on repeated occasions several key participants in Jaramillo's first and second armed uprisings, in the two principal strikes at the cooperative sugar refinery in Zacatepec, in the revolutionary teachers' and railroad workers' strikes of 1958 and 1959, in the founding of the Movement of National Liberation in 1961, in the rural guerrillas under Genaro Vázquez and Lucio Cabañas from 1969 to 1974, in the urban guerrillas of the September 23rd League, in the student demonstrations of 1968 and 10 June 1971, in the land 'invasions' of Michapa and El Guarín in 1960–61, and the successful establishment of the Colonia Rubén Jaramillo outside Temixco in 1974–75. The list is a long one, and we invite readers to consult the notes at the end of each chapter.

Two library grants from the University of Florida and Florida State University provided access to the indispensable secondary and tertiary literature used to supplement our primary sources.

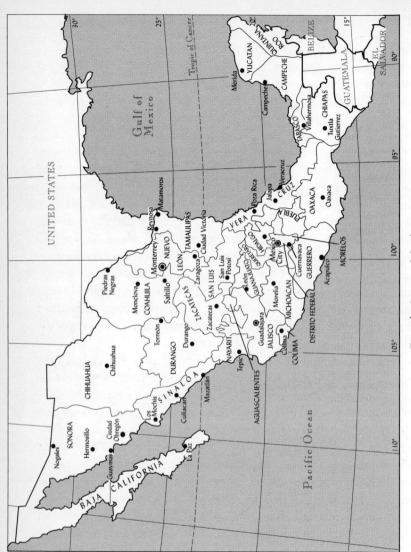

Revolutionary Mexico

✸ Introduction

In his last speech in office on 1 September 1928, President Plutarco Elías Calles called on all revolutionary groups and parties to unite with the intent of transforming the Mexican government from a battleground of political bosses and military caudillos to one based on the rule of law. The new state party in defense of the ideology and policies of the Mexican Revolution of 1910–1919 was formally constituted on 4 March 1929.

The National Revolutionary Party (PNR), as it was called, thus became the official representative and sole interpreter of the revolution. Although reorganized as the Party of the Mexican Revolution (PRM) in April 1938 and then as the Institutional Revolutionary Party (PRI) in January 1946, its monopoly of political power was broken only in the year 2000, after 70 years of veiled dictatorship. Symbolized by a succession of six-year presidents who appointed their successors and ruled like absolute monarchs, the purported rule of law became increasingly marred by violence. The resulting system of presidential despotism smashed all concerted opposition, whether from the political dinosaurs on the Right or the popular forces on the Left.

In this study of the popular resistance to presidential despotism, the authors focus on Mexico's burgeoning sector of the socially discontented who, in conjunction with the privileged elites, eventually toppled the dictatorship. If the resistance failed, it was because the popular forces were too weak and divided to impose their own programs on the divided nation.

Popular resistance to Mexico's presidential despotism responded to the rupture of the social pact written into the 1917 Constitution. The

Constitution that emerged from the Mexican Revolution of 1910 was a program for social change built into the law of the land. It promised the Mexican people that in their struggle for social justice they could count on the government for help. Although it assured the right to private property, individual enterprise, and free competition, the Constitution opened the door to nationalization in the public interest, to the formation of cooperatives, and to collectivist inroads on capitalist production. To the peasants, it promised land reform; to the workers, the right to organize unions, to strike, and to share in the employer's profits. The most advanced constitution of its time, it gave form to the social pact between labor and capital that would be administered by the revolutionary governments that had replaced the old order.

Tampico: Showcase of the Revolution

The port of Tampico during the oil boom of the 1920s provides a classic illustration of how this social pact worked before it was betrayed in the name of the revolution.

When the German anarchist Ret Marut (his real name is clouded in controversy) landed in Tampico in 1924 under the American pseudonym of B. Traven Torsvan, he was amazed to find that there was more socialism in Mexico than under the socialist government of the Weimar Republic. With a death sentence pending for his role in the abortive Bavarian Soviet Republic of April–May 1919, he had lived underground preparatory to fleeing abroad. The anarcho-syndicalist House of the World Worker had been shut down in Mexico City by President Carranza in 1916, but its Tampico branch had not only survived but, in tandem with the anarcho-syndicalist unions, played a leading role in the city's affairs.[1] Labor militancy in Tampico represented a complete departure from the respectable socialist trade unions in Germany, and, far from repressing labor resistance to the foreign oil companies, the local authorities looked on Tampico's strikers with sympathy and even offered police protection.

In Marut's first serialized novels under his third pseudonym of B. Traven, his hero Gales informs a German immigrant hired as a strike-breaker in Tampico that the "police here are not at the disposal of the capitalist but of the capitalist and the worker." The German is uncon-

vinced until he suffers two blows to the head in an "accident". The
police are in sympathy with the strikers. When the injured man is turned
over to the German consul, he is told: "If there is a strike at the electrical
company or the water supplier, there is no technical emergency service
like in Germany or America. There is no water and no power until the
strikers decide.... The government is neutral in these quarrels."[2]

So enthralled was Traven by his Tampico experience that it shaped
his vision of the rest of Mexico. Traven believed that President Calles'
1925 bid to control the foreign oil companies represented a challenge
to the capitalist world order. "It had been Marut's avowed goal to
abolish capitalism, and the novelist Traven had not reneged on this
claim." Because he believed that Calles' confrontational policies
meant a shift of political power to the working class, he decided to give
the President his unstinting support by putting his talents as a writer in
the service of the Mexican government.[3]

Traven's early impressions of Mexico and its revolution were reinforced during his first expedition to Chiapas in 1926. There too he
witnessed the government's intervention on the side of the Indian
peons, the return of communal lands to their original owners, and the
establishment of rural schools and clinics for the indigenous peoples.
His 1928 travelogue, *Land des Frühlings* (*Land of Spring*), is unequiv-
ocal in its support of the revolution and of Mexico's struggle for
political and economic emancipation from the foreign stranglehold.
As Traven initially perceived it, the Mexican Revolution was a class
war on behalf of the oppressed. The central message of his travelogue
was directed to explaining to his German audience (the book has never
been translated) "why the Mexican Revolution had resulted in a
victory for the working class, in contrast to the German experience of
1918, when the [German] revolution had been taken over by
bourgeois politicians and aborted with the connivance of labor and
Socialist party leaders."[4] The Mexican government, he concluded, was
on the side not only of Tampico's workers, but also of the exploited
Indian lumberjacks in the mahogany camps of Chiapas.

Imagine his chagrin when he learned that he had misinterpreted his
sources and had labored under the illusion that what he had observed
in Tampico and Chiapas from 1924 to 1926 was true of the entire
country. Having failed in what he considered his responsibility as a
writer, he made efforts to keep his travelogue out of circulation by

3

blocking further editions. That is not the only reason it has not been translated. It is so full of obvious errors that no publisher would undertake the task.

Yet it was not until his two most important novels, *The Rebellion of the Hanged* (1936) and *General from the Jungle* (1939) that he risked deportation under the Noxious Foreigners Act (Article 33 of the Constitution) by radically revising his earlier assessment. Disillusioned by the further course of the revolution under left-leaning President Cárdenas, he no longer found anything in Mexico worth writing about after the Second World War when his novels were finally translated into Spanish.[5]

Disillusionment and Resistance

Traven's illusions concerning the revolution were shattered by his second and third visits to Chiapas, by his discovery of twentieth-century, post-revolutionary slavery in the jungle. Contrary to his first impressions, the governments of the revolution had yet to change the lives of the bulk of the Indians. His hopes for redemption by "civilized" white politicians had been unfounded. Although only tokens of individual resistance, Traven's novels of rebellion were among the first muffled expressions of the coming popular resistance.

Beginning with his 1931 *Der Karren* (*The Carreta*), the first in a series of six "jungle novels," he ceased to write about down-and-out white proletarians and concentrated instead on describing the conditions of the even more oppressed Indians. As he wrote to his German publisher as early as October 1927, the proletarian Indians' fight for liberation "has no equal in human history. Until today I was unable to make the European working man understand a single part of the fight for freedom." Incensed by what he saw in the mahogany camps of the Lacandon jungle, Traven shifted from writing about workers in trade unions to portraying the guerrilla army, "believing that armed struggle ... was more likely to bring about liberation for the working class."[6]

The Indians marched into the jungle as debt peons to the mahogany barons; then, after rebelling against their bosses, they marched out of the jungle in military formation. They became masters of guerrilla warfare. But did Traven's disguised handbook for guerrillas spring forth untutored from an overactive imagination? Not according to our sources: "Traven drew upon the strategy and tactics of Sandino and Zapata."[7]

Sandino? What had Nicaragua's civil war and struggle against US occupation to do with Mexico? Traven had signed up as a member of the Sandino Liberation Support Committee when Sandino slipped back into Mexico in 1929–30 to rally support for his cause. Although he did not attend the meetings, Traven's personal physician, Dr Federico Marín, testified that his client felt a special bond with Nicaragua's hero. "He knew Augusto Sandino from Tampico during the boom time in oil.... They were both anarchists – Tampico was a big anarchist town in the twenties – and they hit it off." One should beware of taking the physician's words at face value. None the less, there is a definite similarity between the strategy of the general from the jungle in the novel of that name and Sandino's guerrilla strategy. It may well be that, as one Traven scholar writes, Traven's general was "inspired by Augusto Sandino"; his "political program is nearly identical to Sandino's."[8]

The Rebellion of the Hanged

Through the character of Professor Martín Trinidad, the intellectual leader of the lumberjacks and ox-cart drivers, Traven revised and recycled Ret Marut's anarchist philosophy in *The Rebellion of the Hanged*. One cannot rest with half-measures, the Professor warned, because to do so leads to betrayal of a revolution. "If you want to make a revolution, then carry it through to the end, because otherwise it will turn against you and tear you to shreds." That is what happened in Germany during its revolution and during the failed Munich Soviet that followed, when Marut was condemned to death and barely escaped. That is why the revolution of the lumberjacks had to be complete: "We must not do things by halves or believe in promises ... [we must] make a complete revolution and carry it to the farthest corner of the land."[9]

In *The Rebellion of the Hanged*, the Indian peons do not make the mistakes of Marut's fellow conspirators in Munich who, if they were not imprisoned, were murdered on the spot. Describing the lumberjacks' first war council, Traven reminisced: "the discussion was nothing like the lamentable deliberations of those men who, in nearly all revolutions, speak and orate endlessly ... when they should be taking action." The Indians argued over what group should march in the vanguard. Being killed was of little concern to them, as long as they got hold of the enemy's weapons and their comrades continued fighting. To arm themselves and to destroy the enemy were all that mattered. The revolutionary "wants only to overthrow the social system under which he suffers and sees others suffer," said the Professor. "And to destroy it ... he will sacrifice himself and die."[10]

Almost twenty years after the Munich uprising, "Traven produced an anarchist's handbook on how to make a successful revolution," says a Traven scholar and historian of the Mexican Revolution. Having begun his political career as an individualist anarchist in Germany, he had converted to anarcho-syndicalism in Tampico under the influence of the House of the World Worker and the Wobblies. Then, during the 1930s, his anarchism acquired a new dimension in the form of the people in arms. He achieved this tour de force when the Mexican Revolution had lost its impetus and the anarchists in Spain had taken up arms in defense of the besieged Republic.[11]

Traven's jungle novels lead the unsuspecting reader to believe that their setting is the *Porfiriato* and that the dictator is Porfirio Díaz. That was the author's intention, if only to protect himself against the Noxious Foreigners Act. Actually, the novels' underlying targets are the successive governments of the revolution and their betrayal of the Zapatista goal of a workers' and peasants' republic. As the work of an astute observer and interpreter of political events, the jungle novels are a prelude to the popular resistance. Yet more than one Traven scholar has been taken in by the ruse.[12]

Delving beneath the surface, Jonah Raskin shows that by placing key incidents in the past, "Traven made it appear ... that he was writing a historical fiction rather than a novel of contemporary Mexican life [or documentary in the form of a novel, as he repeatedly claimed] – a shrewd and practical move." For the message of *The Rebellion of the Hanged* was "subversive and might provoke a clash with Mexican authorities." When a British edition of the novel appeared in 1950, with a translator's footnote explaining that references to "the dictatorship" referred to the Díaz dictatorship, Traven wrote to his British agent that he intended the "story to be timeless and that's why he refrained from mentioning any dictator."[13] "Timeless," because the novel and its successor *General from the Jungle* objected to the course subsequently taken by the revolution.

General from the Jungle

To have characterized the Cárdenas presidency as a "dictatorship" was unheard of on the Mexican Left. Not until 60 years later did Mexican nationals sharing Traven's political outlook begin to voice the same indictment. On New Year's Day 1994, the Indians erupted from the Chiapas jungle in a performance that recalled Traven's rebellion and march of the hanged. A second edition of Zapata's army, the Zapatista Army of National Liberation (EZLN), took over the Chiapas highlands and its former capital, San Cristóbal de las Casas. The EZLN's First Declaration of the Lacandon Selva announced that all legal remedies against the "seventy-year-old dictatorship" had been exhausted after 500 years of struggle (another of Traven's themes).[14] Once again, Traven had anticipated the course of the future resistance.

To triumph over our enemies, said one of his illiterate lumberjacks, "The best thing would be to do away with everybody who isn't one of us." Otherwise, everything will go on as it was before. "The first task was to kill off the *finqueros* [landowners], the bosses [foremen], and their relatives and children ... to prevent all possibility of a counter-revolution when the rebels should finally have laid down their arms."[15]

To overcome their enemies, it would be necessary to defeat not only the federal army, but "all the defenders of the dictator ... [and] to destroy everything that could be useful to them." That meant all legal documents. Said the Professor:

> Many revolutions have started and then failed because papers weren't burned as they should have been. You can kill all the *finqueros* you like, but later ... their sons, their daughters, their cousins, or their uncles [unless they too have been killed] will come back to confound us with their documents, their registries, and account books ... [therefore] the first thing we must do is to attack the registry and burn the ... deeds, birth and death and marriage certificates, tax records, everything!

The EZLN was the first to take the Professor's lesson to heart. On New Year's Day 1994, when the masked guerrillas under Subcomandante Marcos took over the municipal building in San Cristóbal, "government records and land titles were destroyed and computers smashed."[16]

Traven further hinted that the 1917 Constitution might become an impediment in the struggle for freedom. Liberty, said the Professor, may be lost on the very day you celebrate it. "Don't believe that you'll be free just because your liberty is written in bronze letters and consecrated by law, by the Constitution!" Nothing is forever established; only those among you will be free who "fight every day for their freedom and entrust it to nobody" – certainly not to a hallowed document and its official interpreters. As Rubén Jaramillo, the second Zapata (Marcos became the third), would later declare: "The Constitution has been trampled on in recent years by men in public office who have used their power ... to maintain and enrich themselves in the government." Furthermore, the "Constitution should be immediately revised, so that it may become a practical law and not a bloody trick."[17]

In the lineage of popular resistance, Jaramillo became the link between the old Zapatistas and the new. By the time the resistance had become popular, he was organizing strikes and land seizures against politicians and retired generals who had become landowners. Having observed the creeping bureaucratic control over Morelos' cooperatives and *ejidos* under President Cárdenas, he "smelled a rat." As for Cárdenas' presidential successor, "we have not just a stench but a real plague ... the counterrevolution has begun."[18] Unknown to Jaramillo, both the rat and the government's counter-revolution had already been exposed in Traven's jungle novels.

Although Cárdenas encouraged experiments in workers' self-management and embarked on a mammoth course of nationalizing the foreign oil companies and of collectivizing agriculture in the late 1930s, Traven suspected that nothing would come of the reforms because they came as gifts and were not the outcome of worker militancy and the Indians' sense of community.

General from the Jungle, the last of his six-novel epic, opens on a pessimistic note. How could the rebellion improve the lot of Mexico's Indian peons? "Even if it brought them freedom from their master, Heaven would soon rob them of that liberty." How would they use their freedom? "No one had taught them self-discipline, how to work without being told and supervised.... No one had taught them how to organize their work, in order to be able to form themselves into a cooperative society." The peons' sense of community was so weak [he had previously admired its strength] that "envy, jealousy, and eternal quarrels over leadership would have gradually disintegrated any such organization."[19]

Traven's predictions would soon prove accurate. The Cárdenas experiments with workers' self-management would be discontinued, there would be fewer nationalizations, and land reform would slow down under Cárdenas' successors. His revival of the social pact would end in near-ruin.

What would happen to the peasants once the landowners and bosses were killed and the *fincas* were turned over to them? "The same," says Traven, "as occurred later throughout the Republic: the peons, accustomed for years to masters, tyrants, oppressors, and dictators, were not in truth liberated by the families of peons in little holdings, in *ejidos*." The people remained poor and subservient, the only difference being that "revolutionary leaders were now the wealthy, and that the politicians now used small-holding, ostensibly liberated peons to enrich themselves immeasurably, to increase their political influence."[20]

The words might have been Jaramillo's. Having witnessed how labor militancy had gone down the drain with the eclipse of anarcho-syndicalism and the emergence of government-controlled unions and a Communist party that wagged the government's tail, Traven had second thoughts about Mexico's future.

General from the Jungle ends with the revolution petering out and its original goal abandoned despite the Professor's warning. The rebels become content with half-measures and settle down, refusing to carry the struggle to the rest of the country. While their little village of Solipaz (Sun and Peace) has been mistaken for an anarchist utopia, Traven believed it was more akin to what the *Communist Manifesto* had earlier called "the idiocy of rural life." As one Traven scholar notes, the rebels had become complacent "despite having liberated less than one-tenth of Chiapas." By continuing to live on the margins of the system they had vowed to destroy, the "overall impact of their actions on the state is minimal." The former rebels "limit themselves ... to securing *tierra y libertad* for themselves."[21]

Traven objected to Cárdenas' "renewed emphasis on the central position of the state in national politics." In his inaugural address, the President had declared that "the state alone embodies the general interest ...[and] must continually broaden, increase, and deepen its intervention." For Traven, the effort to bring the workers' and peasants' unions and associations under government control meant that the revolution as he had initially experienced it in Tampico was dead. From being a dreamland, Mexico had become a wasteland where presidential despotism would beget violence, which would in turn beget more presidential despotism, in a never-ending cycle.[22]

Stalemate in the Class War

Traven never accepted the social pact for what it really was – a stalemate in the class war. In Tampico, he expected it to help the workers' step-by-step campaign against the propertied classes with the government in the role of sympathetic bystander. Instead, the social pact led to government interference and arbitration on behalf of industrial peace, not on behalf of change. Conflict resolution became the government's guiding purpose.

So interpreted, the social pact was not a friend but an enemy of organized labor. Traven was right. Lions would never lie down with lambs without eating them first. There would never be peace and harmony among wolves and sheep, among exploiters and exploited, among capitalists and workers, among bosses and servants. Neither individualist anarchism nor anarcho-syndicalism fit the image of the state that Presidents Calles and Cárdenas had built.[23]

The Communist party leader Valentín Campa dates the popular resistance from the end of Cárdenas' term as president. The repressive politics of his immediate successor was indirectly responsible for the massacre of striking workers in front of the presidential palace in September 1941. The outcry against the massacre and the general strike called in protest made the event a *cause célèbre*. Cárdenas' special project of an organized community with everything under control had become a euphemism for a fascist-type corporate state. The "subordination of the organized labor movement to the state apparatus," wrote Campa in his memoirs, "led to the labor bossism [*charrismo*] from which we now suffer." The Marxist-Leninist

Lombardo Toledano had witlessly delivered up the unions to the government on a silver platter, thereby undermining their power of resistance. A decade later, Lombardo would suffer the same fate. Expelled from the leadership of the government-controlled trade unions, he became the victim of his own policies.[24]

As Traven conceded in the second of his jungle novels, *Regierung* (*Government*), the Mexican Revolution had ceased by 1931 to be different from the German Revolution of 1918. Reminiscing on the outcome of the German Revolution, he wrote: "whenever proletarians collaborate with capitalists and bourgeois parties, it has always meant [that] ... the worker will pay the cost of cooperation." To this, he added his reflections on the Mexican Revolution: "It is the same with the Indians. Whenever they collaborate with officials, they will always carry their skin to market." Conflict resolution works among economic and political equals, but among unequals it invariably benefits the stronger party.[25]

Mexico was the first country in the twentieth century to formulate and institutionalize what a later generation of politicians and intellectuals would call a Third Way, the compromise between market capitalism and managed socialism. Also termed the Third Position and the Third Universal Theory, it has been interpreted as requiring not only a mixed economy, but also a political arrangement by which workers and peasants would get half the seats in government and electoral bodies at all levels. The Mexican Revolution opened the door to such an interpretation in its 1917 Constitution. By balancing, counterposing, and harmonizing opposite social forces, Mexico promised to become a beacon of freedom throughout the Americas and the world.

That is not what happened. The experiment with corporatism, a corporate state, and an organized community played into the hands of a veiled dictatorship and despotic presidents, who gave priority first to capital over labor, then to professional interests over the rest of society. The so-called mixed economy was the lie of a republic of equals; the truth was a republic of the privileged.

The resulting popular resistance was two-pronged. On the one hand, workers and peasants mobilized to defend the Constitution against its abuses, to enforce the social pact that had been misconstrued and flagrantly violated by private interests. On the other hand, disillusioned with their efforts to revive the Constitution, they mobilized to make a new revolution. The first prong of the resistance gave priority to trade-union and electoral struggles for political power; the second, to armed struggle.

Notes

1. Philip Jenkins, "B. Traven and the Wobblies," in Ernst Schürer and Philip Jenkins, eds, *B. Traven: Life and Work* (University Park: Pennsylvania State University Press, 1987), pp. 201, 202.
2. Heidi Zogbaum, *B. Traven. A Vision of Mexico* (Wilmington, DE: Scholarly Resources, 1992), p. 13; from Traven's *Der Wobbly* (1926) and *Die Baumwollpflücker* (1925).
3. Ibid., pp. 29, 40.
4. Ibid., p. 40.
5. Ibid., p. 211.
6. Jonah Raskin, "Traven's Revolution in Latin America," in Schürer and Jenkins, *B. Traven: Life and Work*, pp. 226, 227.
7. Ibid., p. 228.
8. Jonah Raskin, *My Search for B. Traven* (New York: Methuen, 1980), pp. 37–8, 38n.
9. Ibid., p. 230; and B. Traven, *The Rebellion of the Hanged* (New York: Hill and Wang, 1952), 215 (quote), 229.
10. Traven, *The Rebellion of the Hanged*, pp. 238, 239, 243, 246.
11. Zogbaum, *B. Traven*, p. 189.
12. See, for example, Robert B. Olafson, "Traven's Six-Novel Epic of the Mexican Revolution: An Overview," in Schürer and Jenkins, *B. Traven: Life and Work*, pp. 141–4; and in the same volume Jörg Thunecke, "Political Satire Mexican Style. Critique of Proto-Fascist Tendencies in B. Traven's *Government*," pp. 234–5, 237–8.
13. Raskin, "Traven's Revolution in Latin America," p. 229; Traven cited.
14. Bill Weinberg, *Homage to Chiapas: The New Indigenous Struggles in Mexico* (London: Verso, 2000), p. 107.
15. Traven, *The Rebellion of the Hanged*, pp. 130–1, 199.
16. Ibid., pp. 199–200, 203; Weinberg, *Homage to Chiapas*, p. 107.
17. Traven, *The Rebellion of the Hanged*, pp. 201–2. See Rubén Jaramillo, "The Plan of Cerro Prieto" in the Appendix.
18. Raúl Macín, *Jaramillo, un profeta olvidado* (Montevideo: Tierra Nueva, 1970), 42–3.
19. B. Traven, *General from the Jungle*, trans. Desmond Vesey (New York: Hill and Wang, n.d.), p. 19.
20. Ibid., pp. 60–61.
21. Zogbaum, *B. Traven*, pp. 201, 202.
22. Ibid., pp. 207, 208.
23. Ibid., p. 58. On Marut–Traven's individualist anarchism at the time of the Bavarian Soviet, see Michael L. Baumann, *B. Traven: An Introduction* (Albuquerque: University of New Mexico Press, 1976), pp. 56–79, 117–27.
24. Valentín Campa, *Mi testimonio: memorias de un comunista mexicano*, 3rd rev. ed. (Mexico City: Cultura Popular, 1985, orig. pub. 1978), pp. 169-171, 136.
25. Zogbaum, *B. Traven*, p. 128; from Traven's *Regierung* (1931).

1 ✸ Background of the Resistance

Historians of the Mexican Revolution generally agree that the year 1940 marks the end of one stage and the beginning of another. The first stage (1910–1940) witnessed a series of social and political changes that ended by transforming the country through agrarian reform and a policy of nationalizing foreign companies. After 1940, revolutionary change gave place to the consolidation and institutionalization of the changes made. Before 1940, the popular forces and the revolutionary governments traveled the same road; afterwards, they went their separate ways. The post-revolutionary period produced its own brand of violence – presidential despotism and popular resistance within the revolution.

Presidential Despotism

By presidential despotism in Mexico is understood not just the method of presidential succession known as *tapadismo* (the veiling of the president's successor) and *el dedazo* (the fingering of his successor), but also the process by which he picks his candidates for government posts in all states of the union, and then has the official party's mass organizations whip up support among workers, peasants, and the so-called middle sectors. If this does not elect all the president's men, the ruling party has the option of fraud, to which it frequently resorts. Winning the electoral count is more important than winning an election! To keep up the appearance of democracy, the official party encouraged token opposition until pressured by the popular sectors after 1968 to institute a "democratic opening," which in the year 2000 finally escaped the control of the official party.

13

The system of presidential succession dates from the founding of the official party, the National Revolutionary Party (PNR), on 4 March 1929. As a coalition of forces representing different wings of the "revolutionary family," it served the interests of the upstart generals who had emerged victorious during the insurrectionary stage of the revolution from 1910 to 1919. The brainchild of General Plutarco Elías Calles, president from 1924 to 1928, it was designed to institutionalize the revolution, to provide for the peaceful succession to power instead of a resort to arms – and to assassination in the case of former presidents Francisco Madero, Venustiano Carranza, and Alvaro Obregón![1]

As the "Maximum Leader" of the revolution in 1929, Calles planned to perpetuate himself in power behind the scenes. For that purpose he chose successors who qualified as loyal, reliable, and responsive to his will. From his example followed a rule that has had very few exceptions: "'Nobody who has a large popular following will be president' because the natural candidate is never the official one."[2]

In the history of *tapadismo*, the outgoing president has invariably appointed a successor he believed could be manipulated. As a result, "one of the most subtle intrigues in the political game for power in Mexico is that in which the capacities, intentions, and interests of the candidates cover themselves behind a veil of irreproachable behavior." Yet only the most astute and Machiavellian seekers of the presidency have been successful in deceiving the one in command to the point of "total blindness." Besides General Calles' failure to detect the real intentions of Lázaro Cárdenas, his choice for president in 1934, in 1970 "Díaz Ordaz did not perceive the occult designs of Luis Echeverría aimed at escaping from his tutelage and paying him back for the grave offences received as his subordinate.'[3]

The President rules through the official party. From the beginning, the PNR came under the control of political bosses supported by armed peasants, the social base of the new political formation. As a confederation of revolutionary generals, it was not only "the formal center of negotiations of the principal political leaders," but also contributed to "subordinating them, whether military or civilian, to the central authority." Beginning in 1929, the bureaucratic state apparatus had at its disposal a state party, "an organization that presented itself as the only legitimate representative of the revolution," of which the President became the chief. All other political organizations were "reduced to the category of "counterrevolutionary" or "reactionary" parties in danger of being declared illegal.'[4]

Ironically, the official ideology was so vague and imprecise that it encouraged the allegiance of people of property in addition to the popular sectors. The PNR's leaders dedicated themselves to "the apologetics of 'the revolution,' which they interpreted in their own interests, that is, as a permanent institution founded on the collaboration of classes of which the ... [President] would be the interpreter." This feature of the official party accounts for those depictions of it as "Bonapartist," as a "coalition of forces that respond to the spirit of equilibrium, to the compromise between the middle class that launched the revolution [Madero, Carranza, and Obregón] and the masses who fought and made it a reality – the compromise embedded in the 1917 Constitution.'[5]

As we sum up the system of presidential despotism in *Mexico 1910-1982: Reform or Revolution?*:

> Since the organization of the first government party in 1929, Mexico has chafed under one-party rule. The party is controlled by the government, and the government is under the President's thumb.
>
> The Mexican President is an elective dictator with power that must turn kings an envious green. All the powers of government together cannot match his strength. He appoints his own successor; he can get rid of elected officials at any level; he interprets the Constitution by enforcing it as he wills. He can direct the army and police to arrest, torture, or kill political enemies.
>
> The law is no barrier to his personal ambition. His office is a racketeer's dream, but the golden opportunity lasts only six years, and he must line his pockets while he can. He often does so. At least half of the six presidents since 1940 took office as bureaucrats living off their salary, but retired as multimillionaires.
>
> Mexican politics at the top shows everyone down the ladder the way to work – the President leads, the rest follow. Corruption is rife. Corrupt bureaucrats translate presidential despotism into a version all their own, no less hateful for its pettiness. Citizens must bribe them to do their jobs. Police use the law to exact their "bite," and enforce the law to their personal advantage.

Mexico has one of the socially most advanced systems of law in the world. The Constitution, a document written in six weeks by revolutionaries, could lead directly to socialism. But the Mexican political system interferes with its enforcement.

Mexico has never been a democracy. The State leans over citizens' organizations like a powerful father watching every move; it keeps independent groups from defending their economic and political interests. The State claims to defend those interests and sometimes does so. But the people do not decide about the matters that concern them. And when large numbers of people swing into motion, some government purpose is usually prodding them on.

The Mexican political system is authoritarian, and this encourages the highhanded use of power. Over the forest of governmental bureaucracy towers the presidency like a giant sequoia. The presidency with all its branches is the one institution that the revolution strengthened. The rest were changed or swept away.

Several critics have likened government after the revolution to the despotic regime of the 19th century. There is the old *Porfiriato*, we are told, and there is the *neo-Porfiriato* based on a new historic bloc of classes. The old and the new differ in substance, but are similar in form.[6]

Under President Cárdenas (1934–40), the system of presidential despotism responded to the interests of the broad masses in meeting their demands for agrarian, labor, and educational reform. Popular resistance to presidential despotism first appeared under his immediate successor, owing to the government's effort to curb the process of revolutionary change and to bring it to a halt. The new President, Manuel Avila Camacho, believed that the outbreak of the Second World War required a more cautious policy. Once the revolution of 1910–40 began to stagnate, the popular forces raised their voices against what they perceived to be government oppression, an emerging state bourgeoisie and union bureaucrats aimed at feathering their own nests. The so-called "revolutionary family" at the head of the official party had converted itself into a millionaires' club. After 1940, the presidents of Mexico took care to defend the club's interests before any others. In defense of its interests, "the people" then began a struggle against the government of the revolution and the union bureaucrats tied to the official party.

Who Are "the People" and What Are "Popular Movements'?

Who are "the people'? In Mexico, they comprise the popular sectors – laborers, peasants, students – and such marginal groups as urban squatters and the indigenous peoples, among others. Besides the three core sectors, they too form part of the popular resistance even if they do not lead it. Mexico's "popular resistance" is a covering term for the various popular movements demanding political change, specifically the overhauling of the system of presidential despotism and the official party's monopoly of political power.

In answer to the question, "What are popular movements?" we are told that they differ from class struggles. "The short answer is that they are defined not so much by their social composition as by their political practices ... they are purely *popular* and not social – mainly because they comprise a struggle to constitute "the people" as political actors.'[7] Although not all popular movements are class struggles, all class struggles involving exploited workers and peasants *are* popular movements.

In his introduction to *Popular Movements and Political Change in Mexico*, Joe Foweraker argues that popular movements can be periodized into those before and those after 1968, when a qualitative change occurred in the relationship between popular movements and the political system, owing to "a new popular leadership, which began with the generation of 1968 ... [and achieved] national expression, first, in the syndical arena of the 1970s, and then in the electoral arena of the 1980s.'[8] To this account we add: the first stage of popular movements dates from the massacre at the presidential palace on 23 September 1941; second, the ten years of guerrilla movements from 1965 to 1975 testify to the continuity between the first and second stages of the popular resistance; third, a final stage begins with the resurgence of the armed struggle following the eclipse of Marxist-Leninist parties at the end of the 1980s.

People's Self-Defense Under Cárdenas

The resistance began as a movement of self-defense of the popular reforms and conquests achieved by the people during the climax of the revolutionary period under President Lázaro Cárdenas. Instead of being directed against the government, the labor strikes and peasant

17

demonstrations during his administration catalysed the greatest wave of popular reforms the country had seen since the great insurrection of 1910–19. These resulted in the organization of new class-conscious labor and peasant associations.

The old, corrupt Regional Confederation of Labor (CROM) gave way to a new revolutionary labor federation founded in February 1936: the Confederation of Mexican Workers (CTM). The nationalization of the railroads followed in June 1937, and the nationalization of US and British oil firms in March 1938. In April the nationalized railroads came under the first direct form of labor self-management in the country's history. At the same time, the Cardenist regime extended the scope of the cooperative sector in industry and gave new life to agrarian reform. Beginning with the wave of strikes in 1934–35, the mass movement gathered to a crest in 1938.[9]

This movement ran into a barrier during the second half of 1938 as a result of the US government's decision to strangle the policy of nationalizations in Mexico. Because of US government and private pressures demanding compensation for US citizens expropriated by the agrarian reform, reactionary elements inside the country decided to confront the Cardenist regime. Within the Mexican Congress, the right wing, headed by General Emiliano Acosta and including the new landowners who had come out of the revolution, launched a demagogical campaign against the cooperatives in the Laguna region of north-central Mexico for the self-styled purpose of freeing the peasants from the "state's yoke." Along with fascist advances in Europe and the imminent defeat of the Spanish republican government by the forces of General Franco, these external and internal pressures encouraged the military uprising of General Cedillo in May 1938. The US government refused to impose an embargo against the sale of arms to the rebels, while the city of Brownsville, Texas, became the temporary headquarters of the oil companies financing the insurrection.[10]

Although the rebellion failed, the rise of reactionary forces throughout the world contributed to paralysing structural reforms within the country. When the National Council of the Party of the Mexican Revolution (PRM) met in autumn 1939, its right wing threatened to split the party should General Francisco Múgica become the official candidate. Múgica represented the party's revolutionary-nationalist wing and the logical continuation of the Cardenist policy of national-izations. Only after this meeting did the party resolve on a more moderate candidate in General Manuel Avila Camacho, soon declared to be the party's only candidate supported unconditionally by the leadership of the CTM.

Unquestionably, the selection of Avila Camacho as the sole candidate of the official party came partly in response to the candidacy of General Juan Andreu Almazán as the representative of the reactionary forces outside the party. This general shared with Cedillo the same strategy of opposition to organized labor. Like Cedillo, Almazán belonged to the clique of generals who had enriched themselves at the expense of the revolution. He had his residence in Monterrey where he had established close ties with some of Mexico's leading industrialists and financiers. He also had ties with US capital. Backed by American companies hostile to the party of the revolution, Almazán presented himself as a conservative candidate. The climate of reaction produced by the outbreak of the Second World War in September 1939 prompted both presidential candidates to opt for the same policy: opposition to social change in the interest of social reconciliation. Cárdenas gave ground before these reactionary pressures.[11]

The partisans of Almazán prepared to struggle on two fronts. In case the electoral means should prove inadequate, the Almazanist generals would resort to a military uprising. For that, they needed the support of monopolist circles in the United States. For the second time, the oil companies, just as they had done during preparations for the Cedillist rebellion, prepared to subvert the civil order of Mexico. In the city of Torreón in March 1940, they met the Almazanist generals Quiroga, Castellana, Martín del Campo, and others for the purpose of arranging the shipment of arms across the frontier. American landowners in the state of Chihuahua converted their estates into arsenals while the city of Juárez across from El Paso became the principal center for recruiting mercenaries.

When the electoral effort failed, the partisans of Almazán waited for the call to arms. But instead of leading an insurrection, the General decided to leave the country. Some say he achieved his purpose even in defeat. For his campaign for the presidency strengthened the conservative forces within the government and the party of the revolution. This showed itself in the government's efforts to co-opt the leaders of the developing labor and peasant movements and to contain their struggle for structural reforms.[12]

The co-optation of the people's leaders dates from the CTM's support of the candidacy of Avila Camacho at the end of 1939. On 22 February 1940, when he declared himself in favor of stimulating US investments in Mexico by all possible means and with every class of guarantees, virtually nobody raised a voice in opposition. Later, in an electoral speech on 8 May in Guaymas, Sonora, he harangued the leaders of organized labor to suspend the class struggle. The next month, in an address to businessmen in the state of Chihuahua on 27 June, he claimed that the moment had come for liquidating the struggle between social classes for the sake of "national unity." For the second and third times, no opposition was voiced.[13]

Mounting Government Repression

The first blow against the cooperative sector and against workers' self-management of nationalized industries caught the labor movement by surprise. As early as 1937 Cárdenas had called for the creation of workers' cooperatives that would permit them to administer the means of production and establish the bases for socialism in Mexico. This project had the backing of the CTM. The law concerning cooperatives adopted at the end of that year provided the legal framework for developing the cooperative sector. In October 1937 Cárdenas created the Labor Bank with the purpose of financing the development of workers' cooperatives. The government helped to organize nearly a thousand industrial cooperatives including cement, rubber, hemp, and textile factories along with sugar refineries. Mixed cooperatives with state participation appeared, such as the one in Zacatepec, Morelos, with 500 workers employed in the sugar refinery and another 10,000 peasants cultivating cane.

Within the framework of private property and competition with capitalist enterprises, this social sector of the economy came up against insuperable obstacles. In most cases the factories acquired by the workers consisted of weak and unprofitable enterprises with exhausted or obsolete machinery. In the case of the railroads, the workers administering them had to pay off a huge debt to foreign capitalists. Although the law specified that the government had the obligation to compensate the former owners, the workers got stuck with the bill. The taxes owed to the government added to their burden. The financial problems faced by the cooperatives and workers' administration of the nationalized railroads led the CTM to conclude that, by and large, the social sector could not afford to pay the same wages as private enterprises. Altogether, these and other difficulties culminated in the eventual ruin of industrial cooperatives and the system of self-management.[14]

Despite their dependent role in the administration of the nationalized sector of the economy, the workers continued to defend the system of self-management and the different forms of mixed administration with government participation. But with a view to economic efficiency, President Cárdenas refused in May 1940 to support the demands of the Oil Workers' Union for an increase in workers' representation on the board of directors of the nationalized oil company Pemex. In August the government put together a mixed administrative council for managing the restructured oil industry, but of the nine administrators five would be nominated by the government and four by the trade union. Shortly afterwards, at the beginning of the new government in December, the Mexican Congress adopted a law that put an end to workers' administration of the railroads. No longer would the workers independently control nationalized industry. The workers suffered a major defeat, although one must admit that the new law also liberated them from a responsibility they could not fulfill within the framework of a capitalist economy.[15]

After this first great defeat, a series of others followed. Besides the reverses suffered by the oil workers and railroad workers, in 1940 the electrical workers took a step backwards. When the US firms refused to satisfy their demands, the workers called a strike throughout the entire industry. But the CTM's leaders denounced the strike, and this action found a sympathetic response in the government. The workers planned the strike for May but put it off until June. Then they postponed it indefinitely because of the position of the CTM and the government's Department of Labor. The government also side-tracked their project for nationalizing the electrical industry until President López Mateos nationalized it twenty years later.

The government's offensive against the workers gained momentum beginning with the six-year term of the new president in 1941.[16] The year began with the reform of the federal law concerning work, the intent being to avoid the so-called "abuse" of the right to strike. In September, in front of the presidential residence, government forces massacred a contingent of demonstrating workers from the nationalized factories producing war materials. Those responsible were not indicted, much less condemned. The next year saw the first strike against an industrial cooperative with government participation – the strike at the sugar refinery of Zacatepec in the state of Morelos. The state governor resorted to fierce repression against the strikers, firing them from their jobs and calling out the judicial police. The local authorities did not stop short of violence.

The ruling political structure since 1929 had begun to show signs of deterioration. Suffocated by the increasing rigidity of the official apparatus, the people's forces started questioning the nature of that apparatus. Until then, the political system could count on the use of those mechanisms that had traditionally served it in confronting revolutionary dissidence: the co-optation and bribery of revolutionary leaders. Now it decided to use more extreme measures: repression carried to the point of assassination of the people's representatives. Thenceforth, the relations between the ruling party and the popular forces would follow a course of escalating violence on both sides.

Objective and Subjective Conditions of Resistance

An analysis of the conditions which launched and helped to perpetuate the resistance can benefit from the sociological distinction between the objective and the subjective conditions of revolution. The conditions are similar in the case of resistance to government repression. The objective conditions emerge independently of the will of the exploited and oppressed classes. Instances of these include government corruption, official terrorism, wage freezes, and increases in the cost of living resulting in a deterioration of the people's livelihood. The subjective conditions appear when the masses acquire an understanding of their situation and resolve to change it. These include the diffusion of populist and revolutionary ideologies, the emergence of revolutionary cadres within the democratic organizations of the people under the influence of a vanguard party, and the examples of successful revolutionary movements elsewhere. Unlike the objective conditions, these have to be created by the workers and peasants themselves.

In Mexico the resistance emerged in response to an offensive by the "moderate" and rightist elements within the government and the official party to undermine the popular and structural reforms achieved under President Cárdenas. We have already shown in what precisely this offensive consisted. Its effects were to line the pockets of the bureaucrats in power, to transform the self-styled guardians of the revolution into a state bourgeoisie, to co-opt the leaders of mass organizations, and to favor the economic interests of the bourgeoisie. These effects, added to the government's offensive against the people's democratic organizations, constituted the objective conditions of the resistance.

Together they characterize the so-called Mexican political system. At the helm is the political bureaucracy which takes the initiative and makes most of the important decisions. Since the president of the republic is the visible head of the bureaucracy, the man ultimately responsible for the government's and the official party's abuse of power and systematic repression of the people, the objective conditions of the resistance have become identified with "presidential despotism.'

The human factor and the role of ideology comprise the subjective conditions of the popular resistance. Three main ideological tendencies have shaped popular movements since 1940: the populist current of agrarian reform launched by Emiliano Zapata wedded to President Lázaro Cárdenas' revolutionary nationalism; the influence of the Mexican Communist Party as a school for militants; and the example of the Cuban resistance against Batista and of the socialist revolution that followed.

Three Contributing Causes of Insurgency

A major source of inspiration for the resistance consisted of the populist and nationalist ideology of the Mexican Revolution. The most important revolutionary currents peculiar to Mexico derive from Zapata's agrarian movement in the state of Morelos and from Cárdenas' nationalization policies. The confluence of these two currents with that of Mexican Communism contributed to catalysing the first great wave of popular resistance against the government – significantly, in Zapata's own state.

The Zapatistas gave preference to land redistribution and to returning the land to those who worked it. They struggled for the division of the great haciendas, for the collectivization of agriculture, and for a decentralized people's government. The Cardenistas, too, opted for agrarian reform. They also called for the nationalization of foreign enterprises, for workers' self-management of nationalized industries, for government support of organized labor, and for a nation-wide program of socialist education.

The peasants influenced by the Zapatistas and the workers who looked to Cardenismo for inspiration were not going to risk their lives or hold out against persecution in the expectation of acquiring only a small piece of land or mere participation in the direction of national-ized industry. The masses would require something more if they were to be mobilized on a grand scale. That "more" was precisely the vision of a new society organized along socialist lines.

The political development of Rubén Jaramillo, instigator of the first people's armed uprising against the government and himself the most important agrarian leader since Zapata, is a case in point. Although he was a prime example of the confluence of the Zapatista and the Cardenist currents, our research revealed a strong dose of communism. There was a long-guarded secret unknown even to Jaramillo's followers: their leader had joined the Communist Party as early as 1938, a datum deliberately omitted from his autobiography.[17] He left the party a year later but rejoined it in 1961.

The second source of inspiration for the resistance came from the Communist Party (PCM). The party underwent a crisis in 1939 from which it did not recover until its 13th Congress in 1960. During those years its most active cadres found themselves either acting in defiance of the leadership, or so alienated by the party's line that they eventu-ally withdrew, or so wanting in discipline that they were finally expelled. David Siqueiros, the party's outstanding muralist, caustically referred to it as the "Mexican Expulsionist Party." Nonetheless, it was the principal vanguard of the left, the only one sharing and benefiting from the experience of Communist parties elsewhere, and in that capacity it contributed to forming some of the best cadres of the resis-tance.

The party was influential in spite of itself. Its leading militants accomplished their best work when they acted independently. But could they and the communists who defected have led the resistance without the intellectual and moral orientation provided by the party? That seems unlikely. The party functioned not only as a school for militants, but also as a pole of attraction for non-communists who eventually joined precisely because of its revolutionary ideology.

Among the rebels inside the party who stayed with it but went their own way until they eventually dropped out or suffered expulsion were top leaders such as Valentín Campa and professional organizers such as Mónico Rodríguez. Expelled for 20 years before being permitted to rejoin the party, Campa founded during this interval a rival communist party and organized the biggest railway strike in the nation's history. After almost 20 years as a party militant, organizer, and collaborator with Campa in mobilizing the railway workers, Rodríguez withdrew from the party following an aborted effort to expel him.

Another group of popular leaders joined the party after having established a name for themselves independently of it. These included Othón Salazar, founder of the Revolutionary Teachers' Movement (MRM) and leader of the great teachers' strike in 1957, and Francisca Calvo Zapata, organizer of the Zapatista Urban Front (FUZ) – the first urban guerrillas in Mexico.

The third most important influence on the resistance consisted of the inspiring example of the Cuban resistance and the social changes that followed. The heroic actions of revolutionaries without a party, notably Fidel Castro and Che Guevara, gave rise to imitators all over Latin America. In Mexico their exploits were copied by the guerrillas who assaulted the Madera Barracks in the state of Chihuahua in 1965. This action gave rise to others. Among the guerrilla movements that emerged in response to the Cuban influence, several made national headlines. These included the Revolutionary Armed Movement (MAR), trained in North Korea, and Genaro Vázquez's Revolutionary National Civic Action (ACNR), an organization both civil and military like the 26 July Movement of Fidel Castro.

Most of the guerrilla groups in Mexico emerged under the influence of both the PCM and the Cuban example. The notorious guerrilla chieftain Lucio Cabañas served as regional secretary of the party in the state of Guerrero, before attempts on his life led him to retreat to the mountains and to organize his own movement of armed resistance. Other guerrilla groups, such as the Lacandones, the People's

25

Revolutionary Armed Forces (FRAP), and the 23 September Communist League – all active during the early 1970s – initially owed their existence to militants of the Communist Youth in rebellion against what they considered to be mistaken policies of the leadership. Despite the fact that the party's new leaders rejected the opportunistic line followed since the mid-1930s, the majority of its youth opted for methods of direct action under the influence of the Cuban Revolution. These three traditions contributed to mobilizing different sectors of the resistance. The populist and revolutionary-nationalist currents appealed mainly to the masses of peasants and workers – the groundswell of the movement. The Communist Party was a key factor in forming the leading cadres of the working class. And the Cuban example had its greatest impact on students and intellectuals. Each of these ideologies performed a different role: the first in defending the interests of the peasants and workers through land "invasions' and the movement for independent trade-unionism; the second in providing leadership in the principal strikes and demonstrations by organized labor against the government; the third in building the student movement and unleashing a decade of guerrilla struggles in Mexico.

Notes

1. Rubén Narvaez, *La sucesión presidencial: Teoría y práctica del tapadismo* (Mexico City: Instituto Mexicano de Sociología Política, 1981), pp. 43, 44–5.
2. Ibid., p. 46.
3. Ibid., pp. 49, 61.
4. Luis Javier Garrido, *El partido de la revolución institucionalizada: La formación del nuevo estado en México (1928–1945)* (Mexico City: Siglo XXI, 1982), pp. 97, 99, 100.
5. Ibid., p. 101; and Enrique González Pedrero, "México, país de contrastes," in Gerardo Davila and Manlio Tirado, eds, *Como México no hay dos: Porfirismo – Revolución – Neoporfirismo* (Mexico City: Nuestro Tiempo, 1971). On Mexico's presidential despotism as a species of Bonapartism, ideologically neither capitalist nor socialist, see Manuel Aguilar Mora, *La crisis de la izquierda en México* (Mexico City: Juan Pablos, 1978), pp. 24–25, 26, and his two-volume *El bonapartismo mexicano* (Mexico City: Juan Pablos, 1982).
6. Donald Hodges and Ross Gandy, *Mexico 1910–1982: Reform or Revolution?* 2nd rev. ed. (London: Zed, 1983), pp. 99–100. On *neoporfirismo*, see Davila and Tirado, *Como México no hay dos*, pp. 75–172.
7. Joe Foweraker, Introduction to Joe Foweraker and Ann L. Craig, eds, *Popular Movements and Political Change in Mexico*, (Boulder: Lynne Rienner, 1990), 5.
8. Ibid., p. 7.
9. On the left turn of the official party of the revolution during the presidency of Lázaro Cárdenas, see Anatoli Shulgovski, *México en la encrucijada de su historia*, tr.

Armando Martínez Verdugo (Mexico City: Cultura Popular, 1968), pp. 109–27; and Adolfo Gilly, *La revolución interrumpida*, 4th ed. (Mexico City: El Caballito, 1974; orig. pub. 1971), pp. 355–66, 376–94. Among the specialized accounts of *cardenismo*, see in particular Lázaro Cárdenas, *Ideario político* (Mexico City: Era, 1972), pp. 65–9; Tzvi Medin, *Ideología y praxis política de Lázaro Cárdenas*, 2nd. ed. (Mexico City: Siglo XXI, 1974), pp. 6–59, 74–87; Arnaldo Córdova, *La política de masas del cardenismo* (Mexico City: Era, 1974), pp. 60–89; Arturo Anguiano, *El Estado y la política obrera del cardenismo* (Mexico City: Era, 1975), pp. 75–81.

10. Shulgovski, *México en la encrucijada de su historia*, pp. 370–76.

11. Ibid., pp. 417–38, 467–74. On Almazán's challenge to *cardenismo*, see also Garrido, *El partido*, pp. 271–7.

12. Garrido, *El partido*, pp. 289–94; Bertha Lerner de Sheinbaum and Susana Ralsky de Cimet, *El poder de los presidentes: Alcances y perspectivas (1910–1973)* (Mexico City: Instituto Mexicano de Estudios Políticos, 1976), pp. 150, 159–60.

13. See *Avila Camacho y su ideología: ¡La Revolución en marcha! Gira electoral* (Mexico City: Partido de la Revolución Mexicana, 1940).

14. Anguiano, *El Estado*, pp. 86–92, 137–9; Shulgovski, *México en la encrucijada de su historia*, pp. 306–20.

15. Shulgovski, *México en la encrucijada de su historia*, pp. 447–53.

16. Nothing is more indicative of the fate of contemporary social movements than labor's share of the national income compared to that of people of property. Near the end of the Cardenist presidency in 1938, for example, wage-earners' share had risen to 30.5 per cent whereas at the end of Manuel Avila Camacho's term in office it had fallen to 21.5 per cent. During that same period – the so-called crossroads of the revolution – the share coming to *empresarios* or entrepreneurs rose from 26.2 per cent to 45.1 per cent, tantamount in economic, if not political, terms to a counter-revolution. See the statistical data from Mexico's *Revista de Economía* (1962), no. 2, p. 49, cited by Shulgovski, *México en la encrucijada de su historia*, p. 491.

17. Hodges' interview with Mónico Rodríguez, Jaramillo's close collaborator, at Rodríguez' workshop in Chiconcuac, Morelos, on 10–11 January 1978; and with Gerardo Unzueta, who confirmed Rodríguez's oral testimony at Communist Party headquarters in Mexico City on 6 February 1978. See Rubén Jaramillo, *Autobigrafía* and Froylán C. Manjarrez, *La matanza de Xochicalco*, 2nd ed. (Mexico City: Nuestro Tiempo, 1973).

2 ✿ Mounting Labor Protests

The resistance began with a series of confrontations and defeats for the working class. In any serious game one has to lose first in order to win later. Without the confrontations with a superior adversary one cannot learn either his weaknesses or one's own mistakes. One must pass through the school of defeats before reaching the final victory.

The first confrontations between the working class and the supposedly revolutionary, nationalist, and popular government took a variety of forms. Local demonstrations were organized to protest the government's imposition of managers on the nationalized industries and cooperatives without the workers' consent. Strikes and work stoppages followed against unpopular administrators. The workers also struck against the government's policy of freezing wages on the pretext of a national emergency and the need for "national unity" during the Second World War. Popular resistance emerged in the struggle for trade-union independence against the labor bureaucrats who had sold out to the official party, against government intervention in union affairs, and against the imposition of labor leaders dependent on the government.

The popular forces began their resistance not directly against the government, but indirectly against its representatives in the nationalized and cooperative sectors. The strikes against the wage freeze during the Second World War went further in questioning the government's policy of stimulating economic development and profits in the private sector when the working class alone was making sacrifices for the country's benefit. The demands for trade-union independence went still further in challenging the government's stranglehold on the labor movement through the intermediary of labor bureaucrats identified with the official party. This last form of resistance led to government intervention against the independent trade unions. Only then did the workers begin to challenge directly the established party of the revolution.

What may we conclude from this development? Considering that the resistance had progressed from local demonstrations through strikes and work stoppages to become a national movement for an independent trade unionism, we may conclude that it had been gaining strength despite its many defeats and reverses.

The Demonstration in Front of the Presidential Palace

The first confrontation occurred in 1941 during a demonstration in front of the presidential residence.[1] How did it come about? General Luis Bobadilla, the government-appointed director of the nationalized factories producing war materials, had implanted a military discipline more suited to a barracks than to a production center. This action provoked the opposition of the workers who insisted that the military chief abide by the established norms in state enterprises and his obligation to consult with union leaders in managing the industry. Since the general refused to consider their petition, the Union of Workers in War Industry (STMG) presented the matter to the Secretary of National Defense, General Macías Valenzuela, who refused to intervene in the dispute on the ground that General Bobadilla had been personally appointed by the President. Frustrated a second time, the union resolved to take the matter directly to President Avila Camacho.

On 23 September 1941, the workers assembled after work and marched toward the Lomas de Chapultepec where the President of the Republic lived. The union's leaders knocked at the gate and asked to be heard. Through the intermediary of a presidential aide they were told to take their problem to the Secretary of National Defense who would be instructed to resolve it directly. The union secretary repeated his request, pointing out that the Secretary of Defense had excused himself from handling the problem. The workers decided not to leave without an audience with the President.

Colonel Maximiano Ochoa, chief aide of the presidential general staff, took command of the situation. He ordered the workers to

29

depart voluntarily or be forced to withdraw by the troops under his command. The union's secretary protested that the colonel had no right to order the withdrawal of workers seeking a peaceful and legal way of presenting their problem to the country's highest dignitary, a right consecrated by the Constitution. Indignant at this response, the colonel retired but returned moments later with soldiers from the presidential guard. Pistol in hand, he ordered them to fire against the union's secretary and the workers who accompanied him. The secretary and eight other workers were killed, and eleven were wounded. The first martyrs of the resistance had made their appearance.

Were those responsible for the massacre indicted? The President did not so much as bother to have the crime investigated. The news media were muzzled, and only the official version of what happened appeared in the press – a story more appropriately aimed at convincing children than adults. Eyewitnesses of the massacre were left with the conviction that the government of the revolution had passed into the enemy camp. Shortly afterwards, the workers responded with a great public demonstration against the massacre.

Successive Strikes in the Public Sector

In April 1942 this action was followed by the first strike against the management of a mixed cooperative controlled by the government, the sugar refinery in Zacatepec, Morelos. The factors motivating the strike date back to January 1940 when the manager designated by the government effectively abolished workers' and peasants' co-participation in management by dismissing Jaramillo, the president of the administrative council, and by replacing the council's elected delegates with his own appointees. But Jaramillo found another way of defending the interests of the workers and the peasants. In March 1942 he threatened the manager with a strike unless the workers got a wage increase and the peasants got a better price for the cane they delivered to the refinery.

Elpidio Perdomo, the governor of the state, responded by detaining Jaramillo and threatening to have him shot should he persist in his project. But Jaramillo remained obdurate, and the strike began on 9 April. To avoid a scandal that might implicate him for his mishandling of the workers, the manager tried to cover up the fact that a strike had occurred. With this purpose he appealed to the state authorities and to his own gunmen to recruit peasants forcibly for the positions temporarily vacated by the strikers. At the same time the peasants were compelled to continue with the harvest and to deliver cane to the refinery. Although the workers remained firm for a month and a half, the peasants gave in because of the official terror. The workers who led the strike were fired. Jaramillo was suspended as a member of the cooperative. Although he continued cutting cane, the refinery refused to buy it. He had to rely on friends to sell the cane for him.[2]

In 1943–44 the workers launched a series of strikes with an even greater impact on the national scene than the explosive movement of masses that had erupted in 1934–35 at the beginning of the Cardenist regime. For the first time, the strikes had for their target not only private Mexican and foreign enterprises, but also the government-managed nationalized sector. The growth in exports, the domestic market, and industry during the Second World War followed the policy of unrestricted accumulation favored by the official party. While the war piled up profits for Mexico's business community, the government put up barriers to the workers' demands through freezing wages. Faced with the increasing cost of living and the loss of purchasing power, workers had no recourse other than to resist the government's policy.

The workers had shown no lack of patriotism in the war against fascism. On the contrary, they had borne the brunt of the sacrifices in the form of overtime. Did the bourgeoisie have to benefit at their expense? Did they have to tighten the screws of exploitation and accumulate wealth in the midst of war? The policy of "national unity" excused the rich from making any sacrifice; it actually made them richer. The Communist Party supported this wartime policy, as did the Confederation of Mexican Workers (CTM). Within the party only mavericks like Mónico Rodríguez, who knew when to break party discipline, supported the strikers during this first stage of the resistance. Meanwhile, communists outside the party led the way.

The strike wave of 1943–44 did not upset the stability of the political system. The labor bureaucrats condemned the strikes in the hope of eliciting government support in the elections of 1943. Some trade union leaders became senators, while the top bureaucracy of the

CTM succeeded in fusing with the state apparatus. At the same time these struggles also helped to shape the growing resistance against the ruling party.

For an Independent Trade Unionism

The resistance of workers against the government and party of the revolution came to a head in 1947 through the struggle within organized labor for an independent trade unionism. Only then did the resistance acquire the character of a self-conscious national movement. Let us consider briefly the events leading up to this new stage, in which Valentín Campa would play the leading role.

On 27 September 1945 the CTM and the Confederation of Industrial Chambers (CCI) reached an agreement formalized in the so-called Industrial–Labor Pact. The CCI represented the interests of small and medium-size capitalists with a pro-government ideology of support for the official party. The pact's objective was to achieve the independent economic development of the country on the premise that the material and cultural conditions of the workers could not be improved by any other means. Among other things, the pact affirmed: "With these higher goals we want to renew, during the stage of peace, the *patriotic alliance* which we Mexicans have created and maintained during the war for the defense of the nation's independence and sovereignty, under the policy of national unity eulogized by the president General Manuel Avila Camacho."[3]

The acceptance of this pact meant an end to protests against the fall in real wages brought about by the increasing cost of living. It meant a moratorium on strikes and popular demonstrations against the government. For the working class it signified submission to the leadership of the governing party. For that reason the independent unions refused to sign the pact, supported by militants within the CTM who began agitating for an independent trade union movement.

The developing conflict between reformist and militant tendencies within the CTM came to a showdown at its Fourth National Congress in March 1947.[4] A confrontation occurred over the election of a new national committee. On one side the Marxist and then secretary-general Lombardo Toledano supported the faction of Fidel Velázquez and its candidate, Fernando Amilpa, for the position of secretary. On the other side Valentín Campa, at the head of the railway workers and the communists outside the party persisted in favor of their candidate, Luis Gómez Zepeda, Secretary General of the Union of Railroad Workers of the Mexican Republic (STFRM). Since the militants were unable to eject the group around Fidel Velázquez from the leadership of the CTM, the STFRM split and organized its own Special Confederation of Workers (CUT). This new labor confederation included the most important industrial unions, not only the railroad workers but also the miners and oil workers who had separated from the CTM during an earlier period. Its purpose was to build an independent labor movement in the conviction that the CTM had become a virtual government agency.

The struggle for trade union independence began within the railroad workers' union and spread from there to other industrial unions.[5] But within the STFRM two opposed lines struggled for hegemony: the independent tendency led by Valentín Campa and the pro-government tendency led by Luis Gómez Zepeda, who later went over to Campa's side. In the trade union elections at the end of 1943 the conflict between these two currents reached boiling point. Because it threatened the union's stability and cohesion, the President was asked to mediate. A compromise was reached in May 1944 in favor of a coalition executive committee: Luis Gómez Zepeda became the new secretary-general while Campa became the secretary of education, organization, and propaganda. The accession of Campa to this important post, which he held until January 1947, signified the beginning of a concerted campaign not only against the government's wage freeze, but also against the general tendency within the labor movement to accept the government's leadership and directives.

Fighting the Labor Bosses

In 1948 Jesús Díaz de León, nicknamed "the *charro*" for his fancy Mexican cowboy dress, emerged as the new secretary-general of the railroad workers, with Campa and his followers in control of the union's vigilance and financial committee. But the Cold War had followed the World War, and the new leadership, encouraged by the government, decided to eliminate the "communist menace" represented by Campa. The government's decision to devalue the peso in

July added to labor tensions, and in August the first demonstrations appeared against the new rise in the cost of living. Besides the railroad workers, the oil workers and the teachers demanded a wage increase and began preparing for a strike. In these circumstances, challenged by Campa's tendency on one side and pressured by the government on the other, Díaz de León decided to take the offensive.

On 28 September he appeared before the Attorney General of the Republic with a petition against Valentín Campa and Luis Gómez Zepeda for alleged embezzlement of 100,000 pesos during their tenure in office. This action met with general disapproval from the union's rank and file expressed through numerous assemblies, meetings, manifestos, and statements to the newspapers. The method employed by de León violated the union's statutes, which required that charges of this kind be brought first to the attention and consideration of the vigilance committee. In a manifesto issued on 4 October, the union's general accounting committee condemned the action of the new secretary for having solicited without authorization the state's intervention in the union's affairs. It declared: "Jesús Díaz de León betrays his union and his class."[6] In the committee's opinion the secretary's offensive had hurt not only his own union, but also other independent unions. This conclusion was shared by the oil workers' and miners' unions, by the CUT, and by the recently formed Association of Laborers and Peasants of Mexico (AOCM), presided over by the Marxist-Leninist Vicente Lombardo Toledano, head of the Popular Party (PP) founded in 1948 in protest against the official party's repressive policies.

On 8 October the newspapers in the capital informed the public that Valentín Campa and Luis Gómez were wanted by the judicial police. The union's executive and vigilance committees responded by accusing the new secretary of "wanting to divide the union in complicity with the government" and by temporarily suspending him from his position. A new secretary-general, Francisco Quintano Madrazo, was chosen to serve in his place.[7]

The battle being waged inside the union was directed not only against the government's intervention in its affairs, but also against the government's wage policy. Thus the newspaper *Excelsior* reported on 13 October that the railroad workers were not disposed to accept wage controls without a new price policy for combating the increasing cost of living and successive devaluations of the peso. The resistance reached a new level when the current headed by Campa with the support of Gómez Zepeda openly challenged the official union position of not demanding a wage increase and then deposed the unpopular secretary, replacing him with a provisional one.[8]

This first great confrontation between the movement for trade union independence and the official leadership came to an abrupt end when the government intervened directly in the dispute by violently replacing the provisional secretary and restoring "the *charro*," Jesús Díaz de León. On the day that Díaz de León was removed by the union's executive and vigilance committees he mobilized his supporters and, with the help of an estimated 100 agents of the secret police disguised as railroad workers, assaulted the STFRM's headquarters and four other union buildings. His *compadre* (the father and godfather of the same child are *compadres* or fathers in common), Colonel Serrano, a senator of the republic and a close friend of President Miguel Alemán, could be seen directing the military operation from a jeep. With the help of an army truck equipped with sound track, "the *charro*" addressed the people who were physically ejecting the union leaders from their headquarters. The assault on the union with the complicity of police and military forces gave rise to the expression *charrismo* to refer to the tendency of "yellow" labor leaders to rely on the government for protection. The term *charro* itself acquired the derogatory connotation of a "yellow" union bureaucrat in the service of the government.[9]

The affair did not end there. Campa and Gómez Zepeda, along with other members of the union's executive and vigilance committees, were detained by the judicial police and indicted for the crime of fraud. Gómez Zepeda was sentenced for having illegally transferred some 200,000 pesos from the union's treasury to the CUT, although he had obtained permission to do so after presenting the matter to the various officers and sections of the STFRM. Campa chose to go underground for a time, and from hiding wrote to the judge that his wages were only 575 pesos a month, that he did not have a house of his own, or a car, or a private business on the side; consequently, that he could not possibly have benefited illicitly from his position as a union official. None the less, when he gave himself up, he was accused and found guilty of fraud and was sentenced to eight years' imprisonment, of which he atoned for his sins during four. Even in jail he was accused of crimes he could not have committed in his condition, such as engineering a supposed act of sabotage resulting in a train collision in Guadalajara on 16 July 1949.[10] This manner of repressing independent trade union leaders may have been "legal," but it was certainly not constitutional.[11]

As a result of this first test of *charrismo*, the leadership of the oil workers' union launched a purge of its own anti-official current. At an extraordinary convention manipulated by the agents of the government within the union's leadership, the militants were removed from key positions.[12] But this coup had no lasting effects, and by 1949 the union was able to recover its independence. The government then intervened directly to change the leadership, as it had intervened against the railroad workers the year before.

A similar fate overtook the capital's tramway workers. In August 1949 their headquarters were taken through a violent assault by the police masquerading as members of the union. That was the end of their independence.[13] Evidently, the offensive of the *charros* against the independent trade unions and confederations of labor was aimed at undermining their influence even to the point of liquidating them.

This process culminated in the coup against the Union of Mining, Metallurgical, and Related Workers (STMMS) in 1950. In May the miners' delegates met to elect a new leadership. But the general secretary, with the support of the government's secretary of labor, refused to recognize the independent delegations and blocked them from entering the convention. The secretary of labor's godson became president of the convention, which then went through the electoral farce of imposing the *charro* Jesús Carrasco as the new secretary. Thus on 16 October, when the 5,000 miners of Nueva Rosita in the state of Coahuila went out on strike against a subsidiary of the American Smelting and Refining Company, neither this action nor the demand for a wage increase could count on support from the union's leadership.[14]

The strike against the American subsidiary made front-page news and awakened the interest of the entire population for being directed against a major foreign enterprise. But the secretary of labor refused to recognize the right to strike for a wage increase and publicly condemned the miners' action. The miners then resolved to take their case directly to the President of the Republic. They began their march on foot from Nueva Rosita on 20 January 1951 and arrived in the capital on 10 March after covering some 1,500 km. Accompanied by their wives and some children, the 5,000 miners in this "caravan of hunger," as the march came to be known, received the almost total support of the working class. When they arrived in Mexico City, they were welcomed with embraces, flowers, and confetti. In the *Zócalo* or central plaza in front of the government palace, they assembled in a giant meeting to ask for justice from the President. But as in the case of the first great demonstration of this type in September 1941, the President did not appear and refused to be interviewed. Instead he directed Secretary of State Adolfo Ruiz Cortines to acknowledge and resolve the conflict. But the workers rejected the secretary's feeble efforts. On 20 April the strikers boarded a special train which returned them to Nueva Rosita without having achieved their objectives.[15]

Despite the assaults of *charrismo*, the workers' resistance was gathering steam. The escalation of the struggle between the pro-government and independent currents in the labor movement had the general effect of making the workers aware of their class interests. Their capacity to act independently of the government and the labor bureaucrats contributed to making the resistance aware of itself.

The Resistance Becomes Aware of Itself

Sociologists make a distinction between a class-in-itself and a class-for-itself. By a class-in-itself is meant a class defined by a particular relation to the means of production, but without the consciousness of being a class; by a class-for-itself is meant both the objective and subjective prerequisites of a class, one fully aware of its own interests. A similar distinction may be applied to the evolution of the popular resistance in Mexico.[16] At its inception it looked upon government paternalism and the trade union bureaucracy as its friends. Only through a series of confrontations with the pro-government forces did it acquire the character of a movement-for-itself.

The confrontation with the government by the workers producing war materials was part of the resistance, but it was not recognized as such. Not until the strike at the refinery of Zacatepec did workers begin to interpret their resistance as a continuation of the Mexican

Revolution in opposition to the official party that had betrayed it. None the less, it was not Jaramillo but Campa who personified the transition of the resistance movement from its early phase of unawareness into one fully conscious and for-itself.

Although Jaramillo knew well the significance of his own actions, the movement as a whole remained unconscious of its aims until several years later. The resistance-for-itself dates not from the wave of strikes for higher wages in 1943–44, but from the struggles to preserve trade union independence against the machinations of pro-government bureaucrats in 1947–48. This phase coincided with the beginning of the Cold War and the generalized offensive against the independent trade unions by the government of Miguel Alemán. The resistance movement did not become aware of itself as such until the working class learned from experience that the government and party of the revolution had become its enemy. As we have seen, this process began with the creation of the CUT in 1947 and reached a crest in 1948–51.

Notes

1. Our account of the massacre at the presidential palace is based on newspaper reports in the Mexican capital on 24 September 1941; on the events leading up to it in Luis Araiza, *Historia del movimiento obrero mexicano*, 4 vols. (Mexico City: Cuauhtémoc, 1965), vol. 4, pp. 233–7; and on Valentín Campa's political assessment of the events in notes from an interview with Campa at Hodges' home in Cuernavaca, Morelos, 10 January 1978. See also the brief summary in Campa's published memoirs, *Mi testimonio: memorias de un comunista mexicano*, 3rd rev. ed. (Mexico City: Cultura Popular, 1985; orig. pub. 1978), p. 169. The popular resistance, according to Campa, began with the mobilizations leading up to the massacre.
2. Data provided by María de Jesús Sánchez Palma, wife of Reyes Jaramillo, the younger brother of Porfirio and Rubén Jaramillo, in Hodges' interview at her home in Tlaquiltenango, Morelos, 20 July 1975; by Porfirio Jaramillo's widow, Aurora Herrera, at her home in Jiutepec, Morelos, 23 July 1975; and by Mónico Rodríguez at his workshop in Chiconcuac, Morelos, 27 July 1975.
3. "Pacto Industrial y del Trabajo" (27 September 1945), in La CTM y la Confederación de Cámaras Industriales, *20 años de lucha* (Mexico City: Confederación Nacional de Industria de la Transformación, 1961), p. 21.
4. Antonio Alonso, *El movimiento ferrocarrilero en México 1958–1959* (Mexico City: Era, 1972), pp. 73–4.
5. For the following historical sketch, see ibid., pp. 70–98; and Valentín Campa's account in *Mi testimonio*, pp. 174–89, 199–204.
6. Alonso, *El movimiento ferrocarrilero*, pp. 77, 81.
7. Ibid., pp. 82–3.

8. Ibid., p. 83; cited by author.
9. Ibid., pp. 84–5, 90–3; and Mario Gill, *Los Ferrocarrileros* (Mexico City: Extemporáneos, 1971), p. 150.
10. Gill, *Los Ferrocarrileros*, p. 151; and notes from an interview with Campa at Hodges' home in Cuernavaca, Morelos, 10 January 1978.
11. On the spread of the Cold War to Mexico and the crackdown on labor insurgency and left trade unionism as communist-inspired, see Barry Carr, *Marxism and Communism in Twentieth-Century Mexico* (Lincoln: University of Nebraska Press, 1992), pp. 144–5, 146–7, 176–7; and Gerardo Davila and Manlio Tirado, eds, *Como Mexico no hay dos: Porfirismo – Revolución – Neoporfirismo* (Mexico City: Nuestro Tiempo, 1971), pp. 112–19.
12. Gill, *Los Ferrocarrileros*, p. 152.
13. Ibid.
14. Ibid., pp. 152–3.
15. Araiza, *Historia del movimiento*, vol. 4, pp. 244–6.
16. This distinction is traceable to Karl Marx, *The Poverty of Philosophy* (1847) in Karl Marx and Frederick Engels, *Collected Works*, 46 vols. (New York: International Publishers, 1975–1992), vol. 6, p. 211. See the discussion of latent and open struggles by classes-for-themselves in Ross Gandy, *Introducción a la sociología histórica marxista* (Mexico City: Era, 1978), pp. 186–200.

3 ✸ The Peasant Movement in Morelos

The peasant movement under Rubén Jaramillo stands out as the single most important keeper-of-the-flame of the Zapatista tradition. He was the first popular figure after Zapata to launch a guerrilla movement in defense of the peasants' interests. Twice he rose up in arms, once in 1943 and again in 1953, each time in response to an escalation of government terror and persecution. It is fair to say that Jaramillo represents the principal link in the long tradition of continuous struggle from Zapata to the guerrilla movements of the 1990s.

Rubén Jaramillo

Jaramillo was born around 1900 in the town of Tlaquiltenango, Morelos. His father, Athanasio Jaramillo, was a miner of gold and silver. When Rubén was 14 years old, he accepted Zapata's revolutionary ideas and, a year later, at the end of 1915, took up arms to fight with Zapata in his home state of Morelos. By 1917 he had so distinguished himself that he was promoted to the rank of captain of the cavalry, in command of 75 men. Following the assassination of Zapata in April 1919 he worked on several haciendas in different parts of Mexico, but returned to Tlaquiltenango at the end of 1920, when he requested land from the government and was allotted a small parcel on a local *ejido*. He continued to struggle to improve the peasants' conditions by organizing credit unions, and in 1927 a cooperative for directly commercializing agricultural products. From the early 1920s until 1929 he followed his father's footsteps by also working periodically as a miner in Mineral de Huaxtla, about 30 km south of

Tlaquiltenango, until the mine succumbed to difficulties because of the Great Depression.[1] Thus Jaramillo became familiar with the conditions of life of Mexican workers as well as peasants.

With the Constitution in his pocket and a pistol in his knapsack, he went from village to village organizing the people in a dozen different ways. He founded his own political party, and on two occasions, in 1946 and again in 1952, ran for governor of the state of Morelos. He coordinated the struggle of the cane growers with two strikes at the Emiliano Zapata Refinery in Zacatepec, the first in 1942 and the second in 1948, and led a third work stoppage by cane growers of the cooperative at the end of 1958 after which a succession of attempts were made on his life. In his last few years he organized thousands of peasants in land "invasions" in the plains of Michapa and El Guarín. He became a master and precursor of other forms of people's self-defense – from expropriations, kidnappings, and armed struggle to the organization of workers and peasants in independent unions and a political party of their own. Only the popular student movement of 1968 seems to have eluded his influence.

Although he rose up in arms on several occasions, he did so only as a last resort. His armed uprisings failed in their objectives, and he obtained more lasting results by organizing his people politically in a labor–peasant party. He learned from bitter experience that recourse to arms tended to isolate the revolutionary vanguard from the day-to-day struggles of the peasants. Jaramillo proposed that workers and peasants should organize themselves independently of the government, but he also believed in working wherever possible within the government's own organizations to stimulate the democratic tendency within them.

When Cárdenas campaigned for the presidency in 1934, Rubén sought his support for a sugar cooperative in Zacatepec that would free the cane growers from their dependency on local merchants and rich businessmen. Owing to his initiative, studies were made and plans were laid leading to the construction of a refinery in 1938. But from that moment forward the government began to intervene in the cooperative's affairs, ignoring its democratic character and appointing its own managers. Because of the huge sums of money at the manager's disposal, his job soon became the booty of politicians and a source of government corruption. From appealing to the federal government to assist the peasants, Rubén turned to resisting the government in the peasants' interests.[2]

At the time the refinery was founded, Rubén's political philosophy was a mixture of Zapatismo and the anarchism of Ricardo Flores Magón. He carried with him a copy of Magón's *Libertarian Seed*, which he discussed with his companions. By 1938, he was also reading the *Communist Manifesto*. That same year, he joined a political study group at the refinery and was recruited into the PCM by the group's leader Francisco Ruiz, who had come to Morelos after organizing the first independent trade union at the sugar refinery of Atlizco in the state of Puebla. Although Jaramillo dropped out of the party a year later, he continued acting under its influence and the advice of its militants.[3]

With Mónico Rodríguez, a machinist by trade who also joined the party with him, he helped to organize the workers at the refinery in a union of their own, thus paving the way for the strike in April 1942. Mónico and Rubén planned the strike together. Mónico mobilized the workers at the refinery and got them to walk out; Rubén incited the peasants to stop producing and delivering cane. Because the peasants were obliged by law to produce for the refinery, the strike was regarded as illegal and its leaders were cast in the role of conspirators.[4]

For his complicity in the strike, Rubén lost his status as a member of the cooperative. But since he continued agitating among its members, the co-op's manager tried first to buy and then to intimidate him. Having failed in both attempts, the manager met with the governor of the state to plot his detention and possible elimination. On 12 February 1943 the state judicial police, joined by the manager's hired gunmen, laid siege to his house – in vain, since he had already been warned of his imminent arrest. Three days later they tried to catch him on his plot where he continued cutting cane, but he escaped a second time. A third attempt occurred on 17 February at the bridge named "La Cantora," which Jaramillo had to cross on the way home from work. Again, friends alerted him in time. After that, he took to armed struggle.[5]

Jaramillo's First Armed Struggle

The first armed uprising by Jaramillo and his followers began in February 1943 and centered on his native state of Morelos. Until then violence against the party of the revolution had come mainly from big landowners trying to safeguard their power in the countryside, from the Church endeavoring to turn back the clock of social change, and from military chieftains hoping to extend the range of their personal influence. In sharp contrast, Jaramillo's armed struggle signified the resurgence of Zapatismo against the representatives of the federal and state governments who had betrayed the revolution.

From the beginning, Jaramillo's resistance took the form of a peasant movement of self-defense. Although the workers at the refinery also played an important role, the initiative came from the peasants in the sugar cooperative and adjoining communal lands. Zapata's own movement had been one of self-defense against the voracity of the big owners seeking to extend their lands at the expense of the peasants. But the popular victories achieved by the Zapatistas and by the revolution of 1910–19 were being subtly undermined under the administration of the new president, Manuel Avila Camacho.

His life menaced by the authorities, Jaramillo looked for refuge in the hills of Morelos. At the same time, his complaints against the local authorities led him to question the role of the federal government and the official party for sanctioning his persecution. As he notes in his autobiography where he says goodbye to his first wife: "You know that I intend to abandon everything and to dedicate my energies only to protecting myself because if I don't, they'll kill me like a dog.... I'm convinced that to speak up in favor of the peasants before this government is a crime, and I believe this is what has happened to me."[6]

By the end of February his guerrillas included roughly 100 men, many of them ex-Zapatistas, mounted and moving from place to place.[7] When they passed through the villages of Morelos and crossed the border into the state of Puebla, they organized "juntas of the people" to explain the reasons for their rebellion. These centered on the continual aggressions against the cane growers by the manager of the refinery at Zacatepec sanctioned by the governor of the state in complicity with the big landowners. But these were not the only "causes." Jaramillo also became the spokesman for the generalized resistance in his state to the military conscription of young men in connection with the Second World War, when they were taken from their homes, villages, and workplaces and lodged in government barracks. Others also rose in arms in protest against this hardship imposed on the peasants by the government. Eventually these forces joined together under Rubén's leadership. Rubén did not oppose military service during the war, but he wanted it to be voluntary and in consideration of the peasants' interests.

The scene of Jaramillo's first actions was an area untraversed by major roads in the south-eastern part of the state on the far side of the Chinameca River. In Peña de la Virgen, close to the village of Zacapalco, the guerrillas received their baptism of fire with the loss of two men. Later, on 24 March, in the village of La Era, he and 200 of his men began preparations for one of the most audacious assaults in the annals of Mexican guerrilla warfare: the simultaneous capture of the three most important cities in southern Morelos – Zacatepec, Jojutla, and Tlaquiltenango. Another 6,000 men disposed to join his guerrillas had armed themselves in the vicinity of Jojutla. They were instructed to divide into two groups for the purpose of attacking the other two cities.

That afternoon, his forces crossed the Chinameca River and galloped northward. Jaramillo succeeded in taking Tlaquiltenango that evening, but the rest of his plan went awry. The other two columns not only failed in their objective, but also dispersed. Jaramillo had to abandon the city and return to the hills in order to elude the pursuing army.

His plan of Cerro Prieto, which he began distributing at this time, was designed to familiarize the people with the purpose of his struggle. Although no copies survive of the original plan, its contents may be inferred from a later edition circulated in preparation for Jaramillo's second armed uprising in 1953 (see the Appendix).[8] The third, fourth, seventh, eighth, and ninth articles attack the monopoly of power and political despotism of the official party for violating the Constitution. The tenth, twelfth, thirteenth, fifteenth, and seventeenth articles denounce the unconstitutional character of industrial and commercial monopolies both native and foreign, and the "bourgeois and capitalist regime that has Mexico in its clutches but ought to disappear." Most striking in the plan is its anti-bureaucratic and anti-capitalist content presented within a populist framework of "power to the people."

The fundamental enemy turns out to be monopoly – both political and economic – in violation of the Constitution. But article 14 notes that the Constitution contains loopholes and is unworkable in its present form. And article 15 adds that the revolution of 1910 did not bring about the social revolution the people wanted. Consequently, the country needs a *new revolution* and a *revised Constitution* so that the land may be collectivized and the factories turned over to the workers under a government of "genuine workers on the land and in the factories." Evidently, this was a program for workers as well as peasants. The Plan of Cerro Prieto was a plan for a socialist revolution in Mexico.

In May, Lázaro Cárdenas, then secretary of national defense, tried to mediate the conflict, but to no avail. In a personal message to the guerrilla leader, he offered safe conducts to all, but Jaramillo rejected them as only paper guarantees.

The armed struggle continued until the ambush by government troops at El Agua de la Peña near Alsaseca, Puebla, on 12 December 1943. Although Jaramillo's men escaped with only two wounded, their morale was broken and they had to disperse. This last action was followed by a respite in the armed struggle and an invitation from President Avila Camacho to visit him at the Government Palace to end the conflict.

The interview with the President took place on 13 June 1944 and resulted in Jaramillo's accepting the amnesties and safe conducts for himself and his followers. Rubén asked that the peasants, the workers, and the employees at the Zacatepec refinery be exclusively charged with its administration, and that the system of forcible conscription be modified to permit the youth to receive military instruction in their own state and municipalities on Sundays and to return home the same day so as to continue with their labors during the rest of the week. Although the government did not release its stranglehold on the refinery, it did modify the system of military conscription. The President also offered to distribute lands to Rubén and his followers in Baja California. But after visiting the area, Rubén concluded that to accept them would amount to an "exile without guarantees."[9] Here ends the first armed uprising of Rubén Jaramillo.

Organizing the Agrarian Labor Party of Morelos

From then until his second planned uprising in 1953, Rubén tried to work within the rules of the political system. With his companions in arms, he founded the Agrarian Labor Party of Morelos (PAOM), and in October 1945 he agreed to run as its candidate for governor. He ran a second time in 1952. This party, which soon had close to 15,000 dues-paying members organized in 29 different municipalities, later established itself on a national scale as the Agrarian Labor Party of Mexico.[10]

Jaramillo's followers who inspected the polls and watched over the final counting claim that he ran away with the elections on both occasions. In 1946 the newspapers momentarily recognized his victory, but subsequently retracted when the official party declared that it had won. In 1952, witnesses reported that soldiers showed up at the polling centers where Jaramillo was ahead and carried off the ballot boxes. On this occasion an allied demonstration in Mexico City's Alameda Park was broken up by federal troops who fired upon the assembled crowd.

Following the first election Jaramillo's followers were persecuted, kidnapped, tortured, and assassinated by the judicial police and the gunmen hired by the manager of the refinery.[11] Under those circumstances an armed clash with Jaramillo's supporters was unavoidable. In August 1946, in an attempt on Jaramillo's life followed by a shootout in the village of Panchimalco, just south of Jojutla, the army was called out and Rubén again fled to the hills. He had no intention of leading another armed uprising, but he had to defend himself against the government and he needed to replenish both arms and ammunition. Thus, on 12 December, he and his men entered the village of Quilamula on the far side of the Chinameca River – the scene of his earlier actions – and disarmed the Rural Defense. After that, and until 1951 when he again prepared to run for governor, the task of clandestinely reorganizing the party became his chief concern.

Jaramillo's most important action during this period was the support he gave in 1948 to the striking workers at the refinery.[12] Having succeeded in removing the old managerial clique and their hired killers, the workers called on Rubén for help when the new manager resisted their demands and confronted them with gunmen of his own. Jaramillo sent his men to back up the workers, and he organized the peasants to demonstrate as well. Workers and peasants presented their demands together in huge assemblies. When a series of partial work stoppages failed to produce results, the workers struck and occupied the factory. With Rubén's support, they also armed themselves. Federal troops intervened, but bloodshed was averted when the workers surrendered and a compromise was reached.

Jaramillo's Second Armed Uprising

The 1952 election also had its aftermath of official terrorism and repression, except that this time Jaramillo resolved to fight the government. In 1952 the PAOM joined the Federation of People's Parties organized by General Miguel Henríquez Guzmán, who campaigned to wrest the presidency from the official party. But the Institutional Revolutionary Party (PRI) assured its victory through the traditional electoral fraud. Henríquez's followers were then hounded and persecuted with the objective of breaking up the popular organizations that had supported him. Under the new governor of Morelos, a rash of political assassinations broke out in which the victims' corpses were dumped along the highways as a means of terrorizing the local population. The brunt of the repression in Morelos centered on Jaramillo and his party. When the protests of the Henriquistas fell on deaf ears, they organized a junta in which delegations from the various states resolved to confront the government's violence with a generalized insurrection. Their plan called for a simultaneous armed uprising in the states of Sonora, Chihuahua, Michoacán, Querétaro, Hidalgo, Veracruz, Oaxaca, Guerrero, and Morelos. Rubén was party to the proceedings. The date set for the uprising was 4 October 1953.[13]

With the backing of the Henriquistas in Morelos, Rubén planned to concentrate his forces on taking the state capital, Cuernavaca. At the same time, a contingent of 350 men under the command of a Jaramillista sympathizer from Guerrero had promised Rubén to take Jojutla and Zacatepec. Jaramillo's followers from the outlying villages of Alpuyeca, Atlacholoaya, and adjacent towns regrouped approximately 1 km north of Zacatepec, near the village of Tetelapa. There about 40 of them waited for the signal to go into action. Although the power plant was taken, they waited in vain. Their man from Guerrero never arrived. Later they learned that the plan had been discovered and the uprising had been called off. They returned to their separate homes.[14]

A similar situation transpired outside Cuernavaca. Early on the night of 4 October, Gorgonio Alonso, at the head of a band of about

47

20 Jaramillistas, seized the police station in his home town of Emiliano Zapata and marched from there on Jiutepec. There they also captured the strategic centers, but by this time the government in Cuernavaca had become alerted to the attack. After reaching the outskirts of Cuernavaca near the town of Atlacomulco, they waited for Rubén before assaulting the penitentiary. While Gorgonio's men assembled at the southern entrance to Atlacomulco, Rubén's men were waiting near the eastern end. The timing was perfect, but the place was indefinite. Through a twist of fate, they missed each other.

At the same time, other groups of Jaramillistas had been directed to seize the government palace, the offices of the judicial police, the telephone and telegraph exchanges. These reinforcements never arrived. On entering Cuernavaca, Alonso's group ran into federal troops and had to disperse. For three days, Gorgonio hid in a *barranca* (gorge) northeast of the city. Then he took refuge in the nation's capital and did not return home until five years later – when Jaramillo and his followers were amnestied through the efforts of the new president-designate, Adolfo López Mateos.

Rubén again went into hiding. But he emerged at the head of 30 guerrillas to attack the village of Ticumán on 7 March 1954. After a quick trial in the central plaza, they executed the town's mayor, the chief of police, and two merchants accused of having participated in the sadistic torture of a local peasant. They had sliced off the soles of his feet and then, to the rhythm of outbursts of laughter and shrieks of pain, had him railroaded out of town. Jaramillo's men also kidnapped Pablo Carrera, a counsellor of the sugar refinery. (In a later action, they kidnapped the refinery's inspector, Angel Abundis, collecting a ransom of 30,000 pesos.)[15]

Jaramillo then marched south with the aim of taking to the hills near Zapata's former headquarters in Tlaltizapán. On the way, his men expropriated the provisions they needed from a local merchant, but in their flight they carelessly abandoned the emptied cans of preserved food. Further south, in the vicinity of El Higuerón, a platoon of soldiers caught up with them. The soldiers were ambushed before they were able to alight from their truck. Approximately 20 of them died in the ambush, the only survivors being a nephew of the previous governor and the platoon's captain, José Martínez, who was badly wounded. Rubén decided to spare their lives in an act of generosity he would have cause to regret. (The captain got his revenge in 1962 when, after kidnapping Rubén, his wife, and three children from their home in Tlaquiltenango, he brutally murdered them in cold blood beside the ruins of the ancient city of Xochicalco.)[16]

During this second armed uprising, Rubén did not confine his actions to the other side of the Chinameca River, but moved throughout the state of Morelos protected by his followers organized in the PAOM. Fifteen thousand of them! They served as his eyes and ears, alerting him to the movements of the army and the judicial police. For a time, his men hid out in the mountains of Tepoztlán and Amatlán, in the northern part of the state. In an interview with Arnulfo Cano, former chief of police in nearby Jiutepec, we were told that Jaramillo stayed in his house with 20 other guerrillas for almost two months. The quarters were cramped, but they served Rubén as his temporary headquarters. There delegations from different parts of Morelos would come to visit him to formulate plans and to discuss strategies for carrying on the resistance to the government. He had another base of operations in Tetelcingo, a few miles east of Cuautla. He also sought to organize sympathizers in other states. Thus, during this period, as during his 1946–51 efforts to elude persecution, Rubén combined legal with illegal forms of resistance.[17]

The government did not take Jaramillo's second uprising lightly. President Ruiz Cortines deployed against him both mechanized units and cavalry, supported by artillery and the air force. Bent on exterminating the guerrillas, he offered neither amnesty nor safe conducts until persuaded to do so by the 1958 president-designate, López Mateos. It was López Mateos who reversed the government's former policy by guaranteeing the security of Jaramillo and his men, by promising to resolve the problems of the cane growers in Morelos, and by nominally agreeing to support Rubén's project for colonizing the plains of Michapa and El Guarín with thousands of landless peasants.

During the political campaign which preceded his election in July 1958, López Mateos met Rubén for the purpose of getting his support. Persuaded by López Mateos' declarations of solidarity with the peasants, Rubén agreed to campaign in his favor. For a brief moment in 1958, Jaramillo found acceptance among members of the ruling party. But his friendship with the president-designate did not last. By the end of the year it had turned into animosity.

From Defending Cane Growers to Organizing Land Occupations

In his appointed role as a special delegate to the League of Agrarian Communities, which had been arranged by the president-designate, and in his new job as supervisor in his native state of the elections of delegates representing the communal villages (*ejidos*), Jaramillo again threatened the interests of the political bosses and the manager of the refinery.[18] The *ejido* delegates or commissioners constituted the peasants' principal lever in their effort to control the administration. The struggle for these positions could be decisive in putting an end to the usurpation of powers and the series of frauds that had transformed the factory's managers into autocrats as well as millionaires. Accordingly, Rubén aimed his strategy at winning these positions for his followers.

The so-called "election" of members of the administrative council of the Emiliano Zapata Cooperative of Workers, Peasants, and Employees violated the most elementary principles of democracy. Its members were not elected directly in general assemblies of workers or peasants, but indirectly by the *ejido* commissioners themselves. On the appointed day, the management would invite them to dinner at a hotel such as the Riviera in nearby Tehuiztla, with plenty of drinks and women to entertain them, and including gifts of money. The next day, the manager would ask them to confirm his own list of candidates. In effect, the delegates were bribed, and their own corruption reinforced that of the management – a vicious circle with no escape except through a change of representatives.

When Rubén succeeded in placing 16 of his followers as *ejido* commissioners, both the manager of the refinery and the governor became alerted to the danger. Their alert turned to alarm when Rubén publicly supported the peasants of the cooperative who demanded an increase in the price of cane. First he helped to organize a committee of struggle to defend their rights; then he began preparing a massive assembly to present their demands. When López Mateos learned of these developments, he asked that Rubén cancel the proposed assembly and stop making trouble.

Jaramillo refused to comply. In a last effort, the governor of Morelos sought an interview with Jaramillo in which he offered, on behalf of management, a gift of 1,500,000 pesos, a residence wherever he wished, and the latest model car on condition that he retire from the struggle. Jaramillo turned down the offer, and the assembly convened on the same day, 2 November 1958. The manager was tried *in absentia* for a series of abuses and errors in administration, for mishandling funds, and for complicity in the assassination of members of the cooperative. Other demonstrations followed, and the peasants refused to cut and deliver cane. López Mateos broke off relations with Rubén. The peasants' cries for justice fell on deaf presidential ears with one exception: the old manager was replaced with a new one.

Next to his defense of the cane growers at the refinery, Rubén's most important action in support of the peasants of Morelos was his project for settlement in the plains of Michapa and El Guarín.[19] Situated at the extreme western end of the state, these lands covered with rocks seemed unsuited to cultivation. But because they lay in the basin of the Amacuzac river with possibilities for irrigating them, a group of millionaires began laying plans to convert them into residential farmlands. Among the millionaires supporting this project were Eugenio Prado, a former manager of the refinery, and ex-President Miguel Alemán. The cattle ranchers in the area held titles to a part of these lands under the false pretext of constituting a half-dozen or so communal villages, and they also stood to profit from the project. The rest belonged to authentic *ejidos* which were not cultivating them because the cattle ranchers had taken de facto possession and would not permit the peasants to work them.

When the peasants of the *ejidos* decided to parcel out and begin cultivating a portion of these tracts, they ran into opposition from the cattle ranchers and the *ejido* commissioners in their pay. At that point early in 1959, they turned to Rubén for help. He agreed on condition that they join a united front with his own followers and landless peasants throughout Morelos with the aim of settling the entire valley. Thus the project received the backing of his Agrarian Labor Party.

In conformity with the prevailing agrarian code, Jaramillo organized the peasants into a group called the Unified Peasants of Morelos and began negotiations with the Department of Agrarian Affairs and Colonization (DAAC) – today the Secretariat of Agrarian Reform (SRA) – for establishing a new settlement of approximately 6,000 families. The projected colony of Otilio Montaño would begin by cultivating 24,000 hectares of virgin land to be parceled out in lots of 4 hectares per family. Accordingly, 80,000 pesos in contributions was raised to have those lands surveyed and their boundaries demarcated by the DAAC, while another 150,000 pesos had to be collected to "persuade" González Lascano, a high functionary of this department, to do his job and to have the project legalized.

Afterwards two assemblies were convoked with representatives of the local *ejidos* and the owners of the uncultivated lands, in accordance with legal requirements: one on 17 May and the other on 23 August 1959. The peasants supported Rubén's project, but the cattle ranchers refused to participate in the proceedings, thus ceding to Jaramillo and his followers the legal right to occupy the lands in question.

In February 1960 the first occupation occurred, involving some 1,000 landless peasants, 800 of whom were armed. They began the work of clearing rocks and building houses. But the ranchers countered with a campaign of intimidation aimed at expelling them. Local peasants were organized and paid to protest the so-called "invasions." Under pressure from the ranchers, the head of the DAAC appealed to Jaramillo to remove his people until the process of legalizing the settlement could be completely resolved. Rubén and his followers complied, but some of the peasants stayed on. The ranchers took over, burning down the houses that had been built and driving out the peasants by force.

Shortly after Jaramillo withdrew his people, the DAAC reversed its earlier decision favoring his project. Rubén attempted to interview President López Mateos to get his support, but the President refused to see him. A year passed before his followers became impatient with the legal obstacles and decided to reoccupy the lands they had been promised. In February 1961, a second land "invasion" began, this one led by 600 peasants of the 3,000 enlisted in the project. Others soon joined them. Gorgonio Alonso assembled a truckload of peasants from Emiliano Zapata, and Arnulfo Cano another truckload from Jiutepec.[20] Across the state, peasants belonging to Rubén's Agrarian Labor Party began descending on the plains of Michapa and El Guarín. This time, the army intervened to eject them.

Jaramillo's Assassination

Jaramillo did not give up the struggle to found his colony, but continued pressing for a legal resolution in Mexico City. But by then his project had become a threat not only to the big landowners in the area, but also to the political authorities. We must not forget that the federal government intervened directly in removing the settlers. It had good reason for doing so. Jaramillo and his peasants had succeeded in questioning the government's commitment to reform and the basis of its popular support. By choosing to operate within the legal system, Rubén had exposed the government's hypocrisy and resistance to social change. That he had twice won the elections for governor in Morelos might be disputed because only the government had access to the final count. But nobody could deny the peasants' right to land under the Constitution and the provisions of the Agrarian Reform. Because Jaramillo's example was extremely contagious, the Supreme Government could no longer tolerate it.

Rubén had not only soiled the populist image of the left-of-center President, but was also guilty of insubordination. He had disobeyed López Mateos' orders not to intervene in the dispute at the Zacatepec refinery, and he had refused to wait for the president's authorization before settling the plains of Michapa and El Guarín. He also threatened to embarrass the government in connection with President John Kennedy's proposed visit to Mexico in June 1962. Rubén intended to ask for credits from the Alliance for Progress to promote the economic development of his new center of population. The agrarian leader had already enlisted thousands of peasants in Zacatepec to petition the US President for aid on the day arranged for him to visit the refinery.[21]

The political authorities also fretted over Jaramillo's projected trip to Cuba at the personal invitation of Fidel Castro. There they expected him to receive not only economic aid for his colony, but also military training for his supporters. On his return to Mexico, he might become an even worse headache for the government. His charismatic personality and simple but fiery speech might easily mobilize the peasants to armed resistance. With his experience as a guerrilla leader, his intimate knowledge of the terrain in his native state of Morelos, and unconditional peasant support, he was in a position to lead a movement of national liberation.

At the time, the international political conjuncture favored the emergence of guerrillas throughout all of Latin America. In January 1962, at the historic meeting in Punta del Este, Cuba was expelled

53

from the Organization of American States (OAS). A week later, on 4 February, Fidel Castro replied with the Second Declaration of Havana, exhorting all the peoples of Latin America to armed resistance against US imperialism.[22] Under those circumstances Jaramillo stood out as a dangerous threat to the system of presidential despotism.

Jaramillo's increasing identification with the Cuban Revolution was cause for positive alarm. In April 1962, in a public meeting in Cuernavaca's *zocalo* or central plaza, he had openly expressed his support for Fidel Castro and Cuban socialism. This was not an isolated act. Early in 1961, anticipating a US invasion such as the one that later occurred at the Bay of Pigs, he and Mónico Rodríguez had organized meetings of solidarity with the Cuban people, in Morelos and in the neighboring state of México. We know that Rubén was planning to visit the Alligator Island because at that time Mónico's wife Adalberta had gone to the town of Zacualpan in the state of México to get the necessary documents for Rubén's passport. In October she made a trip to Mexico City to solicit the return of Jaramillo and 220 of his men into the ranks of the Communist Party. A month later they were accepted. Thus Rubén's sympathies for the socialism of Fidel Castro found further expression in his renewed identification with the communist movement in Mexico.[23]

Evidently, the official party considered Jaramillo to be a far more dangerous man in 1962 than it had in 1943 and again in 1953, when he actually led movements of armed resistance. Since there was now reason to believe that Rubén's trouble-making was directed mainly against the government, it seriously questioned whether he had a right to live! The first attempts against his life had come from gunmen hired by the manager at the refinery of Zacatepec, with the help of the judicial police and the governor of Morelos. Only later had the army become involved, but always in a supporting role. Henceforth, the initiative would come from the Supreme Government.

On 23 May 1962 Jaramillo's house in Tlaquiltenango was surrounded by a group of 60 soldiers and members of the judicial police who had arrived in two army trucks and accompanying jeeps. A machine gun was placed at the entrance and another in the rear. When Rubén resisted, soldiers broke into the house and seized him. Because his wife and three sons insisted on going with him, they too were forced into a waiting car. Hours later their riddled corpses were discovered near the ancient ruins of Xochicalco.[24]

Who had given the order for the executions? Captain José Martínez had led the surprise attack supported by Heriberto Espinosa, head of the state's judicial police. An official investigation of the crime led to the temporary detention and questioning of Captain Martínez, after which he received another promotion. (His first promotion had come in reward for earlier actions against the Jaramillistas.) Months later, in the village of Teloloapan, Guerrero, near the Morelos border, the two of them were kidnapped and questioned by Jaramillo's supporters concerning the real perpetrators of the crime. Before being executed they were tortured to the point of confessing. The orders for Rubén's assassination had come from the Attorney General of the Republic, Fernando López Arias, from the Minister of Defense, General Agustín Olachea, and from the President's private secretary, Humberto Romero.[25]

Was this confession, extracted under duress, at all credible? Rubén's daughter Raquel had escaped from the house on that fatal day to seek the help of the town's mayor. He refused to intervene because, in his words: "We cannot do anything; it is an order from the District Attorney's Office in Mexico, and everything is according to the law."[26] Reporters for the newspaper *La Prensa* later discovered that 10 agents of the federal police under orders from the District Attorney had in fact gone to Tlaquiltenango for the purpose of arresting Rubén. It appears that they directed the entire operation.

The Jaramillista Legacy

A similar fate befell Rubén's brother Porfirio, who had been assassinated some years earlier. A leader of the Jaramillista movement and of the PAOM in the neighboring state of Puebla, he had joined the Communist Party with his brother back in 1938. But he was known to be a better communist than Rubén and did not drop out the following year. Parallel with Rubén's struggle in Morelos, Porfirio struggled to organize the cane growers at the sugar refinery of Atlixco near the town of Atencingo, Puebla. Unlike the cooperative at Zacatepec, it belonged to William Jenkins, a former US consul in Mexico. When Porfirio succeeded in imposing his own council of administration, he entered into a frontal collision with Jenkins, who sought to recover control. The government then intervened by appointing a federal commission to manage the refinery. Since the Jaramillistas resisted this direct intervention by the state, Porfirio ended by confronting the political authorities. He continued agitating among the peasants until in February 1955 he was kidnapped from a hotel in Mexico City and murdered in cold blood. In this case the assassins were Jenkins' gunmen.[27]

The objective circumstances that led to the Jaramillista movement were not peculiar to Morelos: corruption in the public and private administrations of the sugar refineries; open robbery in weighing and paying for the peasants' cane and rice; cultivators without land and land without cultivators; political gangsterism on the part of the state authorities; and systematic repression of the people's leaders by hired gunmen, by the judicial police, and by the army. But while these conditions were present elsewhere, the subjective conditions were not. This explains why Jaramillo's movement did not spread beyond the states immediately bordering on Morelos, and why only in this state a broad movement of peasant self-defense took fire. What Morelos had and the other states lacked was a strong Zapatista tradition for revolutionaries like Rubén to build on. He had at his disposal what other agrarian leaders lacked: a people imbued with the collective experience and ideology of resistance to government repression. This legacy, of which the people of Morelos are the principal heirs, received a new infusion of blood from the new Zapata and his Agrarian Labor Party.

Notes

1. Rubén Jaramillo, *Autobiografía*, in idem, *Autobiografía*, y Froylán C. Manjarrez, *La matanza de Xochicalco* (Mexico City: Nuestro Tiempo, 1967), pp. 15, 21, 23–6; Anon, *Rubén Jaramillo: Vida y luchas de un dirigente campesino (1900–1962)* (n.p., n.d.), pp. 10–12; and Hodges' interviews with Isabel Jaramillo, widow of Rubén's oldest brother Antonio, at her home in Tlaquiltenango, Morelos, 20 July 1975, on Rubén's early life and revolutionary background.
2. Jaramillo, *Autobiografía*, pp. 31–3, 40–3.
3. Based on Hodges' interview with Mónico Rodríguez, Rubén's close companion, at his workshop in Chiconcuac, Morelos, 27 July 1975.
4. Jaramillo, *Autobiografía*, pp. 44–8. The substance of this chapter follows closely the account in Chapter 3 of Juan Vargas Sánchez and Donald C. Hodges, "La resistencia popular en México 1940–1976" (unpublished *licenciado* thesis, UNAM, 1986).
5. Jaramillo, *Autobiografía*, pp. 50–51; and Hodges' interview with María de Jesús

Sánchez Palma, wife of Reyes Jaramillo, Rubén's younger brother, at their home in Tlaquiltenango, Morelos, 20 July 1975.

6. Jaramillo, *Autobiografía*, p. 51.
7. For the following data on Jaramillo's first armed uprising, we have relied on Hodges' interview with Aurora Herrera Jaramillo, widow of his older brother Porfirio, at her home in Jiutepec, Morelos, 23 July 1975. Among secondary sources, see Raúl Macín, *Jaramillo: un profeta olvidado* (Montevideo, Uruguay: Tierra Nueva, 1970), pp. 41–120; and Renato Ravelo, *Los jaramillistas* (Mexico City: Nuestro Tiempo, 1978), pp. 51–81. For Jaramillo's extended account of the events, see his *Autobiografía*, pp. 53–91.
8. There were two plans of Cerro Prieto, the original one distributed at the end of February or beginning of March 1943 (see Jaramillo, *Autobiografía*, p. 77) and a second plan included in the Appendix. The first plan has been irretrievably lost.
9. Jaramillo, *Autobiografía*, pp. 92–6.
10. Ibíd., pp. 102–8; and Anon., *Rubén Jaramillo*, pp. 26–32.
11. Jaramillo, *Autobiografía*, pp. 110–15. The autobiography breaks off in December 1946.
12. The following account of the struggle at the refinery is based on Mónico Rodríguez' recollections. From Hodges' interview at Rodríguez' workshop in Chiconcuac, Morelos, 12 December 1977.
13. Enrique Quiles Ponce, *Henríquez y Cárdenas ¡Presentes! Hechos y realidades de la campaña henriquista* (Mexico City: Costa Amic, 1980), pp. 215–25, 272–89.
14. Ravelo, *Los jaramillistas*, pp. 121–33.
15. Hodges' interviews with participants in the armed uprising: with Gregorio Alonso at his store in Emiliano Zapata, Morelos, 13 July 1975; and with Arnulfo Cano in the central plaza of Jiutepec, Morelos, 23 July 1975. On the assault on Jiutepec, see Quiles Ponce, *Henríquez y Cárdenas*, p. 292.
16. Froylan C. Manjarrez, *La matanza de Xochicalco*, in Jaramillo, *Autobiografía*, y Manjarrez, *La Matanza de Xochicalco*, pp. 140–2, 145.
17. Hodges' interview with Arnulfo Cano in the central plaza of Jiutepec, Morelos, 23 July 1975.
18. Data provided by Mónico Rodríguez at his workshop at Chiconcuac, Morelos, 12 December 1977.
19. On the Michapa and El Guarín land invasions, see Manjarrez, *La matanza*, pp. 147–52; and Anon., *Rubén Jaramillo*, pp. 33–9.
20. Data based on the interviews with Arnulfo Cano, 23 July 1975 and Gregorio Alonso, 13 July 1975 – participants in the land invasions who gave us their eyewitness accounts. For a secondary source, see Ravelo, *Los jaramillistas*, pp. 168–86.
21. Testimony of Mónico Rodríguez at his workshop, 27 July 1975.
22. Fidel Castro, *The Duty of a Revolutionary is to Make the Revolution: The Second Declaration of Havana*, in Martin Kenner and James Petras, eds, *Fidel Castro Speaks* (New York: Grove Press, 1969), p. 104.
23. Ibid. On Jaramillo's reputed sympathies for Fidel Castro and the Cuban Revolution, see the press interview at the beginning of 1961 cited in Manjarrez, *La matanza*, pp. 128–31, 142–5.
24. Manjarrez, *La matanza*, pp. 128–31, 142–5.
25. Ibid., p. 146; and Mario Guerra Leal, *La grilla* (Mexico City: Diana, 1979), p. 178.
26. Manjarrez, *La matanza*, p. 130.
27. David Ronfeldt, *Atencingo: La política de la lucha agraria en un ejido mexicano* (Mexico City: Fondo de Cultura Económica, 1975), pp. 151–3.

4 ⊛ The Revolutionary
Teachers' Strike of 1958

On 6 September 1938, the Mexican government formed the Federation of Workers at the Service of the State (FTSE), which later would be called the Federation of Unions of Workers at the Service of the State (FSTSE). The government did not permit the federal teachers, who were state workers, to join industrial unions or peasant leagues; they were supposed to merge with the new federation of bureaucrats.[1] This plan was carried out during the term of Avila Camacho in 1943. The teachers were integrated into the FSTSE through a single giant organization – the National Union of Educational Workers (SNTE).

In 1915 the sociologist Robert Michels concluded that organization breeds oligarchy, a tendency expressed clearly in the trade union movements of the twentieth century.[2] Between the SNTE's foundation in 1943 and 1958, a powerful group of bureaucrats formed a permanent clot in its heart, diminishing the flow of influence from the base toward the leadership. In Mexico the result of the process of bureaucratization was a disaster because the SNTE belonged to the FSTSE, which in turn belonged to the National Confederation of Popular Organizations (CNOP), and the CNOP was a sector of the ruling Partido Revolucionario Institucional (PRI). The PRI was betraying the Mexican Revolution and relied on the union of teachers (SNTE) to control them. Increasingly, union leaders were sucked into compromises with various state functionaries, resulting in the slow but steady corruption of the union leadership.

"Decency and morality are the watchwords of the nation," said Ruiz Cortines on 2 December 1951. Between 1952 and 1958, these famous words were the slogan of the honest president. They made the

58

teachers in the capital smile bitterly in the last years of Cortines' term, for the corruption in Section IX of the SNTE was intolerable.[3]

The Revolutionary Teachers' Movement

The Revolutionary Teachers' Movement (MRM) was the answer of the teachers at the base to the collaborationist behavior, the corrupt conduct, and the gangster methods of the leadership. The MRM arose in the middle of the 1950s as a spontaneous movement of the great mass of teachers in the Federal District; it was an effort to blow some democratic life into the union. It was a resistance to the corporativism of the SNTE–FSTSE–CNOP–PRI. The teachers at the base, trapped in the cage of the corporative organizations, struggled to escape. From the beginning, the basic demands were the democratization of the union and a salary raise, but there was also discussion of returning to the popular orientation of education prevalent in the Cárdenas period. Current educational policy reflected the freezing of the Mexican Revolution.

In April 1958, Professor Othón Salazar Ramírez, a charismatic leader of the MRM who had dropped out of the Communist Youth but later joined the PCM in the early 1960s, led a teachers' demonstration to the great central plaza in Mexico City – the *Zócalo*. The meeting demanded a salary raise of 40 per cent: prices had risen year after year, while the acquisitive power of the teachers had grown more slowly. The police attacked and broke up the demonstration; this repression was a violation of the right to assembly. Great shouts of protest went up from the parents of schoolchildren, from the students at the Normal School and the National University, and from political organizations such as the Mexican Communist Party.[4]

When the police repression of the MRM occurred during the demonstration on 5 April, our informant Mónico Rodríguez happened to be in the area. Noting that some of the teachers had taken refuge in a building on Bolívar Street, he joined them while they waited for the police persecution to end. Making use of the small auditorium in the building, he identified himself and proposed that they seek support from the schoolchildren's parents, offering to make the necessary contacts in the schools where the teachers had sympathizers.[5]

Mónico Rodríguez

Among the uncelebrated heroes of the working class, Mónico Rodríguez deserves a place as the principal link between Jaramillo and the trade union sector of the resistance. From Jaramillo he learned a particular style of work. He learned that one must acquire the people's esteem before attempting to influence them politically; that it is imperative to share in the miseries and tribulations of workers in order to win their confidence; that agitation is more effective among friends and neighbors than among strangers; that propaganda seldom works through direct exhortation; that it is most effective when applied not all at once but in small doses, one at a time, in a sustained effort; that one must speak the people's language and even appear to think as they do; and that one must adopt a populist rather than an openly communist line in order to be convincing.

During the 1950s Mónico became one of the Communist Party's most popular and effective professional organizers. For the sake of credibility he kept his membership in the Party a secret to those outside it. Jaramillo stopped paying dues and gradually separated himself from the Party when it became apparent that his membership had become more of a liability than an asset in his work of orientation and organization, mainly because of Party interference. And Mónico did the same in 1957 when it became evident that the Party's meddling in his organizing had become self-defeating.

Unlisted as yet in the social register of the resistance, Mónico's work was as big as his notoriety was small. His first major contribution was to organize the workers at the Sugar Refinery of Zacatepec during 1939–42, paving the way for the ensuing strike for which Jaramillo got most of the glory. Later, in 1955–56, he mobilized on a national scale nearly 100,000 railroad workers in defense of their jobs, thereby preparing the conditions for the great strikes of 1958–59, for which Campa and Vallejo alone received acclaim. Finally, he organized and mobilized almost 100,000 parents of schoolchildren in support of the teachers' strike in 1958 and the month-long occupation of the Secretariat of Public Education, for which Othón Salazar took the credit.

What were his antecedents? Mónico was born in Torreón, Coahuila, in 1919. His father was a mechanic who later moved to

Tampico, Tamaulipas, and was there recruited into the CP in 1928 by the charismatic Melquiades Tobías – organizer of the first oil workers' union in Tampico. Mónico came to Zacatepec, Morelos, in 1936 as a machinist commissioned to work for the refinery when it opened in March 1938.

There he met and became a close friend and associate of Jaramillo, who shared his political interests. Both acted mainly under the influence of Ricardo Flores Magón's *Libertarian Seed* – an anarchist tract – but they were not long in turning to Marxism. That same year they joined a political study group at the refinery and were recruited into the PCM by the group's leader Francisco Ruíz. A few years earlier Ruíz and Porfirio Jaramillo, who had joined the Party before returning to Morelos in 1938, had organized the Karl Marx Trade Union at the Sugar Refinery at Atencingo.

Once the union gained governmental recognition, Mónico began pressing for higher wages in conjunction with Rubén's demands for better prices for the peasants' cane. Although in 1941 the Party gave unqualified support to President Avila Camacho's policy of national unity and to the CTM's call for a strike moratorium during the Second World War, Mónico continued agitating among the workers. A rousing speaker and an able organizer, he went his own way and led the workers out on strike when the manager refused to comply with their demands. The Party looked the other way. It hesitated to discipline him because it needed his organizing talents and contacts with the masses. Independent, like Campa, Rodríguez became a professional organizer for the PCM in 1949 and continued in that capacity for eight years until efforts to expel him led to his successful self-defense before a Party tribunal in 1957.

In 1958 Mónico left the Party, disgusted by the treatment he had received and disillusioned by its supercilious disregard for mass work. Although no longer one of the Party faithful, he continued to agitate among the workers as an independent communist. But unlike Campa, he did not rejoin the PCM to be rewarded in later years by an official revaluation of his work and by election to high office as the Party's representative in the nation's congress. As one of its unrecognized militants, he contributed more than his share to building the resistance movement but went unrewarded for his efforts. Glad to be rid of him, the Party abandoned him to his fate until in January 1978 Campa tried to induce him to return. But the rewards were too late in coming, his family discouraged him from rejoining, he still questioned the Party's self-serving tendencies, and he refused to be bought. None the less, he volunteered to assist the Party in an independent capacity during its national membership drive in 1978, during the congressional elections in 1979, and in its trade union work in the state of Morelos.

Launching the Teachers' Strike

When the MRM responded to the police repression with a call upon teachers in the capital for a general strike, Mónico cast his lot with theirs as a private person and parent with schoolchildren of his own. Although no longer a professional organizer for the PCM, he continued his organizing activities supported by his trade as a machinist. The day after the strike exploded on 16 April, there was a meeting of teachers and parents during which Mónico was elected as the right hand of Sr Canales, a member of the conservative National Action Party (PAN) and also the president of the Parents' Front. At this meeting it was agreed that there should be a demonstration at the Monument to the Revolution near the end of April. Rodríguez organized gatherings of the parents and formed groups of teachers to ask for solidarity from workers' and students' organizations.[6]

Soon 90 per cent of the official primary schools of Mexico City were on strike. Meanwhile Enrique M. Sánchez, general secretary of the SNTE, attacked the MRM, accusing it of being a group of professional agitators. According to this compromised union bureaucrat, the movement did not arise from the just demands and economic needs of the federal workers, but was the result of agitation by communist nuclei. In the press, anti-communism blossomed like an evil flower. The SNTE decided that Othón Salazar had unconsciously formed part of a subversive plan.[7]

This campaign did not deceive many. Much more dangerous was the maneuver of the Secretariat of Public Education (SEP), which refused to deal with the teachers' movement because it could not negotiate with "groups that were not legally recognized." But this argument was not successful either, and it became clear that the government was not entirely neutral. On 25 April, the MRM delivered to the SEP the teachers' petition: a 40 per cent raise, supplemental salary with bonus, and 60 pesos per month for travel expenses to and from work.[8]

Occupation of the Secretariat of Public Education

At the end of April, while most of the primary schools were still paralysed, the planned meeting at the Monument to the Revolution took place. During the meeting, some 7,000 demonstrators resolved to march to the SEP to pressure the government educational authorities who had refused to receive Othón Salazar. At two o'clock in the afternoon they forcibly took possession of the SEP's headquarters.[9]

Eighty teachers proposed that the MRM mount a permanent guard in the SEP building until the peaceful resolution of the problem. Salazar began to speak, and the huge courtyard surged with excited and exultant people. At the end of his speech, he announced the proposal of the 80 teachers, urged on by Mónico, who favored direct action. The great mass approved the idea of a permanent guard. On this occasion, Salazar received his nickname: "the little giant."

Mónico Rodríguez helped teachers, parents, and workers build a sort of shanty town in the blockwide courtyard of the SEP. Immediately a headcount was made – 2,000 people were present. Committees were organized to spread word of the strike, to take care of sick people, to set up cooking stands, and to send out brigades to collect money. At midnight the little giant asked the teachers to sing the national anthem.

The various brigades and committees, created spontaneously, came and went through a secret entrance opening on González Obregón Street. The people occupying the SEP slept in tents in an orderly and disciplined fashion, a teacher in one, a parent in another, and a worker in a third. Rodríguez testified that he left the courtyard only once during the first month.

The newspapers carried all these events as front page news on the day after the seizure. Meanwhile, the teachers continued their encampment under the famous revolutionary murals of Diego Rivera, demanding that the authorities grant them a hearing. Every day delegations arrived that declared their solidarity with the teachers. Entire families of poor people joined the camp in the great quadrangle while committees for food and medical aid tended to the needs of those within. Donations both in cash and in kind were not long in arriving.

The big daily newspapers unleashed a campaign against "the communist leader Othón Salazar." They made fun of the "gypsy shanty" and "the hangout of lazybones and beggars" in the courtyard of the SEP. There were also notes of alarm because many of the capital's residents had not seen such a sight in years – the poor defying the authorities.

The teachers knew their rights. Article VIII of the Constitution says:

> Public functionaries and employees will respect the exercise of the right of petition, provided that it is formulated in writing and presented in a peaceful and respectful manner.... Every petition must receive an answer from the authority to which it has been directed, and said authority is required to make it known within a short time.

The Constitution had been violated, for the SEP had refused to respond to a petition, the striking teachers declared. But Article VIII was interpreted differently by the authorities, so that "there was nothing extraordinary in the refusal by the Secretary of Education to receive Othón Salazar."[10]

The atmosphere in the SEP courtyard was one of comradeship and dedication to the struggle: democracy had invaded the solid and enormous walls of the government. Could it be allowed to continue? There was a possibility of contagion; other trade unions were becoming restless. The manifestations of solidarity with the movement revealed the accumulated discontent in many social strata. Side by side with the teachers were to be found groups of unemployed people, peasants from the capital's immediate environs, electrical workers, railwaymen, oil workers, and students from the National University and the National Polytechnic School. Might not the MRM detonate a social explosion?

The President of the Republic decided to negotiate with the teachers. On 10 May talks opened between the Secretary of the President and the representatives of the MRM, while the SEP remained silent.[11] The teachers refused to return to their classrooms until their demands were met, and once more rose the voices of those accusing the Communist Party of subverting the country.

There followed an extremely clever political maneuver on the part of the President. While the talks between the MRM and the Secretary of the President were in progress, Ruiz Cortines presided over the celebration of Teachers' Day in the Palace of Fine Arts, accompanied by the general secretary of the SNTE, Enrique W. Sánchez. President Cortines announced a salary raise for all teachers in Mexico effective 1 July. The raise turned out to be a 17 per cent increase. It reinforced the image of the President as the father of the nation and the incarnation of justice, while the SEP appeared as a hard-hearted bureaucracy which would not even receive a petition. The primary schoolteachers in the capital won part of their demands, but the revolutionary union remained in its condition of illegitimacy.[12]

The MRM decided to continue the strike. It would be difficult, since vacation time was drawing near and salaries had risen. But neither the strike nor the occupation of the SEP would be lifted, said the MRM, until its leaders could have an interview with the President.[13]

The SNTE threatened the teachers with dismissal if they stayed away from classes three more days. There was talk of applying the law against "social dissolution." The strike was slowly weakening. At the beginning of June the MRM decided to lift the occupation of the SEP. On 5 June it ended the strike after two months of struggle, and Othón Salazar invited the teachers to a demonstration in front of the SEP the next day.[14]

Over 40,000 people took part in the great demonstration. Once the problems seemed solved, the President was ready to receive the MRM's leaders. On 6 June they interviewed Ruiz Cortines.[15]

The 6 June demonstration showed the force acquired by the movement. Although the MRM did not achieve legal recognition and remained circumscribed to the Federal District, it came out of the crisis a much strengthened organization. The movement had swept more than 90 per cent of the teachers in the official primary schools into a strike in the capital and had won a 17 per cent salary hike. The teachers interpreted these results as a victory.

The Struggle to Democratize the Teachers' Union

The importance of the MRM's triumph as a showing of popular resistance to the regime lay not only in the satisfaction of its economic demands. The importance of the strike was revealed in its political consequences. The MRM's action had won a raise for all the teachers in the country, and some of them could see the need to democratize their union, the SNTE. The latter struggle would continue. Leading the way, the MRM proposed a change in the rules for Section IX of the union: no member of the Sectional Executive Committee would be able to accept politico-electoral positions without first having renounced his union post, and the re-election of members for consecutive periods would no longer be permitted.

The government, under pressure from the revolutionary movement, was ready to satisfy the economic demands, but the cry for democratic changes called into question the PRI government. The President could not give in easily, and the base of the teachers' movement was exhausted after the partial success of the struggle for the salary raise.

But the MRM knew that it must not lose the momentum acquired by the movement and so began the struggle to win the elections for the Executive Committee of Section IX of the SNTE in the capital. Othón Salazar was elected in August, but the SNTE bureaucracy held another congress in which its candidate Rita Sánchez was elected. Othón Salazar had to get legal recognition from the authorities of the Secretariat of Labor. Rita Sánchez received official approval.[16]

The MRM announced another strike and called a demonstration on 6 September by parents, railwaymen, oil workers, telegraph operators, and the people *en masse*. The police repressed the demonstration and arrested Othón Salazar and the principal leaders of the MRM. No one was killed by the police in the street violence, but several were wounded.[17]

The imprisonment of Othón Salazar and his comrades weakened the MRM for the moment. Some of the teachers on strike were jailed; the rest were threatened with dismissal. Fear spread through the teachers' ranks; many were afraid of losing their jobs. Others chose to return to work because of the salary raise. The September strike did not take hold as had the one in April because a majority of the teachers was not prepared ideologically to continue the struggle in the face of the government's hardening attitude and police repression. The attorney general's office in the Federal District arraigned Salazar and the other leaders for the crime of social dissolution; it accused them of links with international communism and a "conspiracy against the government." In this deft feint the government handed Othón and his friends tickets of admission to prison for a long time. Would the leaders soon disappear behind the grim walls of Lecumberri – the Bastille of Mexico's capital?

The government spoke darkly of more repression, but at the same time the Secretariat of the Interior promised the MRM that if it called off the strike there would be a democratic election in Section IX and that the prisoners would be set free. The MRM ended the strike, and most of the jailed teachers were released. But the Secretariat of Labor refused to recognize Othón as the legal representative of Section IX, and the leaders of the strike remained in prison.

On 19 September the following declaration of the teachers' movement was published in *Excélsior*:

> The MRM believes in the Mexican Revolution and its emancipa-
> tory work and declares that every one of its militants is a soldier of
> that Revolution who should pursue in a peaceful way a better dis-
> tribution of the national income, more bread, housing, and pro-
> tection to the poor, and make great and respectable the Mexican
> Nation.[18]

Far from being a conspiracy against the government, the MRM accused the government of being a conspiracy against the revolution and the Mexican people.

The MRM threatened a new mobilization if all the promises were not fulfilled. A period of negotiations followed. The result was a com-promise: the teachers could elect their leaders, but the imprisoned ones could not be candidates. Consequently, after a massive struggle and a won election, Section IX was at last in the hands of the MRM.[19]

Through the months of October and November, the leaders remained prisoners without trial. It was hardly the first time the Constitution had been raped. Not until the first days of the new President López Mateos did the newspapers proclaim on their front pages that "because of the President's magnanimity the teachers' leaders were at liberty" (4 December 1958). While the 17,000 primary schoolteachers had won another victory, the despot in office presented himself once more as the benefactor of the people, full of the spirit of justice. Six days later, there were more raises in teachers' salaries.[20]

In the growing conflict between the democratic social forces and despotic methods of government, the MRM carried out various actions. It led, for example, a strike lasting 81 days, ending on 31 August 1960, in response to the non-recognition of its Committee of Section IX by the national committee of the SNTE. Although the MRM suffered chronic repression that weakened it, the movement continued to nourish itself on the most combative elements in the teaching profession.

In spite of the efforts of the MRM, the official union managed to maintain itself without any essential changes. Consequently, the MRM had to carry out its main actions outside that structure. Various leaders of the MRM would fall in the struggle, murdered by the repressive forces: Augusto César Manzanaro, leader of the MRM in Jalisco, assassinated by the army in 1971; Joaquín Sánchez, leader in the Tlapa region of Guerrero, murdered by the federal police in that state; Hilario Moreno, leader of Section IX of the Federal District, murdered in one of the dependencies of the chief of police in January 1975. Kidnapped, tortured, "disappeared" – the list is long – but not long enough to persuade the MRM to discontinue its struggle.

Notes

1. Aurora Guadalupe Loyo Brambila, "El conflicto magisterial de 1958 en México" (unpublished *licenciado* thesis, UNAM, 1976), p. 134.
2. Robert Michels, *Political Parties: A Sociological Study of the Oligarchical Tendencies of Modern Democracy*, trans Eden and Cedar Paul (Glencoe, IL: Free Press, 1958; orig. pub. 1915), pp. 312–31.
3. Loyo, "El conflicto magisterial ," p. 130.
4. Ibid., pp. 155, 164–5.
5. The following biographical sketch of our hero is based on oral testimony dating from the first interview by Hodges on 27 July 1975. Among the other memorable visits to Rodríguez's workshop in Chiconcuac, Morelos, we rely on notes from the interviews of 12 December and 21 December 1977.
6. Notes from Hodges' interview with Mónico Rodríguez at his workshop in Chiconcuac, Morelos, 27 July 1975.
7. Loyo, "El conflicto magisterial," pp. 160–2, 164.
8. Ibid., p. 167.
9. This paragraph and those immediately following are from Rodríguez's eyewitness account.

10. Loyo, "El conflicto magisterial," pp. 170–1.
11. Ibid., p. 189.
12. Ibid., pp. 192–3.
13. Ibid., pp. 194–5.
14. Ibid., pp. 195–6, 202–4.
15. Ibid., pp. 205–6.
16. Ibid., pp. 230–2.
17. Ibid., pp. 236–40.
18. Ibid., p. 247; cited by Loyo.
19. Ibid., pp. 252–5, 265–8.
20. Ibid., pp. 268–71.

5 ✸ The Railroad Workers' Strikes of 1958-1959

In order to understand the railwaymen's movement we have to grasp the situation of the railroad systems in earlier years. There was a huge decentralized enterprise belonging to the government: National Railways. And there were three small enterprises also government-owned: Mexican Railways, The Pacific, and Veracruz Terminal.

The railwaymen were more militant than the oil workers because the Union of Railroad Workers of the Mexican Republic (STFRM) contained many Communists. Our informant, Valentín Campa, worked on the railroads from 1922 until the persecution following the 1958–59 strikes. He became the railway union's Secretary of Education in, to the best of his memory, May 1944.

Valentín Campa and Demetrio Vallejo

If Jaramillo was the most popular and the most persecuted leader of the resistance, Campa was next in line.[1] Far from intimidating him, the government's violence made him still more intransigent in his struggle against repression. Like Rubén, Valentín showed the qualities of the new man portrayed by Che Guevara, the inner strength and the indomitable will necessary for revolutionaries to continue working for the people despite official harassment. Again, it is revealing that Valentín came out of the Communist Party.

Consider the tribulations of this notorious labor organizer. Born in Monterrey, Nuevo León, in 1904, he began working for the railroads when he was only 18 years old. He became a national figure because of his struggle against the labor bureaucracy in 1947–8 and then as the leader, along with Demetrio Vallejo, of the big railway strikes of 1958–59. Campa represents a heroic figure within the annals of the resistance movement for his endurance and courage in the face of government terrorism. No labor leader in Mexico had a longer record of imprisonment for standing up to the authorities. Jailed on 12 different occasions under 10 different presidents, he suffered his first sentence between 1949 and 1952, followed by a second long prison term from 1960 to 1970, a total of 14 years as hostage of the Mexican government.

Like Jaramillo, he also ran afoul of the PCM. Having joined the Party in 1927, two years later, at the age of 25, he became the youngest member of its Central Committee. But he refused to be party to Trotsky's assassination, for which the Party finally expelled him along with its secretary-general, Hernán Laborde. Vilified by the Party as a renegade, he did not respond in kind. During his 20 years outside the Party, he steered clear of polemics and public denunciations. He always endeavored to collaborate with it and to engage in common actions with its militants. Only after being indicted and sentenced a second time would he be permitted by the Party to rejoin from his prison cell. This sincere and worthy man became the Party's presidential candidate in 1976.

After his expulsion in 1940, Campa made repeated efforts to return to the Party, but, rebuffed, formed Unified Socialist Action in 1946, followed by a second communist party in 1950, the Worker–Peasant Party of Mexico (POCM). In 1960 this split in the communist movement was finally healed when a majority of the POCM voted to return to, and were welcomed back, by the PCM. Although a minority chose to remain independent, its members joined Lombardo Toledano's Popular Socialist Party (PPS) in 1963 – the successor to his 1948–60 Popular Party (PP).

Demetrio Vallejo too was destined to play an outstanding role in the coming drama. He was born about 1912 in Espinal, a town in Tehuantepec, Oaxaca, and like most people in that economically backward state, he grew up with little formal schooling. He educated himself. In his struggle to change the oppressive society around him, he tended toward "caudillismo" or "leaderism." He became a railworker in 1928, a Communist in 1934, and eventually reached the position of regional director of the PCM in the state of Oaxaca. Expelled in the early 1940s, he joined Unified Socialist Action in 1946 and the POCM in 1950, but after casting the deciding vote to rejoin the PCM in 1960, decided for personal reasons to become independent.

Vallejo, because of his role in organizing the major railway strikes of 1958–59, also suffered a long prison term from 1959 until his release in 1970. Like Campa, he was both incorruptible and self-sacrificing. As an example to other trade union leaders, he renounced his salary of 20,000 pesos a month as a board member of National Railways, a sum due to him under the law. Instead of using it for himself, he requested that it be turned over to the railroad union's treasury. Out of gratitude for his efforts on their behalf, the workers at the Terminal del Valle de México offered to buy him a house in 1959. "He rejected the offer, telling them to use the money for a monument commemorating the struggle in August 1958, a monument symbolic of the railway workers' solidarity" in the first great strike that they won.[2]

Antecedents of the Great Railroad Conflict

The events leading up to the great railroad conflict of 1958–59, in which Campa played a leading role, began with the rehabilitation project aimed at laying off workers in June 1955. The manager of National Railways, Roberto Amorós, wanted to eliminate the activists who were pressuring for a wage hike and fringe benefits. The activists who had assembled in the railway's workshop section issued a summons to the railway workers to throw the compromised bureaucrats out of the union in the Balderas Local in the Federal District. The Communist Party had sent our other informant, Mónico Rodríguez, to work as a mechanic in the workshop for the purpose of organizing Communist cells. During the years leading up to the strike, he was the only party professional to keep up secret contacts with Campa, who had been expelled from the PCM in 1940. He was doing this against the orders of the PCM leadership.

The PCM, therefore, commissioned its general secretary, Dionisio Encina, with Martínez Verdugo, Juan Manuel González, Hugo Ponce de León and Gerardo Unzueta, to take this problem in hand. The Party pushed aside Rodríguez and his co-workers because "they were handling things with their feet."[3] By removing Mónico the PCM lost its camouflage, since he did not operate openly as a party member, while the others did. The immediate result was the denunciation of the participation of Communists in the Railway Union by the union's sell-out bureaucrats. The PCM had made a serious error in interfering in the affairs of the cells already operating under Mónico's leadership. Later, as the railway workers grouped themselves into committees to demand the wage hike, the cell members were forced to apply a line different from that of the Party. Although they had orders not to exchange a word with Campa's group of ex-Communists, the pro-strike current carried them into an alliance with the heretics.

The first strike of 1958 was carried out in National Railways from 26 June to 7 August. Its immediate objective was a wage raise of 350 pesos per week. At the same time, the strikers were struggling for union democracy against the bureaucratic leadership co-opted by President Alemán. Sailing against the wind, the first effort became a triumph for the working class: it obtained a 215-peso raise.[4]

The idea of a pay hike originally arose in February 1958 within Section 15 of the STFRM in the Federal District. A commission proposed a national meeting in order to carry out an economic study to decide the amount of the raise, which turned out to be 150 pesos a month for each worker.[5]

The Great Committee for a Raise was set up on 2 May 1958 in the capital. The president of the Assembly proposed to increase the demand to 350 pesos a month. The general secretary of the sell-out STFRM, Samuel Ortega, threatened the independent delegates of the Great Committee with reprisals. The collective contract would be revised in August of that year, and the compromised union bureaucrats would ask for only a 200-peso raise, the general countersign by which all those willing to play ball with the government would recognize one another.[6]

On 20 May, the independent delegates met union bureaucrats to try to reach an agreement. Demetrio Vallejo told the general secretary that he was opposed to the bureaucracy's making decisions against the base and proposed a preliminary discussion. The proposal for a raise had come out of a collective study based on the real value of 1948 wages, not from the whim of the delegates who had been elected democratically by the different sections in assemblies.

Discontent was widespread, and the bureaucrats provoked the railwaymen. So an assembly of railway workers discussed matters the following day with the manager of National Railways, Senator Roberto Amorós, who promised to study the matter, but only after two months. After this meeting on 21 May, the Great Committee was dissolved. But many union members were dissatisfied and decided to assemble on 24 May to protest the postponement. Among the resulting proposals, the one adopted was Vallejo's Plan of the Southeast. It called for rejection of the 200-peso raise and the 60-day delay; approval of the 350-peso raise; an ultimatum to the General Executive Committee of the union bureaucracy demanding recognition of the new independent leaders and of the raise; and, in case of failure to arrive at an agreement, the threat of scaled work stoppages.[7]

The First Strike (26 June–7 August 1958)

As plans for the proposed ultimatum and strike gained momentum, on 19 June in Torreón, Coahuila, the bureaucrats in Section 27 of the STFRM were disavowed. By 24 June, the railwaymen asked the official union secretary to mediate in their dealings with the authorities. But no agreement was reached, and the Executive Committee postponed the strike. They met again the next day without the railwaymen achieving their objective. The die was cast. Amid all these comings and goings, 26 June arrived, and the workers carried out their first work stoppage of two hours. The second work stoppage on the following day lasted four hours, and the third on the day after a total of six hours. The strike received modest support from the electricians, the oil workers, and the Revolutionary Teachers' Movement (MRM).[8]

In the Federal District, a propaganda demonstration at the Monument to the Revolution was savagely repressed. As Mario Gill recalls in his classic work on the railwaymen: "The demonstration, in which workers from other organizations and the popular masses in general participated, was attacked with a fury comparable to that of the Nazis in Hitler's best times."[9] Rafael Alday and Leopoldo Alvarez were killed; all the union branches in the country were assaulted; Andrés Montaño was murdered in cold blood. The enterprise lost seven million pesos every day. The railwaymen lowered their demand to 250 pesos retroactive to January of the same year, but the authorities refused to accept it.[10]

On 29 June, the fourth work stoppage lasted ten hours, and the next one was of indefinite length. After this show of force and courage, the Senator agreed to pay the 250 pesos provided the future contract be revised. Now it was the workers who rejected the offer as disadvantageous. At last the great arbitrator awaited by all for so long arrived in the person of President Ruiz Cortines. The Supreme Dealer offered to pay them 215 pesos in crude bargaining, without conditioning the November contract. On 1 July the railway workers accepted.

Subsequently, the STFRM defended itself against the attacks of the union bureaucracy and the barks of the bourgeoisie and the authorities. In Guadalajara, the local executive was disavowed on 5 July. In the capital, the Extraordinary General Convention met on 15 July to name its leadership. In this meeting, Demetrio Vallejo was elected; the labor authorities counter-attacked by disavowing him. The railwaymen returned to the fight with work stoppages, carrying through the first on 26 July. The stoppage on 2 August lasted five hours. Some of the strikers were arrested.

All of Mexico was in chaos on 3 August. With urgency Senator Amorós secretly interviewed the strikers and threatened them with 50,000 soldiers.[11] The newspaper *ABC* denounced the repression looming ahead. Some of the workers loyal to the ruling party (PRI) announced their support for the government.

The second secret meeting took place on 6 August and was publicized by *Ultimas Noticias*. National Railways manager Amorós accepted the workers' demands with the exception of their call for official recognition of Vallejo as general secretary of the STFRM. The cry went up from Abe Kramer of the US Embassy that it was time to eliminate the communists. American espionage concerning the role of the PCM and Valentín Campa during the strike had come up with enough evidence to hit at the movement in the best Cold War spirit. But the railwaymen stood united and firm. A show of solidarity came from the telegraph operators, telephone workers, radical teachers, informed peasants, and oil workers from Section 35. The nation reeled from the effects of the work stoppage by 80,000 railwaymen, 7,000 telegraph operators, and 15,000 teachers – altogether, 102,000 people.[12] There was also international support. The bourgeoisie recoiled with alarm.

Confronted with these events, the government accepted the registration of Vallejo's leadership. The agreement contained the following points: democratic elections in 15 days, release of all prisoners, reinstatement of dismissed workers, payment of lost wages, recall of troops from the branches. The workers made manager Amorós sign a little-known promissory letter as an additional seal to the agreement.[13]

With 59,760 votes in his favor, Vallejo won the election; second in command was the Secretary of Organization and Education, Gilberto Rojo Robles. On 7 August, the strikers returned to work satisfied. On the 27th, the new leaders took possession of their offices. Corruption then was as rampant as it is today: according to the files of the STFRM, the manager of National Railways alone spent 50 million pesos in bribes.[14]

On 1 October the Grand Convention for Contract Hiring began its studies. The new manager, Benjamín Méndez, was determined not to make any concessions. The railwaymen argued with proofs in hand that they could be paid more if only the low fares for the Yankee monopolies in minerals were cancelled.[15] So the US Embassy had a second reason for breaking and repressing the strike: the victory of the railwaymen would mean a big loss for the Yankee monopolies protected by the Mexican government.

The Second Strike (24 March–13 April 1959)

In February 1959 it was time to revise the collective labor contract with National Railways. The railwaymen won for the first time the subsidies for housing promised in the Constitution in section 12 of Article 123. They insisted that this right be extended to the other railroad enterprises, all under state management. But since the state refused to comply, strike demands were pressed by the railwaymen of those other enterprises: first The Pacific, followed by Mexican Railways, and Veracruz Terminal.[16] This second strike began on 24 March and ended on 13 April 1959.

As of 24 March no agreement had been reached, and all three enterprises were on strike. The next day, the authorities continued their delaying game and declared the strike non-existent, giving the workers 24 hours to return to work. The officials carried out the dismissals on 26 March, supported by the city police: besides the workers arrested,

8,000 were fired from The Pacific and 5,000 from Mexican Railways.[17] All the sections of the STFRM in National Railways held a one-hour work stoppage in protest.

Their next move was to declare a general strike against the dismissals and the "non-existence" of the strike of the three enterprises. What kind of a system is it that denies the obvious? The bought press and its wealthy buyers returned to the fray with bugles blaring against the "communist menace." The enterprise officials refused to pay the previous raise.[18] In other words, they sought confrontation.

In self-defense, the STFRM reduced its demands to payment for the seventh day of rest and an end to the repression. The cost to the government would have come to about six million pesos, and the proposal was delivered directly to the new helmsman, President López Mateos, on Good Friday, 27 March. Earlier, the President, "a friend of the workers," had accepted the demand.[19] Then he tried to gain time. A hundred thousand people were again on strike, and millions of pesos were being lost.

That Mexico was being threatened by a devaluation imposed by the US did not help matters. President Eisenhower interviewed the Mexican President on 19 February to discuss the issue. It was agreed that the US Treasury and Eximbank would support the Mexican peso. At what price for the Mexicans? The evidence suggests that the price was the breaking of the railroad strike, which was not only causing losses to Mexican industrialists and foreign investors, but also irritating the knights of the Cold War by its communist leadership. The US government had sent Dean Stephanki, a top CIA agent working in Paris, to "advise" the Mexican government on the repression of the strike and the elimination of the "communist danger."[20] As a result, López Mateos back-pedaled from his earlier acceptance of the workers' demands.

The workers in the boxcar shanty town were driven out; the response was a total strike at 2 p.m., 28 March. The railway workers' delegates under Vallejo's leadership were still struggling in good faith to reach an agreement with the President, the Secretary of Labor, and the Secretary of Patrimony. They were ready to persuade the workers to lift the strike if the enterprise reversed its repressive measures and if it abided by the agreement with the President that the rest day would be paid. But the petitions of the workers were rejected. A meeting was arranged with the Secretary of Patrimony, Eduardo Bustamante, at 5.30 p.m. Instead, Vallejo and 83 others were kidnapped by the Federal Police and the army.[21]

Once more, the "defender of the institutions" went into action around the country. In the Federal District alone, several battalions were mobilized: the 2nd, 8th, 21st, and 29th. Some 9,000 strikers were fired from their jobs; more than 10,000 were arrested, mainly the railwaymen, but also professors, peasants, and some activists in the Marxist-Leninist parties. As far as the authorities were concerned, all were communists, "professional agitators," red to the bone. Some of the leaders were tortured, humiliated, and abused in order to make them declare against the movement and the "communist conspiracy."[22] That was how López Mateos showed his love for the Mexican workers. Would the working class take note of what was being done for its "welfare" and decide once and for all to organize itself independently?

One hundred thousand workers were on strike. The nation was in a state of siege; political terror was spreading; and more repression could be expected. The authorities were combing the country for Valentín Campa. On 30 March at Tlalnepantla in the state of México, the police hunted down a hundred Vallejistas. To embellish the repression, the Soviet embassy was asked to send home Nikolai Remisov and Nikolai Aksenov.[23]

On 3 April 1959, the strike was still general when Gilberto Rojo Robles, Vallejo's deputy, sent a telegram to all sections ordering them to return to work. The telegram assured them that a promise had been extracted from the President that their demands would receive attention if the strike were lifted. Later, the government denied that it had made any overtures to the workers and claimed that there had been no agreement. The repression had begun during the talks before reaching a solution. The President continued his persecution, violating his commitment and refusing to meet the demand for the day of rest. Rojo Robles, Alberto Lumbreras, and Miguel Aroche Parra of the POCM were arrested, along with Dionisio Encina, secretary of the PCM. Valentín Campa was not caught until May 1960 after leading the railroad movement from the underground for more than a year.[24] The trials were a lying farce. Ten years later, the student movement finally achieved the liberation of Vallejo and Campa on 27 July 1970.

The railway movement was already divided. Back in 1959 Campa had founded the National Railroad Council to keep alive the democratic tendency in the union. He and his co-workers distributed the underground newspaper *The Railwayman*. But when Demetrio Vallejo was released from prison in July 1970, he did not join the Council, but preferred to organize his own Railwaymen's Union Movement (MSF).

Assessments

There is little disagreement concerning the outcome of the 1958 strike.[25] Its gains for the trade union rank and file were huge: first, the removal of the *charros*, the self-serving labor aristocrats in the service of the PRI government, from positions of leadership; second, the revision of the collective contract, including not only a substantial wage hike, but also the implementation of the 1917 Constitution, according to which employers are obliged to provide comfortable and hygienic housing for their employees (Article 123), an article violated by all of Mexico's presidents from Carranza to López Mateos.

A consensus concerning the 1958 strike, however, is completely lacking. "[S]everal hundred thousand words have been spent discussing the strengths and weaknesses of the tactics employed by the railworkers' union in February and March 1959," notes Barry Carr. The role of communists in the leadership of the union has come under severe criticism for their intransigence in a collective bargaining situation that led to a self-defeating confrontation with the government.

> At issue were the wisdom of the decision to proceed with national solidarity strikes on the National Railways at the end of March; the appropriateness of continuing a union strategy that had become a frontal political challenge to the state by the beginning of 1959; the strike leadership's perceptions of the new López Mateos government … and allegations that the leadership of the union acted precipitously without adequate consultation with the base.[26]

Mario Gill maintains that the movement triumphed because it raised the level of political consciousness of the workers and "the victory as well as the defeat were positive experiences." He claims that, if nothing else, it successfully confronted and defeated the sell-out union bureaucracy.[27]

Antonio Alonso, author of *The Railroad Movement in Mexico 1958–1959* (in Spanish), thinks that the second strike failed because it called in question the despotism of the PRI government, "forcing it to break its own order," to abandon its doctrine of class conciliation in favor of direct repression. In this way, he claims, the bourgeoisie and the Mexican state were strengthened.[28]

According to the evaluation by Lombardo Toledano, the second strike carried the union to defeat because the railwaymen could have won pay for the day of rest, which the government offered in order to prevent the strike explosion. The error of the railwaymen's leaders lay in carrying their demands to a definitive rupture with the public owner. So they lost the battle against the union bureaucracy and momentarily wrecked the hopes of the working class across the country, despite winning the first strike.[29]

Agreeing with the latter opinion in his *Economics and Politics in the History of Mexico* (in Spanish), Manuel López Gallo says that to continue struggling was "counterproductive and negative ... owing to the lack of vision of the railwaymen's leaders ... [and] their inflexibility" that led to a resounding defeat.[30]

Campa and Vallejo, who were closest to the events, admitted to errors of judgment during the second strike, but rejected the notion that the strike was a mistake.

Notes

1. Hodges' interview with Valentín Campa in Cuernavaca, Morelos, 10 January 1978. In his memoirs – Valentín Campa, *Mi testimonio: memorias de un comunista mexicano*, 3rd rev. ed. (Mexico City: Cultura Popular, 1985; orig. pub. 1978), p. 39 – he mentions that he joined the PCM in February 1927.
2. Our profile of Vallejo is based on Hodges' interview with Gerardo Unzueta, editor of *Socialismo*, at PCM headquarters in Mexico City, 6 February 1978. See also Barry Carr, *Marxism and Communism in Twentieth-Century Mexico* (Lincoln: University of Nebraska Press, 1992), p. 204.
3. Interview with Mónico Rodríguez at his workshop in Chiconcuac, Morelos, 12 December 1977.
4. Mario Gill, *Los Ferrocarrileros* (Mexico City: Extemporáneos, 1971), pp. 163–6.
5. Ibid., p. 163.
6. Antonio Alonso, *El movimiento ferrocarrilero en México 1958–1959* (Mexico

City: Era, 1972), pp. 110–11.
7. Ibid., pp. 112–13.
8. Ibid., p. 114.
9. Gill, *Los Ferrocarrileros*, p. 165.
10. Ibid., pp. 165–6.
11. Ibid., pp. 167–8.
12. Ibid., pp. 169–70.
13. Ibid., pp. 170–2.
14. Ibid., pp. 172, 185–6.
15. Ibid., pp. 188–9.
16. Ibid., p. 189.
17. Ibid., p. 190.
18. Ibid., pp. 193–4.
19. Ibid., p. 196.
20. Ibid., pp. 201–2.
21. Ibid., p. 195.
22. Alonso, *El movimiento ferrocarrilero*, p. 151; and Gill, *Los Ferrocarrileros*, p. 201.
23. Gill, *Los Ferrocarrileros*, p. 201.
24. Ibid., pp. 202–3.
25. For a full discussion of the pros and cons, successes and failures of the great railroad strikes of 1958–59, see Campa, *Mi testimonio*, pp. 239–55; Alonso, *El movimiento ferrocarrilero*, pp. 152–74; Gill, *Los Ferrocarrileros*, pp. 211–32; and Carr, *Marxism and Communism*, p. 216.
26. Carr, *Marxism and Communism*, p. 216.
27. Gill, *Los Ferrocarrileros*, pp. 211–13.
28. Alonso, *El movimiento ferrocarrilero*, p. 180.
29. Gill, *Los Ferrocarrileros*, pp. 214–15.
30. Manuel López Gallo, *Economía y Política en la Historia de México* (Mexico City: El Caballito, 1967), pp. 587–88.

6 ✳ Launching the Movement of National Liberation

The origins of the Movement of National Liberation (MLN) can be traced to the founding of the Committee to Promote Peace (CIP) in July 1959, a group started by ex-president Lázaro Cárdenas with the participation of the PCM, the PP, and independent left-wing intellectuals. The Committee's work led in March 1961 to the convocation of the Latin American Conference on National Sovereignty, Economic Emancipation and Peace (CLSNEEP) in Mexico City. The number of Mexican participants in the conference numbered 1,000, not to mention the many delegates from other Latin American countries. The most immediate and urgent aims of the conference were to promote in Latin America the struggle for economic independence against North American imperialism, to win respect for the sovereignty, economic independence, and territorial integrity of Cuba, threatened by the United States, and to ensure the unity of the left in Mexico as a means of pressing the government to return to the revolutionary nationalist road abandoned by the post-Cardenist regimes.[1] Its importance was revealed by the presence in the Cuban delegation of Vilma Espín de Castro, wife of Raúl Castro, commander-in-chief of the rebel army.

By means of the conference, the Mexican struggle was linked with similar struggles throughout Latin America. Support for the anti-imperialist struggle was understood to be necessary for internal reforms in Mexico: the repression of the railway workers was closely connected to the Cold War and foreign pressures on the government to finish off communism inside Mexico. Thus, in a message on radio and television to the Mexican people on 29 March 1959, the Attorney General justified the repression on the ground that the behavior of the railwaymen obeyed "ideologies and interests foreign to those of Mexico ... [aimed at] subverting the public order."[2]

As a result of the conference, the Committee for National Sovereignty and Economic Emancipation was organized; it convoked a National Assembly on 4 August 1961, giving birth to the Movement of National Liberation (MLN). The opening speech at the assembly was given by Heberto Jara, a Cardenist and old revolutionary general. Cárdenas himself addressed the assembly, emphasizing that the organization being formed "does not damage the principles laid down in the Constitution ... [but instead] contributes to the realization of the postulates of the Mexican Revolution."[3] The MLN emerged as a broad front, a kind of amalgamating organism that included the two left-wing (Marxist) parties that sparked it, peasants in the National Peasant Confederation (CNC), trade unions in the Confederation of Mexican Workers (CTM), and even members of the official party in power.[4]

The Program

The MLN maintained that the demands for economic emancipation in favor of the majority were tied to the directing role of the state in the economy. Its program aimed at the acceleration of industrialization mainly on the basis of investments by the state, while justifying the state's role by the demonstrated incapacity of private entrepreneurs to promote sustained and autonomous development.[5]

Although the demands of the MLN were in agreement with the revolutionary nationalist projects of Cardenism, they were tied to the demand of the left parties for the democratization of political life. This demand did not go further than the defense of the Constitution of the Republic, which was constantly being violated. Political democratization was to carry through a basic transformation of the electoral system. Essential conditions would include the democratization of union life and a widening of political participation by worker, peasant, and popular sectors. The corporativist organization and virtual dictatorship of the official party could not but be called into question.

Only through the democratization of the political system could the revolutionary nationalist projects of the movement reach fulfillment: an independent foreign policy, control of foreign investments, preponderance of the public sector, realization of land reform, and redistribution of income to take into account the needs of workers and peasants. But the means for carrying out these projects were never specified. The MLN was heterogeneous in social composition, and this weakness plus the lack of specific tactics led to its eventual demise.

The Split in the Movement

The project of unifying the left failed because of the MLN's breadth and diversity. In the conferences and roundtables, the members of the old and the new left discussed their political and ideological differences but could never reach agreement. The "correct line," the authentic application of Marxism–Leninism, seemed to bear little relation to the realities and needs of the nation. It was endlessly discussable – without a solution – while the partisans of Cardenism were bored with such silliness and gradually turned away.

There was no possibility of agreement when the discussion turned toward immediate strategy. The unity of the left could not be achieved by discussing matters with the wizards of Marxism–Leninism because each wizard had his own version of it. The starting point had to be an agreement between the left parties – the mass organizations and not the groupuscules. Either one begins with plans for concrete action or one never arrives at action. It is the action that makes possible alliances, not the theory of Marxism–Leninism.

Thus the MLN split into different currents. First the two left-wing parties withdrew. Then Cárdenas and his current in the official party moved away, leaving the MLN completely in the hands of the partyless intellectuals of the New Left. Most of these people lived in the capital without ties to the worker and peasant masses; some sold out to the highest bidder by living off the budget of the PRI – González Pedrero and Flores Olea are examples. The movement became not a coordinating committee of the Mexican left, but a quasi-party without a future because of its purely intellectual makeup.[6]

Lombardo Toledano's Popular Socialist Party (PPS), the PP's successor and Mexico's second Marxist party recognized by Moscow, disagreed with the organizational structure of the MLN. It wanted the movement to be a coordinating committee or popular front of the principal mass organizations and left parties, so it demanded a form of organic and functional representation. But the structure adopted permitted individual affiliations with a centralized direction. Thus Lombardo Toledano said that it constituted a new party of the left rather than a representative front of all existing left-wing parties.

The Critical Conjuncture

The critical conjuncture for the movement was the presidential succession of 1964, when it opted to abstain from the elections. This decision was partly a protest against the electoral system in force, a system controlled by the official party, which held in its hands all the means to ensure its own "triumph." But it was also partly a maneuver aimed at containing the partisan differences within the movement, something it certainly could not achieve.

The PCM aspired to participate in the electoral game by means of the People's Electoral Front (FEP), announced in April 1963. The FEP counted on the support of different organizations that also backed the MLN: the Revolutionary Teachers' Movement (MRM), the National Railwaymen's Council (CNF), the Independent Peasant Central (CCI), and the Civic Union of Guerrero (UCG) of Genaro Vásquez. In fact, the program of the FEP did not differ in its fundamental principles from those of the MLN. But the MLN refused to grant it official support, so that the emergence of the FEP marked the beginning of the decadence of the MLN. Even though the MLN decided not to take part in the 1964 elections, various organizations of the MLN disagreed and drifted into conflicts with the independent intellectuals by deciding to support the FEP.[7]

The Cardenists who came at the call of the MLN in 1961 also broke off on account of the 1964 elections. Cárdenas publicly supported the official PRI candidate Díaz Ordaz, thus taking away from the movement the support of the official left. When the Cardenists walked out of the MLN, it lost the support of the masses. Thus the decomposition of the movement set in, and by 1964 it had subsided into a marginal group.

Solidarity with the Cuban Revolution

The MLN adopted a position at loggerheads with the government and the official party. By its solidarity with the Cuban Revolution alone, it won thousands of sympathizers, bringing about an important mobilization. This worried the government.[8] The disagreement between Cárdenas and President López Mateos concerning the Cuban Revolution increased official pressure on the movement. To this dispute was added the question of the political prisoners. The movement called for a struggle to liberate Valentín Campa and Demetrio Vallejo, the chief leaders of the railwaymen, but López Mateos insisted on keeping them in prison. Finally, the President denounced the MLN for succumbing to communist infiltration.

During the term of Díaz Ordaz, the pressures on the MLN increased. When co-option failed, the government resorted to shameless repression. Under these conditions, the MLN slowly weakened until its participation in the popular student movement of 1968 led to the jailing of its leaders. This final disaster was the death of the MLN.

If the movement did not survive, it did at least help to spark the popular student movement and the guerrilla struggles that broke out against the repression of the PRI government. In the last analysis, the importance of the MLN lay not in its efforts to unify the left, but in its solidarity with the Cuban Revolution and indirectly with the methods of struggle that brought Castro to power. The MLN conceived of the road to the democratization of the country in a constitutional manner; that is how Fidel Castro also began.

The two communist currents – the Mexican and the Cuban – that influenced the development of the MLN led toward different objectives. This raised hopes among circles of intellectuals without a party that a group of young fighters might open new political roads for the nation and through a guerrilla war succeed in installing a new government.

The methods of struggle that carried the Cuban left to victory were not officially accepted by the MLN as workable in Mexico; those methods were not even discussed in the documents of the Constituent Assembly. But beside the methods of peaceful and legal struggle within the framework of the Constitution arose others not officially adopted that followed the road traveled by Castro's 26 July Movement. These were the methods that influenced the communists without a party, such as Genaro Vásquez, the PCM militants who had to flee from repression, such as Lucio Cabañas, and the rebellious cadres of the

Young Communists who also took part in the guerrilla wars. The most important guerrilla movements in Mexico, those of Lucio and Genaro, were commanded by old militants from the MLN. And the assault on the Madera Barracks in the State of Chihuahua in 1965 was organized by militants belonging to the General Union of Mexican Workers and Peasants (UGOCM), whose general secretary, Jacinto López, was an MLN national committee member.

Notes

1. MLN, *Programa y llamamiento del Movimiento de Liberación Nacional* (Mexico City: MLN, 1961), pp. 11–18, 20–21. For a full discussion of the MLN and its significance, see Ledda Arguedas, "El Movimiento de Liberación Nacional," *Revista Mexicana de Sociología* (January–March 1977): 229–49.
2. Cited by Mario Gill, *Los Ferrocarrileros* (Mexico City: Extemporáneos, 1971), p. 197; from an article in *La Nación*, no. 912 (5 April 1959).
3. MLN, *Programa y llamamiento*, p. 5.
4. Ibid., pp. 68–71.
5. Ibid., pp. 22–51.
6. David T. Garza, "Factionalism in the Mexican Left: The Frustration of the MLN," *The Western Political Quarterly*, no. 18 (1964): 447–60; and Gerardo Unzueta, "El MLN: una perspectiva para las luchas del pueblo," *Nueva Epoca*, vol. 1, no. 1 (February 1962): 18–19.
7. *La Voz de México* (23 November 1963): 1; and Barry Carr, *Marxism and Communism in Twentieth-Century Mexico* (Lincoln: University of Nebraska Press, 1992), p. 234.
8. On the Cuban connection, see Olga Pellicer de Brody, *México y la revolución cubana* (Mexico City: El Colegio de México, 1972), pp. 85–115.

7 ✸ Assault on the Madera Barracks, 23 September 1965

Two years after the death of Rubén Jaramillo, another guerrilla struggle emerged under the leadership of Arturo Gámiz. The field of action was the mountain range between Chihuahua and Sonora, specifically the town of Ciudad Madera.

The Land Question in Chihuahua

The cattlemen protected by the authorities had provoked, robbed, and murdered the peasants. The Secretary of Agriculture under Ruiz Cortines had authorized the lumber company Bosques de Chihuahua to divide into fractions 400,000 hectares so that they might be distributed among landless peasants. It never came to pass, for both the big and the small owners used their company Four Friends to buy up the land. The poor peasants were hardly pleased by this maneuver, for a single family of cattle raisers – the Ibarras – owned 18,000 hectares of grazing land.[1]

Arturo Gámiz, local head of the General Union of Mexican Workers and Peasants (UGOCM), linked to the Popular Socialist Party (PPS), tried to solve these problems of land tenancy peacefully. But Governor Giner Durán dismissed him with insults. So Gámiz and his followers took to armed struggle. In the last days of 1964, they dynamited a bridge on the properties of the Ibarras family. Eleven guerrillas were involved in the operation.[2]

In Fidel's Footsteps

The last action was the famous assault on the Madera Barracks carried

88

out on 23 September 1965. A mere 17 guerrillas attacked 120 well-armed soldiers. This action in the style of the attack led by Fidel Castro on the Moncada Barracks in Cuba lasted three hours and resulted in the deaths of eight guerrillas.[3]

In the vast manhunt for the survivors, soldiers from the military zones of Chihuahua and Sonora took part, as well as men from the Battalion of Paratroop Fusiliers known for their sadism. To these were added three C–54 airplanes and four T–33 pursuit jets. The troops tried to smoke out the guerrillas; seven peasants from Cebadilla de Dolores, a mountain hamlet, were interrogated under torture by the army. This was the last time that Arturo Gámiz crowned himself with glory, for though he did not fall in the assault on the Madera Barracks, he did succumb in this merciless repression ordered by the PRI government and the local bosses.

His example continued encouraging the survivors and many others. Oscar González and five young people escaped death in Ciudad Madera and carried on the guerrilla struggle in the mountains of Chihuahua and Sonora until they were shot in September 1968 in Tesopoco, Sonora.[4] A third guerrilla experience followed. The Armed Commandos of Chihuahua (CACH) simultaneously assaulted three banks in Ciudad Madera on 15 January 1972, getting away with booty of half a million pesos. This was not the last guerrilla effort influenced by the Chihuahuan experiences. The 23 September League took its cue from the assault on the Madera Barracks on 23 September 1965.[5]

Gámiz and Oscar González separated from the distinguished group of leaders in the PPS and the UGOCM which had organized the land "invasions" in Chihuahua and northern Durango near the end of the 1950s and the beginning of the 1960s. In 1964, this group split into two currents. The one headed by Alvaro Ríos continued the struggle for land within the law and the Constitution. The other, under the direction of Gámiz and González, chose the road of armed struggle and repudiated the strategic line of the PPS and the Lombardist current in Mexican Marxism.

The assault on the Madera Barracks had as its immediate model Fidel Castro's attack on the Moncada Barracks in Santiago de Cuba on 26 July 1953. Gámiz' guerrillas were also influenced by the maxims set forth in Che Guevara's "Guerrilla Warfare" (1960, in Spanish)[6] and by the lesser-known confluence of Castro-communism with North American Browderism. The current led by Earl Browder, until 1945 general secretary of the Communist Party of the United States (CPUSA), favored a popular front strategy that was taken as a model by the Cuban party and was responsible for changing its name to the Popular Socialist Party[7] – the name later adopted by Lombardo for his own party.

The Role of Lombardism

In 1945, Lombardo Toledano founded the Mexican Socialist League, taking as a model the Communist Political Association which Browder had substituted for the old North American Communist Party. Like Browder, Lombardo wanted to found a communist party with populist and democratic currents; he wanted to start from this base to reach a single party of the working class.[8] It was the second time that Lombardo, with Browder's help, tried to pressure the leaders of the PCM to unite with the Cardenist current.

The first time was in 1937 when he called for the intervention of Browder, as Vice-president of the Executive Committee of the Third International, to pressure the PCM to reintegrate its trade unions with the Confederation of Mexican Workers (CTM). In that way, he pushed the line of "unity at all costs." He succeeded, for this was the line approved by the PCM in its Plenum in June that year.[9] But he failed in his efforts in 1945 when leading cadres of the PCM, which had joined his League, left its ranks because of the condemnation of Browderism by the international communist movement. Only one communist party per nation! But if there is more than one, they must find a way to unite!

Lombardo managed to have the National Council of the CTM authorize the creation of the single party with its base in the labor central. Not long afterward, he was expelled from the CTM by Fidel Velázquez and his bureaucratic clique. Looking for another way to support his project, he founded the Popular Party (PP) in 1948. Faced with this new Marxist-Leninist party, the PCM authorized some of its cadres to join it.[10]

This concession to Browder–Lombardism was soon annulled. In its Tenth Congress in 1949, the PCM reaffirmed that the task of its cadres consisted in building their party and no other. But many of the PCM's militants who had joined the PP stayed in its ranks. The PP, which had adopted the new name of Popular Socialist Party (PPS) in 1960, was an independent communist party.[11] Like the Yugoslav party, Lombardo's party had no formal ties to the established Marxist-Leninist parties. The truth is that Browderism was the precursor of Tito's communism and later of Eurocommunism. Thus Lombardism was not alone in its line that communists should seek unity with the nationalist and popular forces.

Arturo Gámiz' guerrilla struggle combined Fidel's rationale for armed struggle with the populism and mass perspective of Lombardo Toledano. His main concern was land reform, and his methods of struggle were Castro's – Gámiz thought that the peaceful and legal road had ended. On 15 October 1965, he expressed his point of view as follows:

> We are convinced that the moment has arrived for us to speak to the powerful in the only language they understand; the time has come for the boldest vanguards to take up the rifle; the time has come to see if bullets can enter their heads since reasons cannot; the time has come to base ourselves on the 30–30 [carbine] ... rather than on the Agrarian Code of the Constitution.[12]

The failure of Lombardism had led him to the opposite extreme of Castroism.

This guerrilla struggle passed from a merely defensive stage to the first efforts at offense. It tried to imitate the desperate deed of Fidel Castro at the beginning of the Cuban resistance. Although the guerrilla leaders had come out of the Popular Socialist Party, the party did not support them. While Jaramillo's guerrillas had been formed out of his sons, *compadres*, and relatives – above all, out of old Zapatistas – Professor Arturo Gámiz surrounded himself with youth, Dr Pablo Gómez being the sole exception. What was the program of Gámiz' guerrillas? They never proclaimed a written program, insofar as we have been able to determine. The program was tied to the demands of the peasants and the PPS, from which the movement sprang.

Notes

1. On the background to the Madera guerrillas, see Victor Orozco, "Las luchas populares en Chihuahua," *Cuadernos Políticos*, no. 9 (July–September 1976): 65.
2. Jaime López, *10 años de guerrillas en México 1964–1974* (Mexico City: Posada, 1974), pp. 16, 21; Prudencio Godines, Jr., *¡Que poca mad ... era!* (Mexico City: n.p., 1968), pp. 39, 52–62, 68–9, 96–8, 106–7.
3. According to the conspiratorial account of the Madera assault by the guerrillas' immediate political adviser, both the PCM and the surviving rump of the MLN were secretly involved in the operation. Godines, *¡Que poca mad ... era!*, pp. 53–4, 59, 68.
4. José Natividad Rosales, *¿Quién es Lucio Cabañas? ¿Qué pasa con la guerrilla en México?* (Mexico City: Posada, 1976), pp. 25, 27.
5. Gustavo Hirales Morán, *La liga comunista 23 de septiembre: orígenes y naufragio* (Mexico City: Cultura Popular, 1977), p. 92; and Luis Suárez, *Lucio Cabañas, el guerrillero sin esperanza* (Mexico City: Roca, 1976), p. 70.
6. Gámiz' guerrillas took to heart the maxim that guerrilla struggle must be a struggle of the masses, a struggle of the people by the people's armed vanguard. "The guerrilla relies, therefore, on the support of the local population. That is its *sine qua non*." Ernesto "Che" Guevara, "La Guerra de Guerrillas," *Obras 1957–1967*, 2 vols. (Havana: Casa de las Américas, 1970), vol. 1, p. 33.
7. Barry Carr, *Marxism and Communism in Twentieth-Century Mexico* (Lincoln: University of Nebraska Press, 1992), pp. 121–2.
8. Ibid., pp. 195, 197–8.
9. Ibid., pp. 55, 120–1.
10. Ibid., pp. 149, 159.
11. Ibid., pp. 189–90, 254–5.
12. López, *10 años de guerrillas*, p. 30.

8 ✸ Student Insurgency and the Tlatelolco Massacre

The CIA's invasion of the Bay of Pigs in Cuba took place on 17 April 1961. While the struggle on the Cuban beach was in progress, 15,000 Mexican students marched toward the central plaza in Mexico City to show their solidarity with the Cuban people; suddenly tear gas and police truncheons fell upon the demonstrators. Repressive Mexico *versus* socialist Cuba – the image was engraved on the minds of many. In 1962, Rubén Jaramillo was murdered on government orders, and in 1964 Díaz Ordaz became president; but there was no amnesty for the previous president's prisoners Demetrio Vallejo and Valentín Campa. The law against "social dissolution" remained in force. In the capital, the students organized marches of international solidarity with the revolutions in the Dominican Republic (1965) and in Vietnam (1967); they read about the new society being born in Cuba.

In 1968, Demetrio Vallejo began a hunger strike to demand his freedom; some students at the National University also began a hunger strike, declaring their solidarity with the political prisoners. The students in the political science department called upon the whole university to strike, their slogan: Freedom for the Political Prisoners! In the 1960s, political repression was mixed with rising radical consciousness: the vapors of this volatile fuel filled the repressive atmosphere. On 26 July 1968 came the spark that set off the student explosion of that year.[1]

The Spark Igniting the Student Explosion in July

In the Juárez Semicircle, the Young Communists and other student organizations from the National University (UNAM) held a meeting to

93

celebrate the anniversary of the Cuban Revolution, while in another part of the capital a demonstration of students from the National Polytechnical Institute (IPN) protested the Grenadiers' invasion of Vocational School Number 5. A group of the demonstrators from IPN moved toward the central plaza, deviating from the route approved by the government. The Grenadiers – military riot police – attacked them with gas and truncheons. The students fled toward the Alameda Park, and there joined the demonstrators from UNAM in the Juárez Semicircle. The Grenadiers overtook and attacked them, resulting in smashed store windows, bleeding students, wailing ambulances, hundreds of people beaten, barricades of overturned buses in the old university quarter, four hours of street fighting with the Grenadiers, the traffic police, the Federal Police, the Secret Service, and the armed police. Two students lay dead; others took refuge in the preparatory schools where the students came under siege for three days.[2]

The police, who should have prevented an explosion, had provoked it. How to cover up their error? By spreading the police theory of history: when some elements of the people rise against their oppressors, it is because criminal agitators are leading them. The agents of the Federal Direction of Security took it upon themselves to give this lesson to the capital. They sacked the offices of the Central Committee of the Communist Party, seized the printing presses of its newspaper, and arrested many of its leaders, including the theoretician Gerardo Unzueta.

"Where is the party in opposition that has not been decried as Communistic by its opponents in power?" Karl Marx's words of 1848 applied as well to the charges of the Mexican government 120 years later. The specter of communism was raised for the thousandth time. Would the people believe it? The students of Mexico did not. There were protest meetings in the provinces, and strike flags rose in the vocational and preparatory schools of the capital. Street fighting between police and students, complete with barricades and Molotov cocktails, were reminiscent of the May Revolution in Paris.[3] Combat soldiers took the schools by storm, breaking down the doors with bazooka fire; the students resisted but were taken prisoner.

Meetings in the schools and departments of UNAM were permanently in session. They protested the hundreds of arrests; they shouted in rage over the wounded and dead. The cessation of all academic activities extended to the Polytechnical Institute, to the Superior Normal School, to the National Agricultural School in Chapingo. On 1 August, the Rector of UNAM led a demonstration of at least 50,000 people as a sign of mourning for the fallen students and the violation of university autonomy.[4] Public opinion, until this moment confused, began to doubt the official versions of events. Were the students really crazy anarchists? Could "criminal communists" march 50,000 university puppets silently through the streets behind the heads of schools and departments? The students were beginning to convince the broad public that the cause of the discontent was provocation by the criminal police.

In order to combat the official lies and the bought press, the students invented a new tactic of struggle: the political information brigades. A brigade consisted of five to ten students with one person responsible for its work. They handed out pamphlets and leaflets; they held lightning meetings to inform the people in the capital about events.

On 5 August, the Polytechnical Institute called all alumni, professors, and students to a great demonstration. The students from UNAM, the Normal School, and Chapingo Agricultural School took part. The professors of the "Poly" headed the march of 100,000 people, carrying placards reading: "Respect the Constitution!"; "Free the Political Prisoners!"; "Worker, Your Cause is Ours!"; and "The Army Learns Nothing in the Schools – Get Out!"[5]

The law against "social dissolution" hung like the Sword of Damocles over the people struggling to change Mexico. The Attorney General arraigned several Communist leaders for "criminal association and sedition." The capital's jails were bursting. The Universities of Sinaloa, Baja California, and Tabasco, the Technological Institute of Veracruz, and the rural normal schools joined the strike.

The Student Strike Council and its Demands

The student movement spontaneously created its directing organ: the National Strike Council (CNH), made up of at least 150 members, two each from most of the 70 schools and universities on strike in different states of the Republic. Among the members of the CNH, elected in the assemblies of the different schools and universities, were many Young Communists.[6] The CNH made six demands:

- Freedom for political prisoners.
- Dismissal of the police chiefs.
- Abolition of the Grenadiers.
- Abrogation of the crime of "social dissolution."
- Compensation for the families of the dead and wounded.
- Determination of responsibility for the repression.[7]

The formulation of these demands reflected the influence of the Communist Party. For example, students had begun by demanding liberation of the arrested students, but the demand was revised as the old communist slogan: "Freedom for political prisoners."[8]

The CNH called for the Mexican people to take part in a student demonstration on 13 August, headed by the Teachers' Coalition for Democratic Liberties, with representation from the schools of the Polytechnic Institute and the departments of UNAM. A column of demonstrators five kilometers long advanced through the capital; the placards carried the demands of the movement. There were 200,000 people in the giant meeting in the central plaza.[9]

The Growing Movement in August

The movement grew. In the following weeks, many institutions and organizations joined the strike or declared their solidarity: the Professors' Council of the School of Chemical Engineering and Extractive Industry, the Student Federation of the Iberoamerican University, the National Music Conservatory (INBA), the Union of Collective Transport Taxi Drivers, the National Organizing Junta of the Christian Democratic Party, the universities and technological institutes of many states in Mexico. The Mexican Electrical Workers Union sympathized with the movement; "as a revolutionary organization," it could not "remain on the margin of any problem affecting the nation."[10]

How could the momentum of the movement be maintained? The CNH planned to take advantage of these expressions of solidarity with a massive demonstration on 13 August. Hundreds of meetings were held in various centers accessible to everyone including Central Alameda Park. The lightning meetings multiplied. There was talk of a monster demonstration set for 27 August.

The CNH always insisted on a dialogue with the authorities. On 22 August, Secretary of the Interior Luis Echeverría made this statement:

> The government of the Republic expresses its readiness to receive the representatives of the teachers and students of the Autonomous National University of Mexico, the National Polytechnic Institute, and the other educational centers concerned with the existing problem, in order to exchange views with them and learn their demands in a direct manner, in order to definitively resolve the conflict our capital has lived through in the last weeks.[11]

The students and teachers answered that they were ready for talks provided that the discussions would be public. The following day, Luis Echeverría told the CNH by telephone that the Executive Power accepted a public dialogue.[12]

What was to be done? To start a dialogue would be to institutionalize the movement, to put on the brakes, to dilute it to haggling. Many students doubted the possibility of an open dialogue with the government and suspected a trick; others wanted to continue the struggle, hoping that the industrial workers would join the movement. Their model was the May Revolution in France. This hard line won support. The democratizing tendency still did not predominate.[13]

The CNH answered that it wanted to see the government's acceptance in writing or hear it announced publicly. Again it emphasized that any discussions must be public, but that no matter what happened it would carry through the demonstration on the 27th. Many preparatory students and some left-wing revolutionaries wanted to turn the crisis into a permanent process that would lead to a social transformation.

The movement neared its climax. The students' political brigades worked the whole city on 26 August without running any serious risks. The CNH announced that it had established new contacts with the Secretariat of the Interior; there was hope that formal conversations would begin on 28 August, after the demonstration.

The day of the great march arrived. The public was invited to the central plaza to take part "in the Great Popular Demonstration in defense of democratic liberties." The parade moved through the broad avenue of the Paseo de la Reforma led by a Coalition of Parents and Teachers. The students shouting "People, unite!" carried photographs and drawings of Hidalgo, Morelos, Juárez, Zapata, Villa, Che, and Demetrio Vallejo. The public applauded from the windows of buildings and threw confetti. Some 400,000 people concentrated in the central plaza, the largest demonstration in the history of the Republic.[14]

The orators appeared. A message from Demetrio Vallejo, weakened by his hunger strike, was read to the multitude. The CNH decided the day and the hour of the public dialogue with the authorities: in the great central plaza, as a continuation of a permanent assembly, on the day of the State of the Union address by the President, 1 September. After singing the national anthem, the huge crowd dispersed. The students remained in the great central plaza camped in tents, waiting for the President, who in five days would have to talk with them in front of the nation.

Mounting Repression in September

The government took this decision as a provocation. The paratroop battalions and the infantry, the armored cars filled with presidential guards, the red trucks full of firemen, the traffic police and the paddy wagons cleaned the students out of the great plaza. Some of the students from UNAM announced the next day that "the demand for a public debate with the students on 1 September, the attempt to establish a permanent guard in the central plaza, and other proposals of a similar nature were part of a grave error that favored political repression."[15]

There would be no dialogue. Instead, the government started the engines of repression that had been idling between 1 and 27 August. In various parts of the city, there were hostile encounters between students and Grenadiers. The army and the Grenadiers dispersed or arrested the political brigades that held street meetings or traveled in requisitioned buses. Sporadic street fights continued for two weeks.

Only a month remained until the beginning of the Olympic Games in Mexico City. In his State of the Union message of 1 September, the President had alluded to the coming Olympics: "We trust that the imminent sports events will not be prevented from occurring," and he had announced "the decision to use all the legal methods at our disposal in order to maintain order and internal peace so that citizens and visitors receive all necessary guarantees."[16]

The movement floated in the air, without aim. The influence of the Communist Party in the CNH slowly grew after 1 September: most of the Young Communists followed a soft line. But they had not achieved control of the CNH. The CNH called for a "Grand Demonstration in Silence" on 13 September. In the silent march, the students walked with a hand in the air making the "V" sign of victory. In the central plaza, the number of students, workers, housewives, parents, public employees, and small-businesspeople barely reached 250,000.

The movement was coming down. As if by means of social telepathy, the middle sectors of the capital's social layers sensed that the great current had lost its direction. Three days passed. The Olympics were drawing near, and the government decided to repress the movement once and for all. The blows of the State's enormous hammer began falling upon the students and continued falling day after day.

18 September: The autonomy of the National University was violated for the first time in 40 years. 5,000 soldiers invaded the University City to arrest 2,000 students, professors, and parents. The army occupied the university campus. The CNH went underground.

19 September: New waves of repression broke. The students stoned the windows at the Secretariat of the Interior. Police arrested dozens of students and bystanders.

20 September: 1,000 Grenadiers battled with 3,000 students near the National Polytechnical Institute. Hundreds of students were arrested.

21 September: Another huge fight between Grenadiers and students took place in the Plaza of the Three Cultures, resulting in several deaths and many wounded.

22 September: Again the army confronted students in Vocational School Number 7. The young people protected themselves with Molotov cocktails and barricades of overturned buses.

23 September: In the area around St. Thomas' Cap, there were violent encounters including gunfights between students and police, exploding Molotov cocktails, burned buses, tear-gas bombs, smashed walls, bystanders beaten up, twenty dead, hundreds wounded, and hundreds arrested.[17]

24 September: This was a day of rest. The streets were full of destroyed buses and the ruins of barricades.

25 September: Sporadic violence broke out between police and students; one person was killed.

26 September: 70 of the arrested received prison terms. The charges against them were robbery, damage to property, and injuries to the government's agents.

27 September: The political arrests were calculated at more than 2,000 people.

29 September: the University City was still occupied by the army.

The *Coup de Grâce*

Was the movement dying? On 1 October, the CNH announced a meeting in the Plaza of the Three Cultures in Tlatelolco. From there, a demonstration would march to St. Thomas' Cap. The student movement was flaring up again! One week before the Olympic Games, the government decided to administer the *coup de grâce*.

The government has succeeded in spreading many official lies about what happened on 2 October in Tlatelolco. After the massacre, the Secretary of National Defense, General García Barragán, announced to the press that the army had intervened to stop a shoot-out between two groups of students. Although in the last weeks of September a few students had obtained light arms in order to defend themselves against the attacks of the repressive forces, the fact remains that the meeting in the Plaza of the Three Cultures was peaceful.[18] The 5,000 people there included not only men and women but children as well. Parents, old ladies, and foreign journalists showed up in significant numbers. The crowd was hardly a collection of combatants, but rather a gathering of innocents. Students were also in attendance, but they provoked no one. They passed out leaflets to the other attenders.

The massacre was an ambush. The government carried it out in a conscious and planned manner. The agents of the police infiltrated the multitude; when the massacre began, they put a white sign around their left wrists so that they could recognize each other. The 5,000 soldiers with hundreds of tanks completely surrounded the plaza: there was no way out or around or through. A helicopter tossed out flares, and the army began shooting to kill.

The intense crossfire lasted 30 minutes. Bullets came from every direction, and it is probable that the soldiers wounded each other. Old people, children, students, and parents fell. Perhaps a thousand were killed or wounded. People ran desperately from one side to the other; some tried to take refuge in nearby apartment buildings. Plainclothes police arrested the directors of the CNH. The panic spread even to the police. But the crossfire continued its macabre dance.[19] The PRI's presidential despot, the heroic army – "defender of the people" – together with the unconstitutional police had carried out their greatest deed by giving themselves a banquet of innocent Mexican blood. For fear of terrible "communism" and "in order to go on being free," they savagely murdered the defenseless populace. They gave not bread but bullets; they handed out blows instead of jobs; not education, but prison; instead of freedom, death. Since the party of the revolution was formally consolidated in power in 1929, there has yet to be a massacre on this scale anywhere in Mexico.

The revolutionary tendency within the movement of 1968 failed. The workers did not join the movement. Some political brigades established contacts with the workers. There were lightning meetings in various industrial zones: Tlalnepantla, San Bartolo Naucalpan, la Merced. A great meeting took place in front of the Electric Company at the corner of Melchor Ocampo and Antonio Caso. But in general the students did not try to explain their demands to the workers, nor did they go into the factories. No one went to present a program of common action to the Ayotla textile factories that were on strike. After all, what did the students have to offer the workers? Some students on the left talked of a total revolution, but the correlation of forces favored the government. There simply was no revolutionary situation: no economic crisis, no political crisis. The workers had no modern arms. The domination of the PRI–CTM over the workers remained unshaken.

Was the soft line of the movement – the democratizing tendency – also a failure? As of October 1968, neither soft nor hard line had achieved anything. The massacre of Tlatelolco was a complete repression; the movement disappeared from the streets; the nation turned its attention to the Olympics.

Post-Massacre Concessions

But within the next three years, some of the demands of the movement were granted. Díaz Ordaz repealed the law against social dissolution;

Demetrio Vallejo and Valentín Campa were freed. After the mini-Tlatelolco of 10 June 1971, Luis Echeverría dismissed the chiefs of police. During the 1970s came a larger amnesty, a democratic opening, and the Political Reform – also in response to the student movement. But this may be seen as tokenism.[20] New political prisoners took the place of the old, and there was no victory in the long run.

The government permitted important changes in the content of education given by part of the National University. In the Department of Economics and the Department of Political and Social Sciences, a Marxist orientation won new converts. A similar situation developed in the new Sciences and Humanities high school system (CCH). The creation of the CCH high schools in Mexico City, a system that occasionally reached into the nearby states, reformed the educational system at the preparatory level.

The Student Movement Analysed

The most profound analysis of the 1968 explosion is that of Sergio Zermeño in *Mexico: A Utopian Democracy* (1978, in Spanish). According to Zermeño, the ruling class had not drifted into a political crisis. The movement could not catalyse protests by the workers into an open confrontation with the authorities that might bring a rupture with the established order. "The Mexican student movement was a protest of emergent middle sectors against the excesses of a fattened ruling class, unreachable and satisfied in its stability, a protest against the closure and rigidity of the political system."[21]

The 1968 student explosion was the response of dissatisfied intermediate sectors constituting a new class, neither bourgeois not proletarian, to "the predetermination of political options ... [by] the impregnable and authoritarian state." Rather than a movement for socialist democracy advocated by the minoritarian sector of the student collectivity allied to organized labor, it was a movement of the technically advanced and professionally qualified sectors incorporated into the developmental project of the modern state. Contrary to most analyses on the left, Zermeño rejected the thesis of a political crisis of the state and of the ruling party tantamount to a revolutionary situation. On the contrary, the main body of protesting students opted for a soft line in favor of political democracy and political reform.[22]

Zermeño was not entirely alone in postulating this interpretation of the events. Leaders of the radical wing of the student movement declared:

> What the student movement achieved was not a reanimation of the class struggle [between labor and capital], but rather the recovery of the possibility of protest for intermediate strata. The massacre of 2 October signified a rupture between the petty bourgeoisie and part of the working class, on the one hand, and the ruling power, on the other.

This view was seconded by the sociologist and former rector of the National University, Pablo González Casanova, who concluded that the student movement "represents essentially the petty bourgeoisie, an ascending class but dissatisfied." As for the students' ideology and its significance, wrote Juan Manuel Cañibe, "their revolutionary ideology does not correspond to the ideology of the proletariat, but rather to that of the ascending middle classes."[23]

The thorny question concerns the identification of students and their movement as "petty bourgeois." What kind of "middle sectors" and "middle classes" did they represent? According to Zermeño, they were not petty bourgeois in the Marxist sense of potential "owners of means of production who do not as a rule employ wage-laborers regularly or in any significant number," nor slated to become for the most part "workers on their own account who do not work for wages and are not owners, but otherwise enjoy a comfortable living." On the contrary, most occupied the bottom rungs of a ladder leading to technical or professional employment at wages above the average. Above the average? By some counts that would place them in the same privileged class as the state bureaucracy and ruling authorities against whom the students were protesting.[24] It was only their incomes that were "middle."

The student movement focused not on the antithesis of bourgeois and proletarians, exploiters and exploited, but on the opposition of power and powerlessness, authority and freedom. Although a minority of student revolutionaries made common cause with organized labor against the veiled exploitation in nationalized enterprises besides that in the private sector, the two struggles should not be confused – nor the two modes of popular resistance.

But if we look at the movement from the perspective of a national resistance gathering steam, it takes on another meaning. "The 68" was a tremendous moment in the rising popular resistance. We can agree with Zermeño when he argues that the social revolution in 1968 was a utopia. But the evidence he presents reveals more than "a protest of emergent middle sectors against the excesses of a fattened ruling class." The explosion of student rage against the social order was more than a crisis in the modernization of Mexico.

Radical students wanted to get rid of the PRI government and revive the revolutionary Mexico of story and legend. The revolution had been disgraced and betrayed; another revolution was necessary. The *anarchizante* combatants from the preparatory and vocational schools lacked ideology, but they knew what they wanted: a new society. University students, who had more ideology than analysis, dreamed of a Mexican May *a la Française*. As a result, Mexico City littered with barricades and smoking buses resembled Paris in the spring.

In the middle of the movement, on 13 September, the National Union of Polytechnical Students analysed the student conflict in a press bulletin that highlights the plight of poor students destined to remain poor:

> The students at the Polytechnical Institute suffer terribly in their efforts to survive and study: 70 percent must have recourse to part-time work; the scholarships are insufficient; absenteeism is rampant among their teachers; failures and drop-outs are increasing every year; the life of a young professional who has finally obtained a degree is turning dramatic: it is extremely difficult to find work.... The young people in this institution want new political and social solutions; they reject the contemporary world as "inauthentic in its lifestyle" because of the power of oligarchies, concentrations of foreign capital, and the existence of administrative corruption.[25]

The Central Committee of the Mexican Communist Party knew that there was no revolutionary situation in August 1968. But in spite of the influence it exercised in the CNH through its young cadres, the Party was unable to impose its realistic line in time. No one could control and channel the social energy that welled up that summer.

The student insurgency was bound to end in utopia. But the heroes and martyrs of the 1968 struggle wrote another chapter in the history of the popular resistance that was *not* utopian. The students ripped away the revolutionary mask of the PRI government and revealed the truth to the nation. This truth would feed and strengthen the popular resistance in years to come.

The student movement not only underscored a historic date dividing sleeping Mexico from the Mexico of the future. Young people were radicalized. Some joined the ranks of the armed resistance. Others thought about the urgent need to make common cause with the peasants and workers; they counseled land "invasions" and independent unions. Much of the momentum acquired by the independent university unions sprang from the movement.

The limited amnesty and the political opening for the left-wing parties during the 1970s owed much to the popular student movement of 1968. The democratic opening of the year 2000 owes even more.

Notes

1. Our main source for the sequence and escalation of student protests is the day-by-day account from 22 July to 2 October in Ramon Ramírez Gómez, *El movimiento estudiantil de México*, 2 vols. (Mexico City: Era, 1969), vol. 1, pp. 145–397.
2. Sergio Zermeño, *México: Una democracia utópica* (Mexico City: Siglo XXI, 1978), pp. 12–13.
3. Ibid., p. 13. The Marx citation is from the "Manifesto of the Communist Party," *Collected Works*, vol. 6, p. 481.
4. Zermeño, *México*, p. 18.
5. Ibid., and Ramírez Gómez, *El movimiento estudiantil*, vol. 1, pp. 191–6.
6. Zermeño, *México*, p. 110.
7. Ibid., pp. 29–30.
8. Ibid., pp. 28–29.
9. Elena Poniatowska, *La noche de Tlatelolco* (Mexico City: Era, 1978), p. 37.
10. Zermeño, *México*, p. 122.
11. Ibid., p. 122 n.3.
12. Ibid., pp. 122, 125–6.
13. Ibid., p. 124.
14. Ibid., p. 125.
15. Gustavo Díaz Ordaz, "Cuarto informe de gobierno (extractos)," Appendix to Ilán Semo and Américo Saldívar, *México, un pueblo en la historia*, 4 vols., ed. Enrique Semo (Mexico City: Universidad Autónoma de Puebla and Editorial Nueva Imágen, 1982), vol. 4, p. 385.
16. Zermeño, *México*, p. 136.
17. Ibid., pp. 180–1.
18. Poniatowska, *La noche de Tlatelolco*, p. 37; and Zermeño, *México*, p. 182.
19. Poniatowska, *La noche de Tlatelolco*, p. 169; and Ilán Semo, "El ocaso de los mitos

(1958–1968)," in Semo and Saldívar, *México, un pueblo*, vol. 4, pp. 132–3, 135.

20. Rosalio Wences Reza, *El movimiento estudiantil y los problemas nacionales* (Mexico City: Nuestro Tiempo, 1971), pp. 51–2.

21. Zermeño, *México*, p. 47.

22. Ibid., pp. 50, 51, 53.

23. Radical student leaders and González Casanova cited by Claude Kiejman and Jean Francis Held, *Mexico, le pain et les joux* (Paris: Du Seuil, 1969), pp. 54, 119; and Juan Manuel Cañibe, "El movimiento estudiantil y la opinión pública," *Revista Mexicana de Ciencia Política*, no. 59 (January–March): 11.

24. Zermeño, *México*, pp. 202–3.

25. Cited by Ramírez Gómez, *El movimiento estudiantil*, vol. 1, pp. 315–16.

9 ✸ The Guerrilla Movements in Guerrero

We have seen that the resistance had a revolutionary as well as a reformist current. Although both were socialist in their objectives, they differed over how to reach the goal. The reformist or democratic tendency hoped to make headway under the existing Constitution by reaffirming and implementing the revolutionary content of Articles 27 and 123, incorporating the basic principles of the Revolution of 1910–19. The revolutionary current – formalized in the Plan of Cerro Prieto in 1943, revised in 1952 – called for a new revolution and for a revision of the ambiguous and double-dealing Constitution of 1917, "so that it might become practical law and not a bloody trick." The two strategies first came into collision when the Marxist parties withdrew their support from the Madera guerrillas in 1965, and subsequently when they endorsed the "soft line" during the days of rage in Mexico City.

The student movement had raised many questions about the government in the minds of young people; the Guerreran Civic Association (ACG) offered them an alternative. If we were to speak of different zones of consciousness-for-itself, then the state of Guerrero would take first place. In that state, Genaro Vázquez and Lucio Cabañas were the catalysts that fused the ingredients of revolution into a flaming resistance.

Once again the soft line was abandoned for the hard line in sheer self-defense. Although Genaro Vázquez and the ACG went into action before the student movement, we only now arrive at a study of his resistance to presidential despotism in connection with its later phase of armed struggle.

Genaro Vázquez

Legend tells us that Zapata came to understand the injustices against the poor when still a child; Genaro Vázquez, who ended by emulating him, might have had the same experiences, for he attended the village assemblies of the peasants from childhood.

He was born in 1933 in San Luis Acatlán in Guerrero; he studied in the rural Normal School of Ayotzinape; he went on to the San Ildefonso preparatory school in the capital, where he received a big dose of positivist education. He decided that it was necessary to know the law in order to defend the peasants, so he took up law studies at the National University. He did not finish them. In 1957, he taught school in the slums of the Federal District.[1]

In the same year, General Raúl Caballero Aburto was looting the state of Guerrero. Who was this merciless general? On 7 July 1952, he had taken part in the infamous massacre of the Henriquistas' political demonstration in the central park of the capital. His propensity to violence was exceeded only by his desire to enrich himself through political corruption. After three years as governor of Guerrero, he had accumulated thirty pieces of real estate in the name of his wife and daughter; two of them alone were valued at 22 million pesos. While the General continued to enrich himself in 1957, Genaro Vázquez and other professional people formed the Guerreran Civic Committee (CCG). Genaro was then 24 years old.

In 1958, he participated in the Revolutionary Teachers' Movement (MRM) during the strike and the seizure of the Secretariat of Public Education. Perhaps this was the reason why he was fired from his teaching job. But since he was in close contact with the peasants of his region in Guerrero, they elected him to represent before the Department of Agrarian Affairs and Colonization (DAAC) the coffee workers, the copra workers, and the palm workers.

On 26 January, he married the teacher Consuelo Solís Morales; by her he would have six children. At about the time of his marriage, he transformed the Committee into the ACG, made up of four peasant organizations.

The Guerreran Civic Association and Repression

On 13 May 1960, Genaro called together his first neighborhood meeting in the San Francisco district of Chilpancingo, the state capital. There it was decided to ask for an investigation of General Raúl Caballero Aburto. But before anything could be done, on 21 October 1960 the student leader Jesús Araujo Hernández unexpectedly led a strike in the state university, demanding a reform of the statutes and the resignation of Chancellor Alfonso Ramírez Altamirano. The authorities called for the army to intervene, and the 24th battalion moved against the students. The students' parents joined the fray, and permanent guards were formed near the university in the Granados Maldonado park.

Two days later, the state's attorney general, Javier Olea Muñoz, decided to hold a dialogue with the students, but the public demanded that the interview be an open one. The state lawyer declared that no one had presented the government with official petitions, but the students showed him that he was wrong by quickly producing copies of the disputed documents.

On 30 October, the ACG led 5,000 people to make a "civic stand-in" in front of the state capitol as an active protest in support of the students. The authorities answered by sending out troops, a squad from the 24th infantry battalion under the command of General Julio Morales. The "civic stand-in," a popular tactic devised by Genaro Vázquez, conceded a few yards of ground and took up a new position in the tiny Nicolás Bravo park.

On 4 November, the federal police and the 50th battalion once more provoked "the civics." This battalion had been mobilized on orders of the "friendly" President Adolfo López Mateos. The provocation united the students with "the civics" against the repression. Students joined the movement in droves to paint walls and pass out leaflets while Genaro moved through Iguala, Atoyac de Alvarez, and other towns asking for support. The demonstrations against Caballero spread. He was threatened with a strike; large businesses were shutting down, and more than 500 small businesses in Chilpancingo plus 23,000 in the rest of the state began to close.

The state government's chamber of deputies announced that there was no reason why the local authorities should not be obeyed. After this pronouncement, the civic movement began to decline, and Genaro once again made the rounds of the villages to whip up resistance with blazing speeches; from this activity arose the Coalition of Popular Organizations. Tourism fell off, and in Chilpancingo the market moved near the university, where the strikers were stationed.

On 30 December 1960, the authorities returned to the attack with stepped-up repression. As people were shopping in the market, machine-guns belonging to the 6th, 24th, and 27th battalions opened up on the crowd. Sporadic fire continued for an hour resulting in 18 dead, including women and children. Genaro, who was on the Costa Grande, went underground as the police launched a manhunt. He secretly returned to the state capital.

Finally, on 5 January 1961, the federal government gave heed to the problem in Guerrero and named Arturo Martínez Adame as interim governor. Then came the government's counter-attack: the newspapers discredited the movement; attempts were made to suborn its leader. But he came back with a legal fight in 1962 as he supported the teacher José María Suárez Téllez for governor. The civics – disciples of Genaro – also set forth candidates for many municipal posts throughout the state and for representatives in the chamber of deputies. In adopting these tactics, Genaro's movement resembled Jaramillo's Agrarian Labor Party of Morelos (PAOM).

The PRI, however, put in as governor Raymundo Abarca Alarcón. Although the Coalition won many offices of the adjutancy in the state, they were not able to survive the state's offensive. One by one, they were pushed out by bureaucratic maneuvers, and the bureaucracy made it impossible for them to purge the lower levels of government. One of these maneuvers took place in Iguala. The civics were disavowed by the authorities, and Israel Salmerón was placed in power. The Civic Committee protested through its local director Gilberto Mota. On 31 December 1961, a year after the massacre in Chilpancingo, the followers of Genaro were once again massacred: 3,000 people were attacked, resulting in 28 dead, dozens wounded, and 156 arrested.

On this occasion the authorities accused Vázquez of killing an agent assigned to watch him. He fled to the north-west, where he worked in the Sonoran and Sinaloan cotton fields as a day laborer.

Before Rubén Jaramillo died on 23 May 1962, Genaro had an

interview with him in the offices of the newspaper *¡Presente!* in Cuernavaca, aiming to formalize an independent organization of poor peasants. In the north he had benefited from similar interviews with other peasant leaders. Thus, he took part in the creation of the Independent Peasant Central (CCI) in 1963, working with Ramón Danzós Palomino, a leading member of the PCM.[2]

The Seven-Point Program

For four years Genaro wandered about, hiding from the police man-hunt and organizing clandestine resistance. In April 1966 he launched the Seven-Point Program with the Self-Defense Council of the People. This organization was formed by the Guerreran Civic Association, the Free Union of Copra Associations (ULAC), the Independent Association of Coffee Workers (ACI), the February 24th neighbor-hood, the Emiliano Zapata Revolutionary Agrarian League of the South, and the Villa de Guadalupe neighborhood.

The Council used peaceful and legal means of struggle against the ambitions of the capitalists and landlords friendly to North American interests. After analysing the socio-economic situation in Guerrero, it noted that civil rights had been abolished, taxes were high, the treasury was being robbed, unemployment was rampant, and nepotism prevailed in government circles; it spoke of the "aggressive attitude of the government's representatives" who thought of the people's rights as a grant from state officials. Therefore, the Program concluded, "we have decided to follow the only correct road open to us, to say ENOUGH ... to the bosses and to the government of Abarca Alarcón."

In order to achieve this objective, the Program set forth Seven Points conspicuous for their nonsectarian character:

- Political freedom and real democracy; resignation of the current government.
- Planning of the national economy to achieve material and cultural progress.
- Freedom and respect for trade unions and the rights of labor.
- Nationalization of the mines in the hands of US corporations.
- Parcellization and redistribution of the great estates and guarantees for the *ejidos*.

- Application of an integral agrarian reform.
- Literacy campaigns and popular culture.[3]

At the end of the document came a call to all honorable citizens, to all religious believers, and to revolutionary radicals to denounce the government's aggressions in leaflets, letters, meetings, and demonstrations. The police continued to look for the propagator of the Program.

Imprisonment, Escape, and the Turn to Armed Struggle

On 9 November 1966, eight members of the secret police attained their objective. Genaro was kidnapped at the office doors of the Movement of National Liberation (MLN) in the Federal District. He was caught by surprise and did not have his pistol with him. The police beat him and questioned him, then took him to Chilpancingo and from there to Iguala. He was formally arraigned on 16 November for seven crimes which carried a term of life in prison. In an interview from his cell, he called on his supporters "to persist in defending their rights and in promoting the people's welfare," and on his friends and comrades "to persist in building the organization of the people."[4] Near the end of the year he asked for federal protection because he feared assassination in the Guerreran jail.

On 22 April 1968, three months before the explosion of the student movement, he was freed by the first armed command of the ACG made up of teachers such as Lucio Cabañas, Roque Salgado, and Filiberto Solís. These last two gave their lives for their friend. Genaro then went to the mountains and began a guerrilla struggle. On 1 August he released his first "Communiqué to the Students" from his revolutionary camp "José María Morelos" in the mountains of southern Guerrero – named after the great guerrilla commander and revolutionary priest who in the wars of independence had freed southern Mexico from Spanish rule.

In the communiqué he warned the students about "the method of systematic political violence used by the forces that govern us," noting that the revolution of 1910 was bourgeois-democratic and that "the rich had taken over its political direction." He restated his thesis that the contemporary Mexican state was a re-edition of the old Porfirian dictatorship with a domestic form of colonialism: repressive methods, institutionalized lies, and institutionalized crime. He urged the students to form "our own revolutionary political leadership" that would take Mexico into socialism through an "anti-feudal, anti-imperialist, and democratic revolution."[5]

Since in Mexico there was no armed proletarian vanguard, he offered the students the chance to create one with the poor peasants of the south. He foresaw repression of the kind that occurred on 2 October, for he called for "the development of an adequate tactic for confronting effectively *armed violence* … [that] one can only answer effectively and victoriously in an armed manner."[6]

Efforts were being made in the meantime to organize national resistance coordinating actions in the towns and the countryside. Genaro also planned to make contacts at the international level. In 1968, the Guerreran Civic Association became the Revolutionary National Civic Association (ACNR), which supported the guerrilla nucleus and provided a base for uniting with other radical groups. Near the end of his life, Genaro would have talks with Lucio Cabañas, who had been a member of the PCM and with whom he had ideological differences: he did not want openly to declare himself a Marxist-Leninist. The aims of his organization were more akin to those of Jaramillo: defeat of the PRI government; formation of a democratic socialist labor government; complete independence; and social justice for all working people.[7]

Genaro's guerrilla movement was made up mainly of peasants. His field of action was the Costa Grande region between Acapulco and the Balsas River bordering on Michoacán. The only ranks were commander and sub-commander. Various indications allow us to deduce that the guerrilla's style of discipline was Guevarist but not their social composition: most of them were peasants who wanted to impose "the Zapatista doctrine" on Mexico.

In spite of the government military force deployed against this guerrilla nucleus, it could not be eliminated easily, for it had massive popular support, especially among the peasants. The Mexican army – "defender of the poor" – used various annihilation tactics against the guerrillas, including that of the "Vietnamese village." This meant moving the dispersed peasant population at bayonet point into "controllable zones." According to official sources, more than 12,000 soldiers (25 battalions) were in Guerrero performing their "social service." To these should be added the air force, the helicopters, and the motorized war *matériel* and personnel: convoys, jeeps, paratroops, scouts, and the rangers who arrived as advisors from the US. By 12 August 1971, the troops numbered over 24,000. Since the army could not catch the guerrilla "cattle thieves," a death squad named "Anonymous Justice of Guerrero" was formed as a secret paramilitary group composed of police protected by the bosses and the PRI government.

Although Genaro implied that various guerrilla actions were carried out, the sources we have consulted speak only of three. The first was an assault on a truck belonging to the Mexican Commercial Bank at the branch located at the corner of Xola and Cinco de Febrero in the capital. It took place on 19 April 1969. This effort failed since the police recovered the three million pesos that had been expropriated. In their flight, the guerrillas were overtaken because of a mechanical failure in the taxi they had seized for the operation. General Renato Vega and his driver were wounded; the guerrilla Juan Antúñez died in this action along with a secret agent. Not long afterward, the guerrilla Florentino Jaime Hernández was arrested in Catalán, Guerrero; but he was soon out of prison and off to Cuba through an exchange of prisoners.

On 29 December 1970 came the second action, the kidnapping of the banker Conaciano Luna Radilla, manager of the Commercial Bank of the South. On 5 January 1971, the guerrillas received a ransom of half a million pesos for his life and released him.

The most famous and the most important operation by the ACNR was the third: the kidnapping of the multimillionaire, owner of a Coca-Cola concession, proprietor of the "Yoli" soft drink factories in Taxco and Acapulco, doctor and PRI politician, ex-mayor of Taxco, businessman and real estate operator married to a US citizen, chancellor of the University of Guerrero: Jaime Castrejón Díez. On 19 November 1971, a commando led by Genaro Vázquez himself snatched this multimillionaire on the highway between Taxco and Chilpancingo. For his life, the guerrillas demanded the liberation of nine political prisoners, the formal trial of peasants held in the barracks, and a ransom of two and a half million pesos.

Although the government did not immediately make arrangements for the release of the prisoners, the kidnapping was a triumph for the

ACNR. The perfumed chancellor was released on 1 December 1971 after the liberated prisoners arrived in Cuba. The entire nation awaited the next action by Genaro Vázquez.

Two months after this brilliant guerrilla action, its leader died on 2 February 1972, supposedly of an automobile accident on the "Thousand Peaks" highway to Morelia. According to the version of José Bracho, the lieutenant traveling with Genaro, the over-confident and inexpert driver "Fidel," was the cause of the accident but not of the death of the guerrilla leader. Bracho claimed that Genaro was still alive after the accident, but fled with a big wound to his forehead. The army located him by chance three days later: he had lost blood and fainted several times. When the police and army medics realized who he was, said Bracho, they let him die. Bracho himself was tortured and beaten.

Genaro Vázquez was not the first to take up arms – Lucio Cabañas had done so a year earlier – but he was the first to focus national attention on the miserable situation of the people of Guerrero. Genaro's guerrilla war resembled Rubén Jaramillo's: after exhausting the legal means of struggle, he took up arms with wide peasant support. Both leaders tried to raise the consciousness of their followers through political parties and electoral struggles, beginning with the PAOM and later the ACNR.

Although they never declared themselves Marxist-Leninists, they were directly influenced by PCM cadres: Jaramillo by his "compadre" Mónico Rodríguez, Genaro by Lucio Cabañas and Danzós Palomino. Anyone who glances at the Plan of Cerro Prieto and compares it with the Seven Point Program or the aims of the ACNR can see that its guiding ideology is Marxist socialism.

Genaro was the creator of the theory of the Mexican state as a new edition of the old Porfirian dictatorship, or *neoporfirismo*. He also invented the "civic stand-ins," a form of Gandhian civil disobedience with popular peasant mass mobilization.

The blood of the peasant guerrillas has watered Mexico's soil since the colonial period, passing through the ten years' War of Reform (1857–67), to arrive at the rural struggles of the twentieth century. Today the authorities want to change their repressive image by injecting money into roads and dams and schools for Guerrero's development. But they will never wipe from the mind of the Mexican people that a popular revolution had begun its march underneath the surface of society. Everything suggests that it will be a long march in Mexico, for every resistance movement seems to be quickly bottled up in its region, as happened with Zapatismo.

Lucio Cabañas

Since the days of Zapata, the most distinguished guerrilla actions in Mexico have been those of the rural schoolteacher Lucio Cabañas (1938–74). His guerrilla struggle, starting in 1967, survived longer than any other – about seven years. With the exception of Jaramillo's *foco*, Lucio's was the only one to confront the army directly. The ambushes he set in June and August 1972 and in August 1974 are still high points in the armed resistance. If the character of Lucio Cabañas had something to do with his guerrilla exploits, we must ask not only what he did and why, but also what kind of man he was.

There are few witnesses concerning the personal life of the guerrilla, and these contradict each other on key points. First, we have the testimony of *El Guerrillero*, written by "Ernesto." Comrade "Ernesto" claims to have participated in one of the simultaneous bank expropriations in Chihuahua City on 15 January 1972. "Ernesto" worked with the Zapatista Urban Front (FUZ) at the beginning of the 1970s, then began cooperating with the 23 September Movement, the guerrilla group made up of the survivors of the attack on the Madera Barracks in 1965. He went into the mountains above Atoyac along with the survivors of the bank assaults in the middle of 1972, remaining with Cabañas' group until 1973.

What does he have to say about Cabañas? First, that Lucio was contemptuous of Marxist-Leninist theory, and, second, that he lacked political wisdom and neither had nor wanted a fully developed doctrine. He did not want to analyse existing social conditions but to carry on an armed struggle. His education, we are told, was rudimentary, and he was ignorant of oratory. He lacked personal magnetism. He had trouble expressing his thoughts. There was little intellectual content in his talk, for he repeated himself often, and usually concerning episodes in the struggle that had little political relevance. He talked with pistol in hand and showed himself extremely mistrustful. Like Pancho Villa, he went to sleep in one place but reappeared the next morning in another. "Ernesto" says that Cabañas "slept with one eye open." He could not stand criticism. He felt himself inspired: nobody could give orders or even advise him. He was so vain that he fomented a cult of personality around himself. Every day, he relived his exploits, singing a romantic song that he had ordered composed. Could this kind of rural schoolteacher lead and carry out a national revolution?[8]

The Lucio of "Ernesto" is completely different from the portrait that emerges from an interview with Lucio's cousin, Atoyac's mayor, Manuel García Cabañas, who described him as inhibited to the point of taciturnity. He was unusually withdrawn. He did not take part in any kind of social events; he did not dance; he had nothing to do with women; nor did he drink or smoke. In short, he was an ascetic, a saint of the revolution. In his behavior as in his talk, he was reflective and calm; he never showed restlessness or irritation. Despite his apparent coldness, he knew how to be friendly. He made a practice of not imposing himself in an authoritative manner on his comrades. As a leader, he demanded little and tried to get an opinion from the group itself. His indecisive and vacillating character did not undermine his political ability to launch slogans and banners that mobilized the Guerreran populace. Most of his ideas were related to immediate local problems. As a man of outstanding agitational and organizational capacity, he managed to build a movement linked not only to the peasants of Guerrero, but also to the student movement there and in the states of Sonora, Aguascalientes, Guanajuato, Tamaulipas, and the Federal District.[9]

What are we to make of these contrary characterizations? To underline their common denominator: Lucio Cabañas scorned abstract Marxist theory and preferred to work toward solving the concrete problems of his own people in Guerrero. Being unsure of himself, he could not stand criticism. That he was mistrustful agrees with the report of his character as withdrawn and inhibited. Possibly he lacked oratorical skill and personal magnetism. But are these qualities indispensable to a guerrilla leader? Lucio's asceticism and dedication to the struggle stand out. He lived to serve his people, and the people knew it. For those qualities, Mexicans still render him homage.

As circumstances change, however, so does people's behavior. The mayor of Atoyac's profile of Cabañas covers only the period when he was a rural schoolteacher and local activist with modest goals and without pretensions to greatness. In sharp contrast, Comrade "Ernesto" gives us the profile of a guerrilla leader whose fame had spread throughout much of Latin America. "His equivalent in the Americas was Fidel Castro" – at least before the latter assumed power in Cuba. But then, Lucio might duplicate that feat as well.[10] By then, he had reason to be vain.

What events in Lucio's life helped to shape his revolutionary character? The main factor was his work in the Young Communists and later in the Mexican Communist Party. As a militant communist, Cabañas became a student leader on a national scale in 1962 when he was elected general secretary of the Federation of Socialist Peasant Students (FECS). A little later, he joined the National Liberation Movement (MLN). In 1964, when he became a rural teacher in Atoyac, he was active in the Revolutionary Teachers' Movement (MRM). In Atoyac he helped to organize the People's Electoral Front (FEP) and the Independent Peasant Central (CCI). He worked in these different organizations as a militant of the PCM, agitating for democracy among the peasants of Guerrero. Finally, he became a member of the regional committee of the Party in his own state, and for a while he received cadre training at party headquarters in the Federal District.[11]

He continued working as a representative of the PCM until the massacre of 18 May 1967 swept away all hope of remaining on the peaceful and legal road. But as he recalled in "How I Went to the Mountains," he continued to distribute the Party newspaper.[12] This experience as a militant helped to form the future guerrilla. Although he ended by breaking with the Party, it had shaped his political development and led to his formation of the Party of the Poor. Lucio also approved the Party's shift from a soft to a hard line at its 16th congress in May 1973. In other words, he accepted the necessity of a new revolution that would carry through and surpass the Zapatista revolution of 1910–19.

Lucio Cabañas' militancy in the Young Communists and later in the PCM makes up the first stage of his political evolution. The massacre of 18 May 1967 at Atoyac marks the beginning of the second stage: there were increasing disagreements with the PCM about the question of armed struggle as the only workable answer for the political fugitive. During this new stage, after leaving the Party, Lucio formed the Armed Commandos of Guerrero and the Party of the Poor.

The Atoyac Massacre

The Atoyac massacre set Lucio on the path of guerrilla struggle. As he says in "How I Went to the Mountains," the common people will put up with poverty and even government repression, but they won't stand for a massacre.[13] The PCM maintained that in order to make a revolution it was first necessary to analyse exhaustively the social reality. But confronted with the massacre, the militant comrades felt no need for a critical examination; they felt the urge rather to take up arms and to kill those responsible for the bloodshed. It did not matter that revolutionary conditions were lacking. At least there existed conditions for striking at the government.

What were the circumstances leading to the massacre?[14] Barely a year after Lucio came to the town of Atoyac as a rural schoolteacher, the state government branded him a communist agitator, and he was charged with the crime of social dissolution. On 21 November 1965, he and another rural schoolteacher, Serafín Núñez, organized in Atoyac a programmatic assembly under the auspices of the People's Electoral Front. A few days later, an order arrived from the governor transferring them to the state of Durango, supposedly to render services in the line of duty, but in fact to stop their agitation.

In Durango, Lucio continued his agitation until the governor demanded that his salary be stopped. He returned to Atoyac and organized a group of parents to demand the resignation of the rural school's principal and his own reinstatement on the grounds that he had been dismissed arbitrarily. On 13 May 1967, there was a strike; the principal was forced out and Lucio was reinstated. But two days later, the government intervened to ruin the agreement. The people returned to the struggle. On 18 May 1967, while a meeting was in progress, the federal police opened fire on the gathering of 3,000, killing 7 and wounding 20. Two police were killed in retaliation, and the rest had to flee. Popular wrath was so great that armed peasants went in search of the attackers. The army occupied the city. Lucio, declared responsible for the massacre though himself wounded and in fact innocent, fled to the mountains.

The PCM and the teachers in the MRM searched for him and finally made contact. They discussed with him the political situation and tried to dissuade him from taking up arms in a guerrilla war. But as a fugitive of the law, Cabañas decided to defend himself by the only means he thought would be successful: arming himself and his comrades from the town of Atoyac and its environs, comrades who had accompanied him to the mountains after saving his life.

The Armed Commandos of Guerrero

Other guerrilla groups supported his determination. Arms and money arrived from various sources. Cabañas recruited additional comrades from the first Castroite guerrilla movement in Mexico, the Armed Commandos of Chihuahua, the 23 September Movement consisting of survivors of Arturo Gámiz' group that had attained national fame for assaulting the Madera Barracks on 23 September 1965. These were the first combat-tested guerrillas to join Cabañas' group.

The actions of the Armed Commandos of Guerrero were initially limited to modest operations of administering popular justice. In a communiqué of 15 July 1970 in the PCM's magazine *Oposición*, the Party of the Poor listed its first exploits: the execution of two army officers and two political bosses whose gunmen had been killing peasants; an attack on the federal police in reprisal for its crimes against the people; armed pressure on a big owner to make him pay the wages of 15 peons he had been trying to cheat; and armed intervention to disrupt the political tour of Luis Echeverría, allowing him to visit only one of the seven towns that form the Costa Grande region of Guerrero.[15]

In April 1970 came the first kidnapping of a rich man. The guerrillas demanded 100,000 pesos for the life of the cattleman Juan Gallardo – and got it. On 2 March the following year, they assaulted the Central Bank of Aguascalientes and made off with 400,000 pesos. Another bank assault followed on 16 April in Empalme, Sonora, against a branch of the Commercial Bank. The second kidnapping took place on 7 January 1972: Jaime Farril, principal of preparatory school number 2 in Acapulco, fell into the hands of the guerrillas. They demanded a ransom of three million pesos. The action failed when the army rescued Farril on 13 April.

Cabañas' guerrillas did not accomplish much during their first two years of struggle. As he himself tells in his last recording a few days before his death on 2 December 1974, he began his struggle in the mountains with only six comrades. The guerrilla band did not grow, and in despair three cadres dropped out. The guerrilla struggle stagnated with only three combatants until 1969 when nine men joined. Then began the executions, starting with two of the main political bosses in Atoyac. The available arms hardly allowed more daring actions. Only after the first kidnapping in April 1970 were the guerrillas able to use 100,000 pesos to buy powerful modern weapons. The bank assaults and the new kidnappings between 1971 and 1972 allowed them to make a qualitative leap from a left-wing groupuscule of nine in 1970 to a force of 30 armed men carrying out an ambush in June 1972. In August 1972, 40 guerrillas took part in a second ambush.

The third and final stage in Cabañas' political evolution began with the document addressed to the Mexican people and published in the newspaper *Excelsior* on 13 January 1972. There we are told that the Armed Commandos of Guerrero were responsible for the kidnapping of Jaime Farril, principal of a preparatory school dependent on the Autonomous University of Guerrero. The document was addressed not only to students at the school, but also to teachers, peasants, and "all working and downtrodden people."[16]

The original name adopted by the guerrillas was an adaptation of the label used by the Armed Commandos of Chihuahua. But when Cabañas' group later claimed national attention, this label disappeared, and Cabañas made reference only to the Peasant Justice Brigade and to the Party of the Poor (PDLP).

Peasant Justice Brigade and Party of the Poor

During 1972, the influence of the Chihuahuan guerrillas was superseded by that of other guerrilla groups. In May, two representatives sent by the Revolutionary Action Movement (MAR) arrived in the mountains and proposed an alliance. In June, these militants began instructing Cabañas' followers in the art of guerrilla warfare; they had learned this art as part of the 50 militants trained in North Korea in 1969. There were four ambushes of the army by Cabañas' Peasant Justice Brigade. Arnulfo Ariza, alias Mena-Mena of the MAR, directed two of them personally. In the middle of 1973, five militants from the new 23 September Communist League arrived. The new League, formed in March 1973, combined members of the old 23 September Movement with members of other armed movements in Mexico. But the resulting group drifted into ultra-leftism and began a hidden struggle to change the political line and leadership of the Brigade and the Party. It was expelled from the Party of the Poor in January 1974.

Fundamental to an understanding of this last stage in Cabañas' politics is the "Ideas of the Party of the Poor" that appeared in March 1973.[17] This document did not restrict itself to pointing out the Party's populist objectives, as in the previous stage, but went on to lay out its socialist tasks. The Party's "Ideas" presented the main targets of the armed struggle as the conquest of political power, destruction of the exploiting bourgeois state, formation of a proletarian state, abolition of the capitalist system, and the construction of a new society without exploiters and exploited, without oppressors and oppressed. The aim was to make a political revolution, a social revolution, and a cultural revolution. "Bourgeois culture, because it is counter-revolutionary and incompatible with the interests of the workers, must be destroyed. The people will develop their own culture."

In order to achieve these objectives, the "Ideas" called for extending the guerrilla war to the whole country until it reached the stage of general insurrection and the conquest of power. It urged the workers to take over the factories, the students to seize the schools and universities, and all the people to mobilize to destroy the repressive police and military forces. Undoubtedly this was a Marxist-Leninist manifesto adapted to the needs of guerrilla struggle, an answer to the massacre of Atoyac and to the massacres that followed it in October 1968 and in June 1971.

On two occasions the Secretary of Defense, General Cuenca Díaz, offered Lucio an amnesty: first on 17 March 1972, then again on 18 November 1972. But Lucio remembered what had happened to Jaramillo after the latter accepted a similar pardon. Once disarmed, he was murdered by the federal police and army elements. Besides, when Lucio went to the mountains, he swore never to make peace with those responsible for the massacre of Atoyac. The massacres on 2 October and 10 June only hardened his resolve. Acceptance of an amnesty would have been betrayal of the struggle he was leading. If he had to die, he preferred to die fighting rather than be murdered as Jaramillo had been.

Again, the money from the ransoms and first bank assaults fueled a qualitative leap in both arms and number of combatants – there were 100 guerrillas by the middle of 1974. So the capacity for action also grew to the most spectacular exploits: the ambushes of the army. On 25 June 1972 came the first, with 10 soldiers dead and 2 wounded. The second took place on 23 August 1972, resulting in 18 soldiers killed, 9 wounded, and 20 captured. On 21 August 1974, the third ambush led to 11 soldiers dead, 6 wounded, and 17 captured. The fourth ambush, on the same day, cost the government 14 dead and 15 wounded. Direct confrontations with the army, such as those on 20 September 1974 (9 soldiers dead, 7 wounded) and on October 1974 (16 dead, 15 wounded), also took their toll.[18]

The bank assaults also increased. On 22 December 1972 the first expropriations were carried out by two commando groups of the Party of the Poor acting simultaneously in two locations, one at the Viking Construction Company offices in Coyuca de Benítez in the state of Guerrero, with a booty of 42,000 pesos, the other at the Mexican Bank of the South in Acapulco, with a take of 230,000 pesos. On 13 April 1973 the Mexican Commercial Bank's branch in the Secretariat of Public Education was expropriated to the tune of two million pesos.

Kidnapping the Governor of Guerrero

Without doubt, the most famous action in Lucio Cabañas' political life was the kidnapping of the senator, multimillionaire governor of Guerrero – Rubén Figueroa, at the time a political candidate put forward by the PRI. On 30 May 1974, the senator fell into a trap. He went to the mountains to negotiate with Cabañas in the hope of ending the violence and achieving social peace in Guerrero, but Lucio refused to let him leave. The senator offered to sign an agreement by means of which 500,000 pesos a month would go to organize and maintain the Party of the Poor if it would surface as a legal party.[19] But Lucio was interested in another matter: freedom for political prisoners, about 300 throughout the nation. While these were in prison, the senator would also remain under arrest. It was then, in his third communiqué of 19 June 1974, that Lucio presented the demands of his Party of the Poor to public opinion and to the federal and state governments.

In exchange for the release of the PRI's multimillionaire and his four friends, the federal government had to begin a military withdrawal from the mountains. Then it would have to satisfy five demands, the four most important of which were:

- Liberation of the political prisoners according to a list and a process that the Party of the Poor was to make known.
- Delivery of 50 million pesos for the people through the Party of the Poor.
- Provision of modern weapons for the Brigade.
- Diffusion throughout the nation of a recording of Lucio and his comrades making speeches and singing guerrilla songs.[20]

From the state government alone, Lucio demanded the liberation of all prisoners, whether political or not.[21] Of course, this demand was impossible to fulfill, as was the demand that the federal government hand over modern arms to the guerrillas. Although Figueroa agreed to free the political prisoners in his own state, he could not free the ordinary prisoners, nor could he count on anything from the federal government, which refused to participate in such deals. The senator's family and friends managed to collect the 50 million pesos. Father Carlos Bonilla acted as an intermediary, taking 25 million pesos to the mountains at the beginning of September 1974. The rest was to be delivered after the senator's release. But on 8 September 1974, the army freed the multimillionaire and recovered 15 million pesos of the ransom already delivered.[22]

Lucio's death was the result of treason. Repression, and guerrilla casualties, increased following the Figueroa kidnapping, demoralization set in, and finally the traitor appeared.

He was José Ramos Ramírez, a coffee grower known as "Chabelo." He recounted events in an interview published in the evening edition of *Excelsior* on 3 September 1975. After joining the Peasant Justice Brigade in October 1974, he learned the following month that some of his relatives had been arrested. This information led him to change sides. Although Lucio still had 10 million pesos of ransom money, Chabelo painted a picture of an armed group reduced in size and demoralized by government repression. Through a cousin, Chabelo informed the authorities of Lucio's hideout near the town of El Otatal. The next day, a military detachment disguised as a group of peasants arrived. The combat lasted an hour and ended the life of the heroic guerrilla.[23]

There may have been a second Judas. Prior to their expulsion by Cabañas, the members of the 23 September League who had joined his guerrillas had made repeated efforts at proselytizing his immediate followers. By their own admission, "For reasons of principle, we have not tolerated nor are we disposed to tolerate, that a number of political deviations we consider to be petty bourgeois [and opportunist] have struck roots in the heart of the movement." Their sole concession was "not to combat militarily such positions at the moment." But that could change, especially after leaving Lucio's camp. According to "Ernesto," Lucio had been betrayed by Mariano Santiago Vázquez. Having been indoctrinated by members of the League, he remained with Lucio in the role of a "fifth column" after the others had been expelled. According to this account, it was Mariano who betrayed him to the armed forces and served as a guide to his whereabouts. If true, then Lucio fell as a consequence of the ideological and factional battles being waged not only between but also within the various guerrilla formations. This is the sense in which the guerrillas were their own worst enemies.[24]

Lessons of the Guerrillas

What lessons does this brief history teach us? Cabañas' guerrilla movement was not ready for the qualitative jump it made with the kidnapping of the multimillionaire senator. In spite of his hundred armed men and the massive support of the Guerreran people, he had to contend with an army that came in from the outside. Revolutionary conditions may have been present in Guerrero, but one state is not the nation. Lucio's mistake was to confuse what he could do in an isolated state with what could be done on a national scale.

There is another lesson. The demands Lucio made on the government were not realistic. It could never have accepted arming the guerrillas and handing them 50 million pesos so they could step up their struggle against the state apparatus. Nor could the Guerreran government free the common prisoners in the state's jails. Lucio's demands were so exaggerated that they gave the impression of weakness, a lack of intelligence, a misunderstanding of the powers and obligations of the federal government. Only much more modest demands had any chance of success. With his unrealistic demands, Lucio gained nothing while the federal government gained time to step up its manhunt.

The kidnapping of the PRI's Figueroa was, none the less, the masterpiece and culminating work of the poor people's guerrilla war. The possibility of negotiating with a distinguished functionary of Echeverría's reformist government opened up. There was a chance of arriving at a political solution concerning two key points of the popular resistance: freedom for the political prisoners, which could have been achieved; and the legalization of the Party of the Poor as the peaceful civil arm of the Peasant Justice Brigade. The senator himself agreed to the liberation of all political prisoners in Guerrero. Besides, as he says in a tape-recording of his first talks with Lucio, he was ready to legalize and sustain the Party of the Poor even though Lucio "wanted to remain upstairs with his armed men," that is, remain in the mountains. This was the road – in his judgment – toward an alliance that could benefit both sides because "a pressure group in Guerrero with a revolutionary sentiment is highly useful for making, as Father Morelos knew, the rich less rich and the poor less poor."[25] Thus Lucio could go on with his armed struggle in the mountains while his Party of the Poor was legalized on the plain. Lucio could have had the best of both worlds. But when this opportunity presented itself, he failed to seize it.

Why? According to "Ernesto," Lucio was overcome by the image of himself as leader of the most consequential guerrilla movement in Mexico since Zapata. Vanity was his undoing. It dissuaded him from accepting the generous terms of peace that would have terminated his life as a guerrilla. He had no lack of money from his various expropriations; he could not be bought. Nor could the opportunity to achieve political power through his Party of the Poor in the state of Guerrero in any way match his fame as a guerrilla hero. So if Figueroa had offered him the job of Federal Inspector of Education in his state, or even to secure a seat for him in the local legislature, Cabañas would have refused.[26]

But "Ernesto" made these reflections in retrospect and they do not explain his break with Lucio, which, according to "Ernesto," occurred because "his movement is [was] not a revolutionary one, nor even a leftist petty-bourgeois one; and by no means, by no path, does it lead to communism." His doctrine boiled down to a few platitudes, that he "defended the poor against the rich ... that the rich must be killed, and that when his movement triumphs ... it will assure that there will be no more poverty, illness, and ignorance." No more poor! Besides, the Party of the Poor was one in name only. Lucio was no Robin Hood. He refused to distribute the cash from his various ransoms and expropriations among the needy in his own state, planning to use it only to buy arms for his pretended revolution.[27]

That was not Cabañas' worst side. "Ernesto" never felt at ease as a member of the Executioner Brigade. He asked himself what kind of party is committed to the ceaseless killing of the rich and concluded, surely not a socialist one. "The name chosen by the Brigade could not be more significant ... that is, a platoon of fusiliers, of killers." It was a name that inspired terror – in reality, and calling things by their right names, "his Brigade was a terrorist one." It smacked of vengeance – little else. Unwittingly, Lucio was following in the footsteps of Sergei Nechayev and the Russian Nihilists, according to whom "everything is permitted in the name of the Revolution."[28]

Death and Resurrection

Vázquez' death, followed two years later by that of Cabañas in 1974, seemed to have closed the door on armed insurgence in the rural guerrillas' main zone of operations in Guerrero. Although a split-off from the PDLP under Carmel Cortés lingered on in the name of the Revolutionary Armed Forces, it too disappeared after a bank expropriation in Cuernavaca in August 1975 and Carmelo's death in a shoot-out with judicial police in Mexico City in September.

Appearances proved deceptive. Contrary to government claims, the PDLP was not wiped out. It went underground, continued with its bank expropriations, and surfaced only in response to the new wave of peasant resistance in Guerrero because of President Salinas' 1991 emendation of Constitutional Article 27 aimed at breaking up the communal *ejidos*. There followed the free trade agreement that opened Mexico to cheaper corn from the US. This double-punch at the peasant class was a near knock-out. While throwing peasant lands on to the market, the neoliberal policy expelled the peasants from the market. Their peaceful protests met with violent repression to which the peasants responded with new guerrilla *focos*.

On 28 June 1995, a peaceful caravan of supporters of the Peasant Organization of the Southern Sierra (OCSS), a legal and reformist movement of the poor in Guerrero, was assaulted by the state police on a road near Aguas Blancas. Following orders from Governor Rubén Figueroa, the caravan was halted. On the presumption that the peasants were armed, the police opened fire, killing 17 of them in cold blood. How do we know the peasants were not armed? The governor had demanded that the police take a video of the operation in order to prove that the caravan had been stopped. An unknown person stole the video from the governor's office and took it to the famous TV journalist Ricardo Rocha, an honest man. Rocha went to Burillo – a 25-year-old millionaire executive at the "totalitarian" television monopoly – and asked him for permission to run it. Burillo, who was tired of the boring newscasts that were nothing but PRI propaganda, told Rocha to go ahead. The world was thus treated to the frightening spectacle of helpless peasants screaming, bleeding, and falling before the murderous gunfire of an unprovoked police attack.[29] President Zedillo immediately ordered the courageous millionaire fired.

The Revolutionary People's Army

On 28 June the following year, a protest meeting was held at Aguas Blancas to commemorate the peasant martyrs. The peaceful gathering with journalists present was suddenly taken over by dozens of masked guerrillas emerging from the forest heavily armed with AK-47s and wearing olive-drab uniforms. Before the astonished video cameras, the new Revolutionary People's Army (EPR) read a manifesto which called for the creation of armed committees of self-defense and for revolutionary tribunals to judge the enemies of the people. That same day, they began cutting down the state police of Guerrero in ambushes.[30]

Who were these new revolutionaries? During the 1960s in Guerrero, the guerrilla movements of rural schoolteachers such as Genaro Vásquez and Lucio Cabañas were responses to the ferocious repression of their legal organizations. Cabañas fell in combat in 1974, and his Party of the Poor went underground to organize the Union of the People's Clandestine Workers' Revolutionary Party (PROCUP). PROCUP set up a secret urban guerrilla group that kept a low profile in the 1980s. In 1994, it kidnapped the billionaire banker Alfredo Harp Helú and obtained a ransom of tens of millions of dollars to finance the uprising of the new EPR. Its ambushes of the Mexican federal army have continued, and the EPR's survival shows that it has support from the general population.[31] A government research body, el Centro de Investigaciones de los Movimientos Armados, has documented the history of the EPR.[32]

The EPR's *Manifesto of the Eastern Sierra Madre* (in Spanish) was formulated on 7 August 1996. The Mexico City newspaper *Corre la Voz* distributed it on the Mexico City subway for several hours before the government suppressed it. According to the *Manifesto*, the EPR was organized on 1 May 1994, and on 18 May 1996 it gave birth to a political–military party, the Revolutionary Popular Democratic Party (PDPR). The *Manifesto* contains the Party program. It calls for a new provisional government representing the revolutionary democratic forces, a new Constitution for a Popular Democratic Republic, and a reordering of the economy to benefit the backward regions. It would transform into national property the strategic areas of the economy and the nation's natural resources as well as the native and foreign monopolies, and nationalize banking in order to facilitate the development of small and medium business. Among the immediate demands are respect for the autonomy of the Indian peoples and their cultural rights, elimination of the *latifundios* and the changes in Article 27, distribution of lands, respect for the rights of women, freedom for political prisoners, work for all with adequate wages, public health programs, punishment of those carrying on the dirty war of repression. A socialist program, it nowhere uses the word *socialism*.[33]

Because of the ambushes, the Mexican government has denounced the EPR as a terrorist organization. In underground interviews with the leaders, published in video form by Canal 6 de Julio, there appear red stars as emblems, and the discourse is hard and uncompromising, recalling the revolutionary movements of the 1970s and 1980s. The guerrillas are always masked in the videos, and no one knows the identity of the leaders. Although peasants and indigenous peoples are present, the spokespersons seem better educated and more articulate than the average peasant.[34] We suspect that rural schoolteachers are at it again.

The Revolutionary Army of the Insurgent People

The PDPR–EPR is an expanded version of PROCUP, comprising 14 different armed organizations, some with an anarchist pedigree. Besides the legacy of Cabañas, it embraced the "lessons of anarchism" and paid homage to the father of anarchism, Pierre Joseph Proudhon. But the movement soon divided when the anarcho-populist tendencies it nurtured surfaced in June 1998 as the Revolutionary Army of the Insurgent People (ERPI). The motives behind the split were clarified in an article in *Proceso* (28 June 1998) in which the Autonomous EPR, as the ERPI was originally known, accused the EPR leadership of being dogmatic, intolerant, and anti-democratic. Reporters from *El Universal* (14 June 1998) believed that the split represented a generation-old difference between the Maoists in PROCUP and Cabañas' followers. The EPR advocated armed struggle as the only path without any possibility of dialogue with the government, while the ERPI defined its role as an armed wing of the popular struggle.[35]

The ERPI's first internal document, *Thesis for Change (Our Basic Principles)*, rejected the messianic role of a political–military vanguard and called for its subordination to an insurgent popular assembly as the seat of popular power. "For this reason," the document declared, "we do not aspire to be a vanguard marching before the people, but to march together with the people in the struggle for democracy, justice, and liberty."[36] Viva Zapata! That was the program and strategy, not only of the indigenous people of Guerrero and the Sierra Madre del Sur, but also of the indigenous people of Chiapas in communiqués by the charismatic Subcomandante Marcos and the Zapatista Army of National Liberation (EZLN).

In the wake of the dissolution of the Soviet Union in December 1991 and the end of its support of revolutionary movements in Latin America, Jorge Castañeda's *Utopia Unarmed* (1994) proclaimed the death of Latin America's armed struggles while advocating the return trip to reformist politics, from communism back to social democracy.[37] Ironically, its publication appeared on the heels of the EZLN's New Year's Day 1994 armed takeover of four towns in the Chiapas highlands: Los Margaritas, Altamirano, Ocosingo, and the state's former capital and major tourist attraction, San Cristóbal de las Casas. Next, the EPR appeared in 1996 and the ERPI in 1998 in the mountains of Guerrero, and guerrilla organizations proliferated throughout Mexico's central and southern states in the most spectacular development of armed struggles since the early 1970s. The insurgencies of the PDLP and the EPR have proved contagious. From the bloody swamp of Mexican politics, guerrillas have risen like a cloud of mosquitos to sting the gigantic tiger of the Mexican army. Armed groupuscules are operating in the countryside in half the states of Mexico; they have an alphabet soup of revolutionary acronyms and programs. They have no chance of taking over the government. But military roadblocks are everywhere, and the 14,000 Mexican millionaires have an order from the National Police to ride around only in armored Mercedes-Benz limousines protected by bodyguards.

Notes

1. For these data and the following biographical sketch, see Orlando Ortiz, *Genaro Vázquez* (Mexico City: Diógenes, 1973), pp. 73, 79, 188, 190, 273; Jaime López, *10 años de guerrillas en México 1964–1974* (Mexico City: Posada, 1974), pp. 33–64.
2. Based on the recollections of Cristóbal Rojas, editor and publisher of *¡Presente!*, in an interview by Hodges in the newspaper's offices in Cuernavaca, Morelos, on 10 December 1977. Rojas had been among Jaramillo's close collaborators and supporters.
3. Baloy Mayo, *La guerrilla de Genaro y Lucio: Análisis y resultados* (Mexico City: Diógenes, 1980), pp. 57–8.
4. López, *10 años de guerrillas*, p. 50.
5. Ortiz, *Genaro Vázquez*, p. 196.
6. Ibid., p. 198.
7. López, *10 años de guerrillas*, p. 61. See the discussion of the "Four Points" and its programmatic implications in Ortiz, *Genaro Vázquez*, pp. 187–219.
8. Camarada "Ernesto," pseudonym of the author of *El Guerrillero* (Guadalajara: Graphos, 1974), pp. 61–2. An accomplished guerrilla in his own right, his book is about not only Cabañas but also several other guerrilla movements in which he participated. For a devastating critique of the Mexican guerrillas by a fellow guerrilla, this book is indispensable. See the autobiographical data on pp. 65, 97–108, 114, 118–19, 127–8, 157, 171, 193–6.
9. See the interview on 9 July 1975, "Habla Manuel García Cabañas, presidente municipal de Atoyac y primo de Lucio Cabañas," in Luis Suárez, *Lucio Cabañas, el guerrillero sin esperanza* (Mexico City: Roca, 1976), pp. 34, 45, 48, 49.
10. "Ernesto," *El Guerrillero*, p. 220.
11. On Lucio's early life before taking to the sierras, see José Natividad Rosales, *¿Quién es Lucio Cabañas? ¿Qué pasa con la guerrilla en México?* (Mexico City: Posada, 1976) pp. 29–76.
12. Suárez, *Lucio Cabañas*, pp. 65–6.
13. Ibid., p. 55.
14. Interview, "Habla Manuel García Cabañas," in Suárez, *Lucio Cabañas*, pp. 34–8, 44.

15. Partido Comunista de México, *Oposición* (15 July 1970).
16. Suárez, *Lucio Cabañas*, p. 86.
17. Ibid., pp. 87–92.
18. For an account of these and other actions from June 1972 to June 1974 in the Mexican press, see Juan Miguel de Mora, *Lucio Cabañas: su vida y su muerte* (Mexico City: Editores Asociados, 1974), pp. 17–150.
19. Suárez, *Lucio Cabañas*, p. 267.
20. De Mora, *Lucio Cabañas*, pp. 148–9.
21. Ibid., pp. 149–50.
22. Suárez, *Lucio Cabañas*, pp. 304–8.
23. Ibid., pp. 28–31.
24. "Ernesto," *El Guerrillero*, pp. 73–4, 76, 219.
25. Suárez, *Lucio Cabañas*, p. 267.
26. "Ernesto," *El Guerrillero*, p. 210.
27. Ibid., pp. 64, 68.
28. Ibid., pp. 65, 67, 68–9, 71–2.
29. "La matanza de Aguas Blancas," video produced by Canal 6 de Julio, Medellín 33, Col. Roma, México, D.F. This is the address on the video. These radical journalists have 300,000 videos circulating in Mexico City, where half the families have a VCR. (Television is heavily censored, and this is the fightback of the opposition to the dictatorship.) The left video journalists have been beaten and their cameras smashed by the police, so they keep a low profile.
30. "EPR: retorno a las armas," video produced by Canal 6 de Julio.
31. "El EPR sigue evadiendo al Ejército," *Reforma*, 17 July 1998, Mexico City.
32. "EPR: retorno a las armas," video, "El EPR de cerca," video by Canal 6 de Julio, containing interviews with guerrillas in the underground and also with Carlos Montemayor, a leading Mexican authority on the history of guerrilla warfare.
33. *Corre la Voz*, 5–11 September 1996, Mexico City.
34. "EPR: retorno a las armas," video, "Habla el ERPI," video by Canal 6 de Julio.
35. Bill Weinberg, *Homage to Chiapas: The New Indigenous Struggles in Mexico* (London: Verso), pp. 287–9.
36. Ibid., pp. 291–2.
37. Jorge Castañeda, *Utopia Unarmed: The Latin American Left After the Cold War* (New York: Vintage, 1994), pp. 427–76.

10 ✿ Resurrecting the Student Movement

In the 1960s and 1970s, the despotic federal government shaped student politics in the public schools and universities in Mexico City through representatives of the student associations under the wing of school authorities with close ties to PRI politicians. These student representatives seldom went to class because, in their own words, they were "busy taking care of student affairs." Yet they invariably passed to the next grade with high marks, or, if they chose not to graduate should graduation not be in their interest, they remained in the preparatory schools and university programs as "fossils" in order to continue controlling student politics.

Mexicans have a name for these fake students: *porros*. This word is slang for student provocateurs and lumpen youth subsidized by government or private agencies. They are young toughs who receive special training in military arts such as judo, and in street fighting. Why do they work against their classmates? What is their origin? How were regular students converted into *porros*? What is the role of the teachers, principals, and chancellors who support them? How are they organized? Why do they kill, rape, blackmail, and steal?

Student *porros* on Government Payrolls

In 1940, the official party decided to recruit young people from the Schools for Children of Workers, founded by Cárdenas, for certain political tasks. Fifteen-year-olds were selected and trained to break up political meetings and smash election stands that were rallying support for the reactionary presidential candidate General Juan Andreu

Almazán. When Almazán's partisans defended themselves, special commandos of youth and adults, protected by the police, went into action. The man organizing them was General Alfonso Corona del Rosal.

Ruíz Cortines and López Mateos used these pseudo students to repress protests. During this period, in the Citadel of the Federal District, they were known by their wristbands of adhesive tape and by their brush haircuts. In the railroad and oil conflicts, they were known by an ID card with a tricolored band and a badge reading "PRI Police."[1] The thugs at the National University took their orders from the engineer and university professor Sergio Ramiro Ramírez, alias "The Fish." His colleagues in the Department of Chemistry, aided by young soldiers, helped him to form his shock brigades. The student leaders of these shock brigades received money from the private secretary of López Mateos for breaking up popular demonstrations and student marches that were supposed to be "against the government," although this interpretation of student activities was often an invention of the government. The *porros* were simply student gangsters led by the Fish. During the term of López Mateos, they were trained by the Chief of Special Services for the capital's police.[2]

In the mid-1960s under President Díaz Ordaz, they received their training in the Venustiano Carranza park in Mexico City. The capital's mayor entrusted them with the task of cleaning up the main streets that were crawling with penny vendors. The vendors and beggars were thought a scandalous sight for the blue eyes of the American tourists beginning to arrive in droves, and the government wanted to hide these ugly signs of poverty and lagging development. So these *porros* went to work on the unfortunate of society. After bloody attacks and petty robberies, the marginalized poor disappeared from downtown Mexico City.[3]

Different chancellors of the National University have required the services of the *porros*, and so have many in the provinces, along with the directors of all the preparatory and vocational schools and superior educational centers throughout the nation.[4]

Toward the end of the 1960s, the brigades of thugs at the National University were called *porros*. Some of these poor and hungry young people were also called "hawks"; they worked in the Special Services of the Central Department of the Federal District. In the capital's

University City, they got money from the Chancellery and from the principals of every department and preparatory school dependent on the National University. They sold marijuana to the students and mugged them. They received 2,000 pesos per month from the Central Department for guarding the subway installations and for breaking up political meetings. They also assaulted and robbed citizens in the streets.

In a candid interview published in *Excélsior* (19 October 1969), Pedro Eduardo Guzmán Maldonado (alias El Chabelo) explained why the *porros* disguised their real activities and identities. He should know. As the student head of the López Mateos Cultural Association at the National University, he was directly responsible for the beating of striking students in 1968. "Because we attacked the leftists to the point of exterminating them," he explained, "they now target us." By "leftists," he meant "communists who want to destroy the country, to harm the government ... [and] to foment chaos." Although he began by denying that his *porros* acted in conjunction with the government's hawks, he ended by admitting their collaboration in 1968. Indeed, the government had paid him 1,000 pesos and each of his confederates 500 pesos a week to defend what he called the government's "rightist line." In response to the question, "How do you know that the money came from the government?" he replied: "Because it gave us the green light ... which is why we never had problems with the police."[5]

After the massacre of Tlatelolco in 1968, they took advantage of the fear, exhaustion, and demoralization of the student masses to pressure them back into the classrooms. They did not hesitate to spill the blood of students who resisted them: under the protective wing of the authorities, they shot and stabbed people, they machine-gunned schools like Vocational number five in the Citadel, and on several occasions they used dynamite or home-made bombs to break up assemblies. On 13 August 1968 and again on 10 June 1971, they tried to provoke the students into violence so that their demonstrations could be repressed. "To war! Let's take on the State!" they shouted among the marchers. They would just as soon shout "Viva!" for President Echeverría as for Che Guevara. Blackmail, rape, threats, and violence were their way of life.

Of all the *porros*, the hawks were the most vicious. The infamous General Corona del Rosal gave them military training. The Market

Office hired them. They were paid off in various government offices; but on the payroll they were always listed as "auxiliary services" under the codes R1, R8, and R10. They had different training camps: Ixtapalapa, San Juan de Aragón, and the Cuchilla del Tesoro. The best equipped was at San Juan de Aragón, where commandos were trained: it had pits, tracks, hanging bars, wooden stairs, vehicles, and a military academy. They received instruction in the morning and afternoon. When they were not acting as bodyguards for Díaz Ordaz or Luis Echeverría, they were busy looking for "terrorists" in the subway, in the Merced or Jamaica markets, in downtown Mexico City.

They practiced judo, karate, kendo – all the martial arts. But they stripped them of the mysticism that often accompanies such disciplines and learned them only to kill. They studied the use of firearms, from the simplest to the M–2. To conceal all this training, their camps were surrounded with barbed wire, and police guards kept bystanders away.[6]

Like the famous Nazi assault troops of Heinrich Himmler, they had to be at least 1.7 meters tall. They were aged between 18 and 23. They had to show a graduation certificate from primary school and a military service card in order to be admitted to the hawks. Once recommended by a politician, a military man, or another hawk, they had to endure three successive runs around an obstacle track. The hawks were also recruited from criminal gangs: the Fish's *porros* working in the National University, "the mummies," "the nazis," the bad boys of Peralvillo, the market boys from Jamaica, and soldiers who had been court-martialed. The justice of the government promised impunity to all these lumpen elements.

Entering the group was relatively easy, but leaving was another matter. The army gave the training through "professors" and subordinate leaders called "Spaniards." According to Gerardo Medina V., a member of the conservative National Action Party, the hawks were divided into groups at the base level. Each group had 16 members. The password was changed daily. All the police knew it, and the hawks could resort to a secret telephone if they needed police aid. The parents of a young hawk had no idea what their son was doing for a living. The "professors" received training from the FBI, and 12 of them went to Japan and South Korea for more practice in the art of repression. In England, they took courses in criminology!

Many professors and Spaniards belonged to the infamous Olympic battalion in 1968. They were cynically referred to as "the guerrillas," but they had other nicknames like "godfather" and "role-player." They made 70 pesos a day when the peso was still worth something, not to speak of the bribes they picked up along the way. They hired a Japanese instructor to teach them karate and judo. Díaz Ordaz and Echeverría were so pleased with the hawks that they raised their pay. Paid training courses abroad lasted three months.

They were in action on 2 October 1969 to stop the commemoration of the Tlatelolco martyrs at the great cathedral and at St. Thomas' Cap. In April 1970, they had a workout during the repression of the Deportivo de la Magdalena Mixhuca in Mexico City. On 4 November 1970, they rampaged in the towns of Celaya, Irapuato, and León. On 27 January 1971, the journalist Félix Fuentes claimed that two million pesos a month of the public's money was being spent on these killers.[7]

Initially, there were approximately 400 hawks, not including PRI shock groups, but they grew at a cancerous rate. A reliable source told us that every high official had three bodyguards paid 30,000 pesos a month. Perhaps that is only gossip. But all of this is excellent background for understanding what happened on 10 June 1971. The events leading up to that tragic day began in the Autonomous University of Nuevo León.

The Gathering Storm in Monterrey

The "Monterrey Group" of northern industrial millionaires has great influence in Mexico. Governor Eduardo Elizondo of Nuevo León had placed his cronies in the Autonomous University in order to control it. They were rich boys from private enterprise with political connections to the state organization of the PRI, committed to driving out the democratic students and teachers from the administration of the university.

In September 1969, the Department of Philosophy and Literature in the university went on strike, demanding a new plan of studies.[8] The authorities imposed an anti-student Governing Popular Assembly, which was legalized in a PRI-like way by means of the University Organic Law. This law was unpopular, for the teachers and students neither took part in its elaboration nor were asked to approve it: the governor and his servile Congress, who would later betray the law, endorsed it. Article 11 of the law placed at the head of the university administration 31 people completely foreign to the institution's life, and allowed only three students and three teachers into the top offices.

Thus all the departments joined the strike and demanded respect for university autonomy and the right to internal democracy. They won a partial victory when two decrees conceded them democracy. In March 1970, the university council elected Dr Oliverio Tijerina F. as Chancellor. It then presented the draft for another Organic Law, drawn up by the new chancellor, to the state Congress, which rejected it. The law students, favored by the state government, seized the chancellery. The state subsidy was cut off. On 16 December, the Chancellor bowed to pressure from the government and demanded the resignation of the General Secretary of the university, a man widely respected by the students. This action undermined the Chancellor's prestige; he resigned on 13 February 1971.

On 20 February, the university council handed the reins to Ulises Leal Flores, but the state government refused to recognize the new Chancellor. The university's patrons threatened to cut off the money they were giving, and the institution asked for an increase in the government subsidy in order to pay the teachers. On 23 March, the University Workers' Union denounced the anti-university policy in a political meeting. Two days later, the university council called for a demonstration. The next day, the anti-university "New Organic Law" was published; the students and teachers rejected it. On 4 June, the state Congress took 15 minutes to give the law its stamp of approval.

On 2 April 1971, the fake "Popular Assembly," protected by the new law, elected as chancellor a confessed anti-communist, a partisan of the PRI, Dr Arnulfo Treviño Garza. The university had two Chancellors! The governor ordered the government committee to name heads of departments and schools who would obey. The mass of the students formed a solid front of university resistance and prevented the PRI's appointee from taking possession of the Chancellor's office on 13 April. Ten days later, all the buildings of the university fell into the hands of the students, and the workers joined them in a strike on 26 April.

Mexico City Students Declare Their Solidarity

On 14 March 1971, seven schools and departments of the National University in Mexico City declared their solidarity with the students in Monterrey. While the police and the *porros* in Nuevo León attacked both workers and students, the ex-hawks in Mexico City, having been removed from the payroll of the Administrator of the Federal District, assumed once again their role and began to work over the National University. The National Strike Council (CNH) of 1968 had changed its name to the National Council for Struggle (CNL) and had taken into itself all the committees of activist students formed at the National University and the Polytechnical Institute. The ex-hawk *porros* of the Fish were ordered to intimidate the leaders of the CNL.

In self-defense, the students at the Polytechnical, the National University, the Chapingo Agricultural School, the Iberoamerican University, and the Superior Normal School formed an alliance under the umbrella of the Coordinating Committee of the Committees for Struggle (COCO). Its primary aims were support for the Monterrey students and liberation of the political prisoners of 1968. This movement lost momentum due to the attacks by the various groups of *porros*: those of the Fish, of Francisco Villa, of the MURO, and of the chancellery of González Casanova. Echeverría's government also took the wind out of the students' sails by a phased release of the political prisoners in stages, on 9, 24, and 26 April 1971.

On 15 April, leaflets were distributed supporting the University of Nuevo León in Monterrey, and information assemblies were held. At the beginning of June, the various departments discussed the question of carrying through a demonstration on 10 June 1971. On the 4th, the Department of Medicine decided not to take part in the demonstration, followed by the graduate Department of Economics in the Polytechnical Institute. Four days later, COCO brought together the 16 schools and departments in favor of the strike. Meanwhile, in Mexico City, federal police agents worked with the traffic police to remove from the walls painted announcements of the demonstration. While the feds scratched off the paint, the cops blocked off the area to traffic so that the public might not witness the government's first moves against the students.

The demonstrators were to march from St. Thomas' Cap to the

Monument to the Revolution in Mexico City. Its organizers demanded support for the students in Nuevo León, freedom for the political prisoners, and democratization of education and of the unions. The Independent Union Front (FSI), born on International Labor Day in 1971 and embracing 14 different associations, called upon the public to be present at the demonstration and voiced its full support "for union democracy and against the labor bureaucrats." This front included the MRM, the revolutionary CCI, the UGOCM, the National Railway Council, and the Poor People's Organization of Netzahual-cóyotl (the giant shanty town east of Mexico City).

Organizing the Repression

Shortly before 10 June, the Fish – professor at the National University and chief of the *porros* – took an aid with him on a secret trip to Monterrey. There the two had a fateful meeting with the president of the formal businesspersons' association COPARMEX, with the banker Eloy Ballina, and with others of the infamous Monterrey Group of industrialists. Who was the go-between? A certain Garza Leal, known as "The Elbow," we are told by Antonio Solís, the ex-hawk who revealed everything in his *Jueves de Corpus Sangriento*. The big money in Monterrey was scared of communism and desired the services of the proven shock brigade. A deal was made in an automobile moving through the streets of Monterrey – an old Mafia trick that avoids prying ears. We do not know how much money changed hands, but it must have been a huge sum, for in the third chapter of Solís' book we learn that the Fish handed his aide 20,000 pesos, not as an advance, but as a gift.[9]

The *porros* began preparations for their illicit deed. The first meeting was on the slopes of the Ajusco mountain range in Mexico City at an isolated place called Fuentes Brotantes. Sixty-four killers showed up as well-dressed students. Many innocent young people imagine the *porros* as rough-and-tumble hooligans who are always whipping up public brawls. Yet often these innocents have a *porro* sitting beside them in a classroom, waiting to identify student radicals in order to betray them. They are not just lions relying on sheer strength; they are also cunning foxes. They stepped up their training in *el sabate*, the Spanish name for the Korean martial art *taekwondo*, under leaders called Centurions because they had one hundred hawks under them.

The business group in Monterrey promised the hawks a great future. Said the Fish himself: "We will no longer be despised *porros*, but chiefs of a powerful political movement that will overturn the government itself."[10] President Echeverría had enraged the Monterrey group by intervening against its interests in the Bosques de Chihuahua lumber company, and he had humiliated the group on other occasions. The business association COPARMEX had pressured Governor Elizondo to use the army to calm down the Autonomous University of Monterrey; but Echeverría, by partially solving the university conflict as the Great Arbitrator, had swung the balance of power in favor of the bureaucracy against the big money. The only thing left to the super-rich was the provocation of violence on 10 June. The great industrialists had also promised the hawks to shut down their plants in a great protest strike against the massacre, so that the Mexican people would believe the government responsible. This promise was never fulfilled.

The above are the main events leading up to the massacre. On the morning of the fateful Thursday, in a pension on the Maestros Avenue, the Fish's henchmen waited.[11] At 2 a.m., the finishing touches were put on the plan of action. In plotting their conspiracy, they were advised by the people financing them, one Mexican and one American.

At 8 a.m. on the day of the student march, the hawks decided to attack the demonstrators en route to the Superior Normal School. At noon, they checked the long halls in the tenements and the roofs overlooking nearby streets in the area of Maestros Avenue. The hawks then took up positions with kendo clubs and battery-charged sticks. Arms and ammunition were distributed, including five machine-guns, eleven pistols of .38 caliber, four of .22. They were ordered to attack journalists as well as students.

At 4 p.m., small groups of hawks with placards were in front of the Superior Normal School and the surrounding streets shouting *viva*s to Che Guevara and chanting slogans against the repression in Nuevo León. There were 70 hawks in this group masquerading as students: their hair was cut short, they wore tennis shoes and light shirts. On the roofs, they greeted other snipers, probably from other commands. In the Cosmos movie house waited the Fish with 37 extra men. The anti-riot tanks of the army and the Grenadiers along with the urban police arrived early for the fun. Since noon, they had been watching the National University, the Buenavista subway station, the Technical Institute, St. Thomas' Cap, and Mexico–Tacuba Avenue. The trap was set. The passwords for entering and leaving the encirclement were "hawk" and "shell" for federal police and other agents. The traffic police were kept busy trying to isolate the students. By 3.50 p.m., the sector was thoroughly cut off from normal traffic.

The Corpus Christi Massacre

A few minutes before 5 p.m., the demonstration began to march through Plan de Ayala Street toward Mexico–Tacuba Avenue. It moved in groups: in front, the Economics Department of the National University, next the Popular Preparatory School, then two vocational schools, the sciences, and so on. From St. Thomas' Cap started the Department of Philosophy, the Department of Dentistry, the Ayutla Textile group, and scores of other organizations. There were more than 5,000 people marching. The crowds began to roar the chant, "Mexico! ... Freedom!" This was how they chose to celebrate the religious holiday known as Corpus Christi!

Colonel Emanuel Guevara T. halted the march because it did not have a permit; he threatened to break it up. But the Grenadiers let the marchers through – there were a lot of demonstrators – and then cordoned off the entrances to the streets to the east of the walls of the Normal School. Colonel Angel Rodrìguez C., chief of the Police General Staff, spoke with the leaders about calling off the march because "in the Cosmos movie house there is a group of young people armed with clubs and guns who are going to attack you."[12] The students shouted: "The Constitution permits us to march, and it is the highest law of the land!" They broke out in the National Anthem. They marched forward for ten minutes while through the Puente de Alvarado Avenue rolled four more buses of hawks commanded by Rubén Navarrete.

Suddenly, a burst of machine-gun fire rudely interrupted the demonstrators' singing. The hawks in the sidestreets and those who had mixed with the marchers pulled out their guns and clubs. In terror, the students fled toward the Superior Normal School and Mexico–

Tacuba Avenue, where more hawks awaited them. The students were welcomed with clubs on the streets and with gunfire from the rooftops. Desperately the students and the other marchers tried to break out of the ambush, but all the streets to the south were blocked by anti-riot tanks and Grenadiers. By 5.15 p.m. the chaos was so great that the hawks and other aggressors from the Fifth Company attacked each other. The Federal Police covered the backs of the hawks by firing from their cars at those who had escaped the encirclement. Some took refuge in the Cosmos movie house but were pursued by the furious hawks. The Grenadiers and the police looked on 30 minutes later as the streets ran with blood, some perhaps wondering if they did not have a son or acquaintance somewhere in the desperate crowds.

As agreed beforehand, many journalists were attacked, but the ones who dared to tell the truth were the foreigners. At around 7 p.m., the police supported the hawks with tear gas. Some students managed to find a way out through Malobor Ocampo Street, but their attackers caught up with them. Meanwhile the Fish and his group went into action on Carpio Street. A couple of hawks who had been hurt in the struggle were taken to hospital, so Rubén Leñero organized an attack to "rescue" them in an effort to keep the whole operation secret. He and his hawks entered the hospital hitting and shooting. Within seconds, they had searched the hospital from top to bottom in the best traditions of Hitler's SS, discovered their comrades, ripped the bottles of blood serum from the other wounded, and exited the hospital. Wounded students were dragged off to military camp number one. It was raining, and battalion No. 40 began moving from the Laredo Highway toward the central plaza. From 8 to 10 p.m., the army was combing the zone from the Monument to the Revolution to the central plaza, but shots could still be heard.

Gerardo Medina of the National Action Party reports that according to Colonel Alfonso Guarro, the public forces taking part in the repression numbered 900, with the hawks numbering 1,500. Official sources admit to only 11 dead. But one hawk testified that he had seen more than 30 dead, 100 wounded, and 1,000 beaten. The wounded were distributed in various hospitals, including the Xoco Hospital in the south of Mexico City, where witnesses say that there were more than 150 injured. This figure from one hospital would suggest that there were hundreds of wounded. The Eighth police station, among many others, was jammed with arrested persons.

Unlike Díaz Ordaz, President Echeverría tried to control the demonstration from Los Pinos, the Mexican equivalent of the White House. With the President were Hank González and Leandro Rovirosa Wade, officials who were discussing various matters of state. One witness claimed that the President wept when he heard the news of the massacre. Those directly responsible – Martínez Domínguez, the Administrator of Mexico City, and Rogelio Flores Curiel, chief of the capital's police – were removed from office on 15 June. This shows that the top leaders differed with those directly responsible about the method of repression and the bloodshed. Echeverría was clever enough to realize that the government could not allow a repeat performance of the sort of repression that had occurred in 1968.[13]

Although we know that intermediate government officials paid and ordered their hawks to break up the demonstration, another kind of hawk is exemplified by the Fish and his *porros* who took orders from the Monterrey Group and tried to undermine rather than support the government. So these two groups of hawks were working at cross purposes. This can hardly surprise us, for we have already seen the same thing happening in the National University in clashes between *porros*.

Finally, a lesson of this bitter experience is that the hawk–*porros* were to the students what the co-opted labor bureaucrats were to the industrial unions, what the rural political bosses were to the peasants, and what the government bureaucrats were to the people in general. All of these parasites were in collusion against a popular union of workers, peasants, and students. So we must not underestimate the important role of the *porros* in the repression.

Notes

1. Gerardo Medina Valdés, *Operación 10 de Junio* (Mexico City: Universo, 1972), p. 210. For the following account of student hit-men we are indebted to Juan Vargas Sánchez and Donald C. Hodges, "La resistencia popular en México 1940–1976," (unpublished *licenciado* thesis, UNAM, 1986), pp. 150–61.
2. Antonio Solís Mimendi, *Jueves de Corpus Sangriento* (Mexico City: Talleres Alfaro Hermanos, 1975), p. 95.
3. For this information we are indebted to Juan Vargas Sánchez' interviews with sociologist Lorenzo Ismael Vargas Sánchez and Licenciado Ernesto González at the Procuradería General de la República y Ministerio Público de la Delegación

Cuauhtémoc, Mexico City (December 1979 and January 1980).

4. Solís Mimendi, *Jueves de Corpus Sangriento*, pp. 37–38.
5. Cited in Gerardo Davila and Manlio Tirado, eds, *Como México no hay dos* (Mexico City: Nuestro Tiempo, 1971), pp. 210–12.
6. Medina Valdés, *Operación 10 de Junio*, p. 220.
7. Ibid., p. 235.
8. For the following account of the student rebellion in Monterrey and its impact on the student movement in Mexico City, we are indebted to Vargas and Hodges, "La resistencia popular en México 1940–1976," pp. 162–73; and to Vargas' interviews with Leopoldo Ayala, teacher at the Vocacional No. 5 del I.P.N. in the Ciudadela (21 October 1977), and Salvador Dueñas, teacher at the Vocacional No. 5 (15 March 1978). Both interviews took place at the school in Mexico City.
9. Solís Mimendi, *Jueves de Corpus Sangriento*, p. 95.
10. Ibid., p. 105.
11. For the sequence of events on "Bloody Thursday," see Medina Valdés, *Operación 10 de Junio*, pp. 74–106.
12. Ibid., p. 87. On the intervention of the "Hawks," see also "Dos horas de angustía, de terror y de sangre," Davila and Tirado, *Como México no hay dos*, pp. 191–2.
13. Armando Ayala Anguiano and Fernando Martí, "Díaz Ordaz vs. Echeverría," in *Contenido*, no. 173 (October 1977), p. 39.

11 ✸ Urban Guerrilla Warfare

In answer to the repression of the popular student movement on 2 October 1968, there appeared for the first time in the post-revolutionary epoch the phenomenon of urban guerrilla warfare. This new guerrilla struggle was of two kinds. The first consisted of the guerrilla movements organized by old cadres of the Young Communist League (JCM) or, in the exceptional case of the Revolutionary Action Movement (MAR), by cadres of communist sympathizers trained and financed initially by the North Korean government. This type of guerrilla struggle embraced the Lacandones, the 23 September Communist League, and the Revolutionary Student Front (FER). When the FER was reorganized as the People's Revolutionary Armed Forces (FRAP), it became the most consequential organization, the one that enjoyed the most success. The second kind of guerrilla struggle was made up of people who lacked the political experience of the JCM cadres, who were repressed in a short time and disappeared from the field of action. Among these, the guerrillas who received the most notoriety were undoubtedly the Zapatista Urban Front (FUZ).

The Lacandones

David Jiménez Sarmiento, a young student in the Department of Philosophy and Literature at the National University and a member of the JCM, had taken part in the organization of the popular student actions that suffered repression on 2 October 1968. Disillusioned by what he saw at Tlatelolco, he gathered around him other comrades from the Young Communists who decided to form guerrilla

146

commandos without previous approval from the PCM. They finally formed three groups: Lacandones, Patria o Muerte, and Arturo Gámiz. The first was the most famous, named after the Indians of the Chiapas jungle who, as primitive hunters, resisted Spanish colonization for centuries and were pacified only in the 1940s. The influence of the Cuban Revolution was obvious in the selection of the second group's name, for it was Fidel Castro's slogan during the height of the resistance to North American imperialism. The last group's name also showed Cuban influence, for Gámiz' guerrilla movement was the Mexican counterpart of the 26 July Movement and the assault on the Moncada barracks. Che Guevara's well-known *Guerrilla Warfare* also gave a political orientation to these commandos.[1]

They began their actions in Mexico City, Monterrey, and Chihuahua. The Lacandones specialized in assaults on stores and businesses from 1969 until 1975. On 18 January 1973, they carried out an expropriation of the Bimbo Bakery – the Mexican front name for Wonder Bread. During this action, they lost their best cadres. But they replaced them and reappeared in 1974–75 as members of the 23 September Communist League.

"Juche" and the Revolutionary Action Movement

In immediate response to the fusillades at Tlatelolco, there arose an urban group made up of Mexican students with scholarships at the Patrice Lumumba University in Moscow. This group was the creation of the ex-schoolteacher Fabricio Gómez Souza, 36 years old, who was studying in that special university for Third World students. When he heard what had happened in Tlatelolco, he held a meeting in his dormitory with a dozen Mexican students who decided to join him in preparing a guerrilla war. They formed the Revolutionary Action Movement.[2]

As the movement's leader, Gómez Souza interviewed representatives of the Soviet, Cuban, and Vietnamese governments in order to get help in creating a guerrilla *foco* in Mexico. For diplomatic reasons, these governments refused to become involved. In November 1968, Gómez Souza journeyed to Pyongyang, capital of the Democratic People's Republic of Korea (DPRK), where he got what he wanted. On his return to Moscow, he received from the DPRK Embassy

US$25,000 to travel with comrades to Mexico to gather at least 50 revolutionaries for training in the DPRK.

Gómez Souza arrived in Mexico at the beginning of 1969 and recruited a student from the JCM in Morelia, one Angel Bravo Cisneros, who took over the leadership of the first contingent of youth. It included Marta Maldonado, daughter of Braulio Maldonado, ex-governor of the state of Baja California, a young woman from the upper class who would become the Patty Hearst of Mexico. Two more contingents followed them to the DPRK for training. After long and hard workouts at a camp 50 km north-east of Pyongyang, they returned to Mexico in September 1969.

In Korea, they received strong communist indoctrination. In keeping with the concept of *juche*, as conceived by DPRK leader Kim Il Sung, the Mexican guerrillas would maintain themselves by their own means: they would get their arms from raids on the soldiers and police, their finances from bank assaults. Each of the 50 guerrillas would recruit 10 others until there were nearly 550 ready to begin the armed struggle. Then each of these 550 should recruit 10 more, and these still others in geometric progression. They immediately set up training centers in Mexico City and in the states of Michoacán, Querétaro, Jalisco, and Guerrero.

Their first guerrilla action was an assault on a cashier from the Commercial Bank of Michoacán carrying over a million pesos from Morelia to Mexico City. The assault took place in the Tres Estrellas bus terminal in the capital on 19 December 1970. On 10 September 1971 came the second attack, an assault on a branch of the Bank of London in León, Guanajuato. That year, 40 members of the organization, including Bravo Cisneros, Gómez Souza, and 17 others trained in the DPRK, were captured. But the movement survived repression until it united its cadres with the 23 September Communist League when the latter was founded in March 1973.

Guadalajara's Revolutionary Student Front

The guerrilla movement third in importance came out of the Revolutionary Student Front (FER) at the University of Guadalajara. The FER made its début on the political scene in September 1970, when it confronted the mafia of bureaucrats, professors, judges, and politicians who controlled the university with the help of an armed fist: the reactionary Guadalajara Students Federation (FEG). The reactionary organization's connections with the state government was obvious to all, for it functioned as a springboard to political posts.[3]

In these circumstances, the FER carried out its first action on 24 September 1970, when it expelled the tramps and freeloading carousers from Student House by seizing and holding the place. After the building was surrounded by soldiers and police, it was attacked by the army. The day before, there had been a shoot-out between members of the FEG and members of the FER, resulting in three dead and dozens wounded. The FEG gangsters had started the fight; while none of them went to jail, members of the FER were put behind bars. The embryonic FER decided the best tactic was to go underground to begin a clandestine armed struggle against the student hawks.

The violence was not confined to the university. Gunfights and vendettas between the two student factions wound up with the FER carrying out bank assaults and kidnapping VIPs. The first bank assaults occurred a year later. On 25 November 1971 came an attack on the Zamora Bank with a booty of 130,000 pesos, followed on 23 December 1971 by an assault on the Refaccionario Bank of Jalisco with a take of 100,000 pesos. At the end of 1972 and the beginning of 1973, there were raids on several banks and businesses. The driving force in this group was the Camaña López brothers: Carlos, Alfredo, Juventino, and Ramón. The first two were students at the university and members of the JCM.

Feats of the People's Revolutionary Armed Forces

For these assaults, Carlos and Alfredo were arrested along with two other comrades in the group. It was then that Juventino, who went by the nickname Ho Chi Minh, founded the People's Armed Revolutionary Forces (FRAP). On 4 May 1973, he kidnapped the US Consul in Guadalajara, George Terrence Leonhardy, and asked for a ransom of one million pesos. In exchange for the consul's life, Ho asked for the release of 30 political prisoners including his brothers Carlos and Alfredo. Once freed, they were flown on a special flight to Cuba.[4]

Ramón, the fourth brother, along with some comrades, kidnapped the industrialist Pedro Sarquis Morrows on 2 June 1973. That action got them a ransom of 3 million pesos. In August, Juventino was caught, and later Ramón was also arrested. But the FRAP continued its struggle. On 28 August 1974, it snatched General José Guadalupe Zuno, brother-in-law of the President of Mexico. This man was a progressive identified with Cardenismo. A ransom of 20 million pesos was demanded for his release, but the government refused to negotiate with "terrorists." The only concession given was the playing of a tape against the government and in support of the guerrilla war. Two days later, the women's commando named Che Guevara and belonging to the FRAP kidnapped the millionaire Margarita Saad. Her family handed over a total of 4 million pesos, but Margarita was found slain, with no explanation. This deed caused the national press to turn against the guerrillas.[5]

While the Lacandones and the MAR joined the 23 September Communist League at its founding in March 1973, the FRAP refused to do so. Instead, one of the original members of the League and of the JCM, David López Valenzuela, went over to the FRAP. He left the League because he was opposed to its tactics of spectacular deeds and to the murder of police as a means of raising public consciousness.[6] The FER, which became the FRAP, was one of the few urban guerrilla movements that was born with links to the masses. But mass support gradually vanished once the armed struggle was launched.

Promise and Perversion of the 23 September Communist League

Our treatment of the important guerrilla movements would be incomplete without a discussion of the 23 September Communist League. It arose as a result of the work of Raúl Ramos Zavala, ex-leader of the Young Communists. Raúl left the JCM at the end of 1970. He interviewed the representatives of other revolutionary movements to try to overcome their divisions and to fuse them into a single nationwide movement.[7]

He made his first contacts with the Professional Student Movement (MEP), a Christian communist movement counseled by Jesuit priests in the Monterrey Technological Institute. In this movement, Ignacio Salas Obregón, the future maximum leader of the League, distinguished himself.[8] Later, Raúl Ramos journeyed to Chihuahua, where he contacted Diego Lucero Martínez, a survivor of the attack on the

Madera Barracks who belonged to the 23 September Movement. Just as Fidel Castro and his comrades took as homage to the assault on the Moncada Barracks the name 26 July Movement, so the survivors of the attack on the Madera Barracks named themselves after the date of their assault.

When Ramos returned to Mexico City to work as a professor in the National University, he established contact with David Jiménez Sarmiento of the Lacandones. Following up his project of unifying the left, he then went to Guadalajara and there, with the mediation of Diego Lucero, interviewed Fernando Salinas Mora, also of the 23 September Movement. The Movement had collected all those members of the FER who had disavowed their leaders and taken to guerrilla warfare under the name "The Vikings"; they were directed by Juan Manuel Rodríguez.[9]

In this way, Ramos brought under one executive command eight movements with a guerrillaist tendency: the former members of Monterrey's Young Communists, Monterrey's Professional Student Movement, Chihuahua's 23 September Movement known as the Armed Commandos of Chihuahua, Mexico City's Lacandones, and Guadalajara's guerrilla group The Vikings, containing the rebel group from the FER. Unity was achieved with the argument that a divided guerrilla movement would not be able to withstand repression, much less smash the system.

Linked together, they went into action with two bank assaults simultaneously in Monterrey on 14 January 1972, and three more the next day in Chihuahua City. The aim was to build funds for the formation of a guerrilla organization on a national scale.

The first guerrillas fell in Chihuahua and Mexico City. In Chihuahua, Diego Lucero and two comrades were killed while eight more went to prison. Raúl Ramos, the maximum leader of the organization, died in a shoot-out with a police patrol in Mexico City. New leaders emerged – Ignacio Salas and an ex-member of the Young Communists in Monterrey, José Angel García Martínez. These two met in the Pantitlán neighborhood in Mexico City, where they decided to continue Ramos' project: the formation of a national guerrilla organization.

On 15 March 1973, the first national meeting to found the future League took place in Guadalajara. The various representatives met in the house of Fernando Salinas Mora, alias El Richard, a member of the 23 September League. Besides the representatives of the five initial movements brought together by Ramos came delegates from five other movements: the survivors of the MAR, "the Sickies from Sinaloa," the Spartacus Communist League, the FUZ, and Lucio Cabañas' Peasant Justice Brigade. Cabañas thought he would be proclaimed chief of a new national movement that would take the name of his Party of the Poor. But the name adopted at the Guadalajara meeting – the 23 September Communist League – honored the first Cuban-type guerrilla movement led by Arturo Gámiz. A national coordinator with a directing bureau of five people was chosen; Lucio Cabañas was not included.[10]

In Guadalajara, a second national meeting of the League convened in July–August 1973. The delegates agreed to: support the mass movement; liberate political prisoners; expropriate arms; expropriate banks; and kill not only prominent chiefs of police and army officers, but also union bureaucrats who had sold out to the bosses and the government.[11] Because it objected to this last point, the FUZ left the League. Disagreements also caused the exit of the MAR, the Spartacists, and Lucio's Peasant Justice Brigade. As a result of internal dissensions, the League was reduced to its initial members plus the Sickies of Sinaloa, whose political weight increased with time.[12]

Let us see, then, how the League "sickened" under the influence of the Sinaloans, on the one hand, and the Jesuits, on the other. The directing bureau under the control of the revolutionary Christians formed one faction; the group operating in the Autonomous University of Sinaloa formed the other. The struggle inside the League took up much of its attention. Each faction accused its rival of petty-bourgeois opportunism, and each became increasingly leftist in response to the other's criticism.

The League differed from the other urban commandos in guaranteeing to each guerrilla a monthly salary. This amounted to 3,000 pesos at predevaluation value. Later, the guerrillas got a raise of 23 per cent, so that the police worked for lower wages than did the members of the League.[13]

Unlike other guerrilla groups, then, the League was made up of mercenaries of the revolution. It preached the tactic of killing police and soldiers for the simple reason that these were instruments of the bourgeoisie. Of the 76 police killed by various guerrilla groups in a two-year period, the League could claim credit for most of the deaths. The League murdered police in cold blood, not even trying to seize their arms. It hated the police. It hoped to demoralize them, create panic among their relatives, and cause them to seek other jobs.

At the beginning of its struggle, the League embraced between 200 and 250 militants. Three and a half years later, it was as strong as when it began. By December 1976, 21 heads of the organization were at large. Since each commanded a dozen cadres, the repression clearly had failed to crush the League.

The first action of the League was an abortive attempt to kidnap Monterrey industrialist Eugenio Garza Sada in September 1973. Because of the resistance he put up, he was killed. On 10 October came the second action with the double kidnapping of the Monterrey businessman Fernando Arguren and the British consul in Guadalajara, Anthony Duncan Williams. Since the government stated that it would not negotiate with "criminals," the League killed the businessman and freed the consul. After the failure of these two efforts, the League dedicated itself to bank assaults, which were more successful, until in 1976 it resumed kidnapping, obtaining 5 million pesos in ransom for the daughter of the Belgian ambassador. But it failed in its attempt to seize the daughter of the President-elect, José López Portillo. In this action David Jiménez Sarmiento, the former Lacandón and ex-militant of the Young Communists, died.

The events leading up to the birth of the League lay at the heart of the JCM. In *The 23 September Communist League: Origins and Shipwreck* (in Spanish), Gustavo Hirales Morán tells the story. In the 1970 elections, the JCM had chosen to abstain from the voting. This was hardly an aggressive answer to the Tlatelolco massacre and to the repression of the popular student movement in 1968. So at the JCM's Third Congress in December 1970, it lost a radical current commanded by Raúl Ramos Zavala.[14]

Valentín Campa told us in an interview that Ramos' current in the JCM gained the backing of the majority at the Congress. The situation of the Communist Party was so grave that Campa and Martínez Verdugo debated against this current for four days and nights – in vain.[15] Ramos built up the confidence of the rest of the rebels in the new revolutionary project of confrontation with the existing political system. A few months later, whipped into a fury by the second violent repression of 10 June 1971, they prepared and carried out the first armed strikes.

It was not that these political theorists were hypnotized by *foquismo* or guerrilla militarism. On the contrary, they defended the view that there was a permanent need for ideological struggle. At the same time, Salas developed an interpretation of the economic character of the university, based on the concept of the production and reproduction of capital in the educative process: the thesis that a student proletariat nestled in a factory university. From this perspective, the student struggle was interpreted as a revolutionary struggle of the proletariat, a struggle that "only the opportunism, myopia, and cowardice of the democrats had stopped ... from turning into an armed insurrection to destroy bourgeois power."[16] These radical theses were hardly new. They had first been spread by Students for a Democratic Society (SDS), the New Left in the US.

As theoretical positions, they were articulated in the mimeographed documents "Madera I, II, and III"; as political views, they appeared in the "Manifesto of the Student Proletariat." The manifesto was elaborated by Hirales Morán, signed by the coordinating commission of the Student Federation of the University of Sinaloa, spread among the students of the whole country, and known to its enemies as the declaration of principles by the "Sickies of Sinaloa."[17] What kind of sickness did they suffer from? They were victims of the "infantile leftism" criticized by Lenin in his *"Left-Wing" Communism: An Infantile Disorder*.

Behind the tactical and strategic conception that talked of permanent harassment of the bourgeois state and a struggle to the death against the petty-bourgeois opportunism in the heart of the League itself, there lay a non-Marxist, religious conception of the world. The proletariat was seen not only as a social product of human history, but also as "the avenging and executing arm called to destroy injustice, secular evil and sin, and to regenerate a corrupt society through an inevitable bloodbath."[18] These ideas had a revolutionary Christian ring to them, but Salas took them from anarchists old and new, from Bakunin and Cohn-Bendit, and from the SDS and Marcuse as well.

The Zapatista Urban Front

Concerning the lesser guerrilla bands, mainly the FUZ, there is little to add. In December 1969, the FUZ assaulted a supermarket in Mexico City, and in October 1970 it attacked a branch of the National Bank of Mexico. The FUZ became famous by carrying out one of the most spectacular kidnappings in Mexican history. On 27 September 1971, it snatched Julio Hirschfeld Almada, a government bureaucrat and millionaire, from his post as General Director of Airports and Auxiliary Services. The sum demanded for his release was 3 million pesos.

In June 1972, the magazine *Punto Crítico* interviewed Paquita Calvo Zapata, a militant from the FUZ, in prison. She told her interviewer that the Front was made up of both an underground armed commando and an open, legal one. The first wing took care of politico-military action while the second carried on organizational and recruiting work. In the case of the kidnapping of the millionaire, the aim was to raise public consciousness, "to show that private-enterprise millionaires and reactionaries are also government functionaries." The FUZ wanted also to unify the revolutionary forces, to bring about the "political and military coordination of all the urban and rural guerrilla organizations as a first step toward unification in a great organism of armed struggle on the national level."[19] This proposal was a forerunner of that of the League, with a difference: the FUZ always emphasized the need to link up guerrilla actions with the popular resistance and the peaceful and legal democratic movement.

Notes

1. For an accurate albeit unsympathetic account of Mexico's Lacandones, see the investigative reporting of Elsa Robledo, "Toda la verdad sobre los terroristas mexicanos," *Contenido*, no. 163 (December 1976), pp. 34–5; and Jaime López, *10 años de guerrillas en México 1964–1974* (Mexico City: Posada, 1974), pp. 105, 118.
2. Our data on the Revolutionary Action Movement (MAR) is also taken from Robledo, "Toda la Verdad", pp. 35–42.
3. Ibid., pp. 43–4. On the Revolutionary Student Front (FER) in Guadalajara, see López, *10 años de guerrillas*, pp. 91–9, 108.
4. Robledo, "Toda la verdad," p. 43; and, for a series of prison interviews with members of the People's Revolutionary Armed Forces (FRAP), pp. 51–7.
5. López, *10 años de guerrillas*, pp. 140–2, 146–7; and Ramón Pimentel Aguilar, *El secuestro: ¿Lucha política o provocación?* (Mexico City: Posada, 1974), pp. 137–40, 144–7.

6. Robledo, "Toda la verdad," p. 44.
7. For an inside account of the 23 September League, see Gustavo Hirales Morán, *La liga comunista 23 de septiembre: orígenes y naufragio* (Mexico City: Cultura Popular, 1977), pp. 11–25, 91–102. For additional data, see López, *10 años de guerrillas*, pp. 110–11; and Robledo, "Toda la verdad," pp. 43–5, followed by a prison interview with Hirales Morán, pp. 46–50.
8. On the role of Jesuit priests in the formation of the League, see "Ernesto," *El Guerrillero* (Guadalajara: Graphos, 1974), pp. 145–9, 159.
9. Ibid., pp. 146–7.
10. Ibid., pp. 148–50.
11. Ibid., pp. 150–2.
12. Ibid., pp. 153, 157, 159–60.
13. Robledo, "Toda la verdad," p. 44.
14. Hirales Morán, *La liga comunista*, pp. 11–15.
15. Hodges' interview with Valentín Campa, Cuernavaca, Morelos, 10 January 1978.
16. Hirales Morán, *La liga comunista*, p. 18.
17. Ibid., pp. 18–19.
18. Ibid., pp. 21–2.
19. On the Zapatista Urban Front (FUZ), there is a prison interview with its spokesperson Paquita Calvo Zapata, *Punto Crítico* (June 1972), pp. 28–9, reproduced in abridged form in López, *10 años de guerrillas*, pp. 111–14. See the more readily available translation, "Urban and Rural Guerrillas Have the Same Importance," in Donald C. Hodges, *The Legacy of Che Guevara: A Documentary Study* (London: Thames and Hudson, 1977), pp. 130–2.

12 ✸ The Democratic Tendency of the Electrical Workers

Alongside the armed resistance of rural guerrillas and urban commandos in the big cities, the workers' movement against government repression underwent a revival. In 1971–72 a new wave of peaceful resistance began, but in this phase it was not the student struggle that prodded the masses into action. Just as the railway workers were the vanguard during the previous stage, so during this new period of mass movements, the electrical workers took the lead. The role played earlier by Vallejo and Campa was taken over by Rafael Galván, General Secretary of the Electrical Workers' Union of the Mexican Republic (STERM) from 1960 to 1972, and then leader of the Democratic Tendency within the new United Union of Electrical Workers of the Mexican Republic (SUTERM).

Rafael Galván

Like Vallejo and Campa, Galván came from the ranks of Mexican communism. On 20 November 1935, as a member of the Young Communist League, he took part in a shoot-out with the fascist Golden Shirts. Like Othón Salazar of the Revolutionary Teachers' Movement – another product of the Communist Youth who made a name for himself independently of the Party – Galván challenged the stranglehold of the union bureaucracy on the rank and file.

After his stint with the Communist Youth, Galván came under the influence of Lombardism. He then joined Cárdenas' Party of the Mexican Revolution (PRM) and remained in its ranks when it became the PRI in 1947. In 1968, he even rose to become a senator. Only after the repression of the Democratic Tendency in July 1976 did he move back toward the PCM.[1]

The Independent Unions of the Electrical Workers

As the 1959 railway strike and the independent unions directed by the railwaymen were repressed, a new independent union arose among the electrical workers. In 1960, President López Mateos bought up the stock of foreign companies to nationalize the electrical industry, and the STERM emerged within it. Its forerunner was the National Federation of Workers in the Electrical and Communications Industry (FNTICE), also led by Galván. The labor policy of the STERM sprang from the same current running through the FNTICE. It fought to enforce democratic principles in union life, calling for active participation of the electrical workers in their assemblies and local sections. Its aim was to reduce the power of the national committee, promoting decentralization and workers' initiative at the section level. Such participatory mechanisms were thought to be the only way to guarantee that the union leadership would represent the workers' interests.[2]

This labor policy of the FNTICE and the STERM made them conspicuous among the federations of Mexican unions, most of which were highly centralized, with unlimited power residing in their national committees. Even so, before 1960, the FNTICE did not play an outstanding role in mass struggles because the electrical workers did not labor in the nationalized sector of the economy as did the railwaymen and the oil workers. This meant that the electrical workers never drifted into a direct confrontation with the Mexican state, except for their struggle against the state's Federal Electricity Commission (CFE), a government enterprise that tried to weaken not only private industry but also the unions in the private sector.[3] Their principal enemy was not the boss state but the big owners in private industry. Only after the nationalization of the electrical industry, only after the reorganization of the FNTICE into the STERM, did the electrical workers behind Galván become a vanguard of the resistance to the national tendency toward bureaucratization in the unions and to the co-option of bureaucrats by the corporate state.

When the CFE was founded in 1937 to run the tiny nationalized sector of the electrical industry, a labor union was created from above by the PRI government: the National Union of Electrical Workers and Similar and Related Workers of the Mexican Republic (SNESCRM). The government favored the state sector in order to weaken private industry, to increase its dependence on the state in matters of finance, pricing, and energy. And the growth of the SNESCRM gave the CFE no labor problems.[4] As the state picked up enterprises from the private sector, it gave preference to this union as the representative of the workers of the nationalized enterprises. The state disavowed collective contracts with unions in the private sector and with the corresponding workers' rights, including the right of free union affiliation.

Labor problems mounted during the 1950s when the electrical workers in private industry presented a common front against the CFE, the SNESCRM, and the labor bosses by raising the banner of democratic and independent unionism. The electrical workers formed alliances with other independent unions, such as the railway workers and the oil workers, that also wanted a new labor central in the years 1957–59. But the electrical workers did not show enough solidarity with the railwaymen's movement, and the effort failed. There were two big unions of electrical workers within the private sector, and these failed to reach an agreement. Besides the FNTICE, there was the Mexican Union of Electrical Workers (SME), the oldest union and the one with the most members. Created in 1914, it was the union of a single business: the Mexican Light and Power Company, the oldest branch of the electrical industry, founded during the days of the dictator Porfirio Díaz. The electrical workers of the private sector, divided between these two unions, could not play a decisive role in the workers' struggles until they either united or became integrated into the state sector.

Nationalization of the Electrical Industry

In 1960, the state practically ended foreign interests in the electrical industry, mainly the US-owned Mexican Light and Power Company and the American and Foreign Power Company, founded in 1924. The state acquired 90 per cent of the stock of the first and everything in the enterprises belonging to the second. These enterprises were nationalized, but Mexican Light and Power as well as its labor union (SME) was not integrated with the CFE. In 1963, Mexican Light and Power was restructured as a so-called decentralized enterprise, the Central Light and Power Company, which meant that it continued functioning as a private business although 90 per cent of its stock passed into the hands of the state. In 1968, this stock became the property of the CFE, and its general director became president of the company. Thus the electrical industry remained only formally divided into two state organizations, one nationalized and the other not.[5]

Why wasn't Mexican Light and Power nationalized at the same time? The workers in the SME and the FNTICE then made up 65 per cent of the organized work force in the industry. They were a political force independent of the labor policy of the CFE and its union; they were a threat to its hegemony.[6] The nationalization of the entire industry could mean a confrontation between the government and the independent majority sector of the electrical workers represented by the SME–FNTICE, or it might result in a rectification of the government's labor policy against the old pattern of co-opting union bureaucrats. Since either alternative was politically unacceptable, the government decided to incorporate the FNTICE's workers into the nationalized sector under the patronage of the CFE, leaving the SME's workers with their old collective contracts in the private sector. To divide and conquer was the government's game.

On 27 September 1960, the electrical industry was nationalized by modifying Article 27 of the Constitution. The modification declared that "the state alone can generate, transmit, transform, distribute, and supply electric energy aiming to serve the public."[7] Since the FNTICE's electrical workers ceased working for private companies and faced for the first time the state as boss, they decided on a reorganization to protect their acquired rights. But because the FNTICE was a federation of 52 organizations with autonomy at the local level, there was resistance to integration in one big union.

There was no choice. The 52 organizations were facing the enormous power that the CFE would acquire by controlling a basic industry that absorbed one-eighth of total public investment, and the rival union favored by the CFE could take away from the independent unions the collective contract at any minute. The 52 had to unite. In the last of four national assemblies called to discuss the matter, they decided to form a new union. In 1960, each of them became a section of the STERM, thus keeping its independence before the national committee. The STERM became the first national industrial union effectively to limit the centralization of power in an effort to preserve the active internal democracy of its members.[8]

Jurisdictional Wars

From its beginning, the STERM placed in doubt the SNESCRM's sway over the workers in this branch of the nationalized industry. It demanded the additional nationalization of the Central Light and Power Company in order to facilitate the integration of the electrical industry with other electrical workers, most of them organized in independent unions. Its new banner for struggle bore the slogan "A single collective contract for the industry!" So the government delayed nationalizing the whole industry while it pushed for union integration under the hegemony of the SNESCRM. The CFE's tactic favored the development of the SNESCRM in order to control a large majority of the electrical workers. Although at the time when the enterprises belonging to the American and Foreign Power Company were nationalized there was about the same number of workers in both unions, the CFE's labor policy aimed at the yellow union's domination by 1970. It was then that SNESCRM began to compete openly for the collective contract of the STERM.[9]

Following the nationalization, the government was thus faced by three unions of electrical workers. The situation hardly favored the workers. To ameliorate it, the unions associated with the CFE signed an agreement on 6 July 1966 to heal the split while continuing to observe their respective contracts with the nationalized enterprises. On 28 January 1969, a second union agreement aimed at the integration of the SME with the other unions and finally with the CFE.[10] But, as we have seen, the CFE wanted to deal only with the SNESCRM, breaking away from the agreements of 1966 and 1969.

During the 1960s, the CFE had prepared the future destruction of the STERM by taking work away from it and by stopping the inflow of new members. In 1971, the co-opted bureaucrats of the SNESCRM dealt the decisive blow by stripping it of its right to a collective contract. In January, Francisco Pérez Ríos, General Secretary of the SNESCRM and a PRI senator, demanded the right to the STERM's contract for his own union from the Federal Committee of Conciliation and Arbitration. The other big bureaucrats of the CTM immediately declared their solidarity with his aggressive maneuver. Months later, in October 1971, the STERM was stripped of its contract by an arbitrary judgment of the government umpire.[11]

The result of the arbitrariness was not what the government expected. Far from collapsing, the STERM mobilized its base to protest the adverse decision. Enraged by the repression of 10 June 1971 and encouraged by the retreat of the government that followed the atrocities, the popular sectors poured into the streets to support the electrical workers. For years, the main organ of the union, *Solidarity*, had been denouncing the government's maneuvers and explaining democratic alternatives to state control and repression: this had prepared the ground for popular defense of the workers against the offensive of the co-opted union bureaucrats. On 14 December 1971, with the support of the Railwaymen's Union Movement (MSF), the STERM initiated a week of national demonstrations for union democracy. This consisted of public demonstrations in 40 cities attended by thousands of workers from other industries, by peasants, and by students. The electrical workers took to the streets in a way reminiscent of the ill-fated demonstrations of 1958–59, when the railwaymen stood in the vanguard of the popular struggles.[12]

The demonstrations by the electrical workers and those who joined them had important results, for they kicked off the longest wave of worker insurgency in the history of Mexico. During the following years down to 1976, the independent electrical workers headed the democratic tendency against union bureaucratization and corporatist control of the labor movement.[13] Since they turned into a center of attraction for other resistance movements, they began to unfold a program for workers in other industries and for other sectors of the population ready for popular struggles. Thus Galván, the leader of the democratic tendency, replaced Vallejo and Campa as enemy number one of the union bureaucracy and the corporate state.

The journal *Solidarity* set forth the movement's program in January 1972. The article "Why We Struggle" defended the right to the collective contract, the struggle for democratic union solidarity, and the Popular Program. The Program expressed the outlook of the Coordinating Committees for Popular Action (CCAP). These Committees for union democracy had first appeared in the factories, but during the demonstrations of 1971 they turned into broader organisms trying to spread the democratizing struggle to other sectors. The Program called for basic reforms: union democracy, enforcement of the laws, reorganization of the nationalized enterprises to allow workers' participation in management, continuation of the Cardenist policy of nationalizations, liquidation of the great estates, and education managed by the people. All of this implied a worker–peasant–student alliance. Not even Demetrio Vallejo's South-east Plan of 1958 had set forth propositions so essential to the democratic restructuring of the nation.[14]

The Unification Pact

Faced with the STERM's answer to repression, the government was forced to recognize and mediate in the conflict, to contain it with concessions. In September 1972, it instigated a move toward unity between the STERM and the SNESCRM. On 20 November 1972, there was a unity congress in which the two organizations reached a unity agreement to form the United Union of Electrical Workers of the Mexican Republic (SUTERM). This was a triumph for Galván if only because he gave the new union a democratic structure, using as a model the statutes of the STERM.[15]

The creation of the new union in December 1972 grouped together all the electrical workers in the nationalized industry. But it was carried out behind the scenes in secret negotiations and imposed from the top down. Since the unification pact permitted the leaders of the old organizations to remain in their positions, the democratic tendency coexisted with the bureaucratic tendency in the SUTERM. Besides the fact that Pérez Ríos remained in the post of General Secretary, the new organization joined the labor central, the CTM. Of course, these agreements meant a victory for the SNESCRM and the government. Still, the STERM shared the leadership at both the national and the local level, participating in the key posts. And Rafael Galván remained president of its Commission for Vigilance and Prosecution.

The unification with the SNESCRM took by surprise various sectors of the New Left, which saw it as a sellout. To be sure, the popular resistance led by the STERM lost in part its role as a gravitational center for other unions with democratic tendencies, and that meant a gain for the government. But Galvanismo had gained a powerful position inside the CTM from which it could carry on the struggle for union democracy. A determined movement, boring from within, can sometimes be more effective than an isolated critic shouting from outside.

Boring from Within

On 31 August 1972, a *Solidarity* article began the task of boring from within. The central thesis of the democratic tendency was made clear: the proletariat has its own ideology and interests that carry it toward the workers' state and not toward a third state form, neither capitalist nor socialist. "The revolutionary nationalist state is not a finished form of restructured state but a *capitalist* state still, though deeply influenced by the Revolution," declared the article,

> in which the measures of the state, even without proletarian direction, weaken the capitalist system through nationalizations, statifications, land reform, etc.... All these conquests must be defended by the workers ... in order to finally realize fully *their own historic interests* by arriving at socialism. The condition for all this, of course, is the *political, ideological, and organizational independence* of the working class. That is our point of view.[16]

The task was to work inside the CTM, but without losing the organizational independence of the new democratic tendency of the SUTERM.

From this point on, the conflict with the electrical workers was carried on within the single union of state workers. This internal conflict sharpened steadily. Finally, on 22 March 1975, in a congress manipulated by the bureaucratic leadership with delegates chosen from above and with the intervention of the CTM's boss Fidel Velázquez, the national leadership of the Democratic Tendency was expelled from the SUTERM along with a hundred of its militants, including half of its National Executive Committee.

The Revolutionary Union Movement

But this maneuver failed as surely as had the previous ones. The democratic tendency once more responded with public demonstrations which reached a climax on 5 April in Guadalajara. Then in a giant meeting 30,000 workers approved the Declaration of Guadalajara, which became the program of the new Revolutionary Union Movement (MSR), the heir of the struggles carried on by the SUTERM's democratic tendency.

The new program was even more advanced than the STERM's program set forth in *Solidarity* in January 1972. It called for: reorganization of the workers' movement in a reorganized labor central; unionization of all salaried workers; a general wage hike with a moving scale to keep pace with increases in production; action against inflation through price controls; enlargement of the system of state food stores with prices subsidized by the government; workers' housing, rent controls, and municipalization of collective transport; a state monopoly of foreign trade; and an alliance with all underdeveloped nations to defend their raw materials against imperialist exploitation.[17] It was indeed a program that could better the living conditions of most Mexicans.

The new Revolutionary Union Movement, led by the democratic tendency of the militants expelled from the SUTERM, represented the most thorough alternative movement for the workers during 1975–76. As we shall see, it was the immediate forerunner of the National Front for Popular Action, the most important mobilizing center of worker insurgency, created a year later in May 1976.

In November 1975, the largest demonstrations of workers, students, and middle sectors since 1968 took place in Mexico City. The MSR's campaign for union democracy culminated in the great demonstration of 15 November with 150,000 marchers moving through the downtown area. Besides the electrical workers in the vanguard role, the left-wing political parties and the independent unions took part. Once more, Galvanismo was the gravitational center of a rising struggle.[18]

Galván then announced the plan of the Democratic Tendency to call a national strike in order to get back into the leadership of the SUTERM. The government replied that the strike would be illegal and that the state would take legal proceedings against its leaders. A few months later, on 20 March 1976, the MSR held a huge protest meeting at the Monument to the Revolution in Mexico City. The demonstration was a protest against the treacherous union bureaucrats and their

165

manipulation of the labor movement in the interests of the bosses and the state. The demonstrators planned to march from the Monument to the Central Plaza, cutting a swath through downtown Mexico City. But the demonstrations at the end of the preceding year had put the government on alert. It fielded 27,000 "guardians of order" to prevent the march. Faced with that much muscle, the workers opted to go home. Clearly, the state was ready for another great confrontation with the popular resistance.

The National Front for Popular Action

The polarization of forces lurched forward. On 14 May 1976, 300 delegations to the first National Congress of Worker, Peasant, and Popular Insurgency met to represent hundreds of thousands of workers throughout the country. The Congress created a popular front of support for the electrical workers excluded from the SUTERM – the National Front for Popular Action (FNAP). This was to be the heir of the MSR with a common program similar to the old one. Once more Galvanismo was in the vanguard of the formation of a new resistance movement.

The Front backed the electrical workers' national strike planned by the Democratic Tendency. Galvanismo was ready for the strike because it sensed that it had the support of the organizations attending the Congress. The first date picked for work stoppage against the CFE was 30 June 1976, four days before the presidential elections. The so-called progressive forces in the government showed no sign of making concessions until 22 June, when President Echeverría called for reconciliation with the electrical workers. The National Council of the Democratic Tendency postponed the strike to the middle of July.

Although the Galvanistas hoped that the President and the nationalist sectors of the PRI government would resolve the conflict, the presidential elections reinforced the government's position: it no longer felt pressured to reach an agreement. Galvanismo had been using the strike as a threat to the government, but the state no longer feared the response to massive repression of the strikers. The talks with the government were bogged down when the strike day arrived. The Galvanistas' demands were scarcely excessive: recognition by the CFE of the representatives elected by the union; cessation of CFE intervention in the internal affairs of the SUTERM; reinstatement of the 300 workers fired for belonging to the Democratic Tendency; and reform of the electrical industry administration with worker participation.[19] Only the last demand was perhaps overambitious.

Initially, the government agreed to reinstate the fired workers and to stop CFE interference in union affairs. Then the government backpedaled. But conditions turned unfavorable for a strike when on 15 June 1976 the expected support from the Mexican Union of Electrical Workers (SME) melted away, just one day before the planned confrontation. The general secretary of the SME dealt a serious blow to Galván's plans, declaring that his union was not in sympathy with the struggle of the Democratic Tendency. He recognized the sold-out union bureaucrats in the SUTERM as the SME's legal representatives.

When the day of decision arrived, Galván's hope that the government would respect the strikers' rights was dashed as the bureaucracy notified the public that it was going to fight the strikers. The government had to back its co-opted union bureaucrats, who made up an important sector of the ruling party. Before the time designated for the strike to begin, the sold-out SUTERM leaders, backed by their own thugs and by the army, seized the CFE's offices throughout the nation. They prevented the electrical workers from going to work until they signed a document recognizing the bureaucratic leaders as the only authorities within the union. The strike was being repressed before it could begin.[20]

The Galvanistas thought that the CFE would be unable to keep the electrical system going without the striking electrical workers and that the situation had to change in favor of the Democratic Tendency. They were mistaken. Although there were blackouts in some cities, huge losses, and chaos in the administrative system, the government kept the electrical system going. Faced with this unexpected development, desertions began, and the retreat turned into a rout. On 27 July 1976, the leaders of the Democratic Tendency in Puebla and Jalisco abandoned the struggle by recognizing the executive committee of the sold-out bureaucrats. Finally, the union bureaucracy attacks, the government pressure, the army intervention in the electrical industry, the poisonous campaign against Galvanismo in the mass media all combined to break the resistance of the electrical workers.

Only after the defeat of the Democratic Tendency did the government decide to appear as the great benefactor. On 31 July 1976, the Attorney General notified the dissidents that they could return to work without reprisals, without losing the autonomy of their sections, and without having to sign the document imposed by the sold-out bureaucrats. The government did more than assume a paternalistic attitude: it stooped to shameless demagogy, assuring everyone that it accepted the just demand for reinstatement of the fired workers. At the same time, it suggested that the strike threat had been unnecessary for reaching an agreement. After all, the government was accepting the reinstatement of fired workers and discussing the other pending questions.

What were the facts? Three days later, the sold-out bureaucrats signed a collective contract with the National Institute of Nuclear Energy that excluded the combative nuclear sections of the Democratic Tendency, expelling them from the union. The sections of the Democratic Tendency in Puebla and Jalisco did not recover their independence. Galván and other expelled members of the SUTERM's Executive Committee were reinstated neither in their posts nor as members of the union.

The Fundamental Enemy

Only through such experiences did the Galvanistas realize that the government had turned into enemy number one of the Democratic Tendency. After these defeats, there were changes in the analysis of social reality and adjustments in the strategy of the workers' movement. From the moment the leading cadres of Galvanismo were excluded from the SUTERM, they stopped believing in the so-called left wing of the ruling party and in the possibility of democratizing the bureaucratized unions by the method of boring from within. A new direction was taken. The new strategy called for independent organization of the workers and for alliances with left-wing parties. Galván decided that only by systematic opposition to the government was there any hope of building a democratic and popular alternative to the PRI's corporative cage. This was also the position defended by the Mexican Communist Party within the National Front for Popular Action.

It was a strategy of convergence. But did the Galvanistas think along the same lines as the members of the PCM? On the contrary, they were miles apart. Of all the popular movements, Galvanismo had the most acute analysis of the correlation of social forces and of the unique predicament of labor in nationalized industry under conditions of Mexico's system of presidential despotism and the PRI monopoly of political power. Consequently, they were also the best prepared to respond intelligently to the veiled dictatorship of Mexican democracy.

The Galvanistas' unmasking of this dictatorship can be briefly summarized. It was the only tendency on the left to underscore the new, post-bourgeois modes of exploitation in the public sector: first, by the inept management teams relying on graft and other corrupt practices for supplementing their already inflated salaries; second, by government bureaucrats concerned with providing an investment climate attractive to the multinationals through a policy of subsidized prices at the expense of workers in the public sector; third, by the *charros* or union bureaucrats who lined their own pockets by keeping a lid on wage increases. These three modes of exploitation were beyond the ken of Marxist political economists, the Lombardist allies of the official party, and the PCM.[21]

As *Solidaridad* summed up the predicament of workers in the public sector, they were not just exploited but super-exploited. Beginning with the presidency of Miguel Alemán, the nationalized industries were made to serve the propertied interests that years earlier had capitulated to the revolution, "to serve them at the *expense* of the workers – the sole producers of the usurped wealth." For "the subsidies that the State conceded to capitalism were a deduction from wages not paid to the workers."[22]

Owing to the comparative backwardness of the Mexican economy and the counter-revolutionary policies of the Mexican state, the existing division of labor made the production of oil, electricity, and other primary goods the job of the public sector, "while foreign investment reserved for itself the production of finished industrial and agricultural products on a grand scale that included their commercialization both domestic and foreign." Such a mutual arrangement advantageous to both parties had a nether side conducive to "super-exploiting the national workforce." None the less, "to keep the workers in tow a simple semantic trick sufficed ... an appeal to the 'national interest' [in the case of underpricing goods in the public sector sold to the multinationals] ... to 'revolutionary development' [in the case of policies favoring the development of the private sector] ... and to 'democracy' [in the case of the PRI's monopoly of political power]." Thus, the mission of the officially recognized political parties was "to detect, distort, falsify, and finally to dissolve every social complaint, every authentic ground for uneasiness": first, by means of systematic bribery of individuals and dissident groups; second, by "a vast network of technically sophisticated internal espionage for aborting conspiratorial activity as understood by the upholders of [law and] order."[23]

For the first time on the Mexican left, the phenomenon of *charrismo* was defined in depth as the governmental imposition of a spurious trade-union leadership for the purpose of controlling and repressing the workers, of simulating a classist defense of their interests, and of dissimulating the super-exploitation of which they were victims. How to explain it? "*Charrismo* emerged as the bastard outcome of *State–labor class* relations, first, because only the State with its revolutionary aura backed by the prestige of the Constitution was in a position to humble the workers, and second, because labor problems were concentrated in the public sector." *Charrismo* became a dissolvent factor of the class struggle where labor insurgency was strongest – among teachers, railroad workers, oil workers, and the electricians whose Democratic Tendency became the cutting edge of resistance to the labor bureaucracy.[24]

Behind the *charros* were the bosses in the nationalized industries who relied on them to keep the workers at bay. As Rafael Galván targeted these new enemies of the revolution hiding behind its cover, "in the nationalized industries the private entrepreneur is replaced by a new type of manager who, without being an owner or a representative of private property, nonetheless shares in the surplus in the form of elevated salaries, commissions, bonuses, contracts, [etc.]." Consequently, the class struggle involves more than a confrontation between bourgeois and proletarians. For the workers, it means not only "defending the social property of the nationalized enterprises against raids from the private sector," but also a "class struggle between the administrators of nationalized enterprises and the workers."[25]

This explains the rhetoric of revolutionary nationalism instead of socialism on the part of the Democratic Tendency. Socialism becomes possible simply through the defense and recovery of the public sector by the people acting within the law and the Constitution. The popular sectors are not ready for a new revolution, nor do they need one: "Revolutionary nationalism is the station of transit toward a socialism that in Mexico has the exceptional advantage of being protected and foreseen by the [country's] fundamental law." Since the economy is still dependent on foreign investment, on so-called imperialism, the road to socialism begins with what Lenin called the struggle for national liberation.[26]

Notes

1. Barry Carr, *Marxism and Communism in Twentieth-Century Mexico* (Lincoln: University of Nebraska Press, 1992), p. 247; data on Galván's political trajectory from Hodges' interviews with Valentín Campa (10 January 1978) and Gerardo Unzueta (6 February 1978).
2. Silvia Gómez-Tagle and Marcelo Miquet Fleury, "Integración o democracia sindical: El caso de los electricistas," in idem with José Luis Reyna and Francisco Zapata, *Tres estudios sobre el movimiento obrero en México* (Mexico City: Colegio de México, 1976), pp. 165–8, and 167 n.13.
3. Ibid., pp. 162–3.
4. Ibid., p. 152.
5. Ibid., pp. 166–7, 169.
6. Ibid., p. 167.
7. Ibid., p. 166.
8. Ibid., pp. 152, 166, 170, 174-175.
9. Ibid., pp. 170–2.
10. Ibid., pp. 169, 190.
11. Ibid., pp. 187, 190, 197–8; and "Política antiobrera en la CFE" (30 November 1971), from the articles in *Solidaridad* published under the title *Insurgencia obrera y nacionalismo revolucionario* (Mexico City: El Caballito, 1973), pp. 385–8.
12. "¡Los trabajadores, otra vez, ganan las calles!" *Solidaridad* (31 December 1971), ibid., pp. 392–95.
13. Rodolfo F. Peña, "Prólogo," *Insurgencia obrera* , pp. vii–viii.
14. "¿Por qué luchamos?" *Solidaridad* (January 1972), ibid., pp. 299–303.
15. "Nace el SUTERM," *Solidaridad* (30 November 1972), ibid., pp. 490–2.
16. "La revista *Debate* y los agujeros sin queso," *Solidaridad* (31 August 1972), ibid., pp. 455, 456–7.
17. "Declaración de Guadalajara" (April 1975), Appendix to Ilán Semo and Américo Saldívar, *México: un pueblo en la historia* (Mexico City: Universidad Autónoma de Puebla and Editorial Nueva Imágen, 1982), vol. 4, pp. 343–5.
18. Américo Saldívar, "Una década de crisis y luchas (1969–1978)," in Semo and Saldívar, *México*, vol. 4: pp. 210–11.
19. Ibid., p. 211.
20. Ibid.
21. "Los trabajadores del sector nacionalizado," *Solidaridad* (editorial), in *Insurgencia*

obrera, pp. 87–8.

22. "La guerrilla y la histeria anticomunista," *Solidaridad* (editorial), ibid., pp. 112–13.
23. Ibid., pp. 114–15.
24. "El charrismo en el sector nacionalizado," *Solidaridad* (editorial), ibid., pp.210–12.
25. Rafael Galván cited by Manuel López Gallo, *Economía y Política en la Historia de México* (Mexico City: El Caballito, 1967), pp. 573–4. However, Galván rejects the thesis that the new bosses, not to mention government bureaucrats and the trade-union mafia, constitute what he calls a "special class." See Robert Michels, *Political Parties: A Sociological Study of the Oligarchical Tendencies of Modern Democracy*, trans. Eden and Cedar Paul (Glencoe, IL: Free Press, 1958; orig. pub. 1915), pp.21, 399–400.
26. Peña, "Prólogo," *Insurgencia obrera* , pp. xiv.

13 ✹ Peasant Land Seizures and Committees of Self-Defense

Basing themselves on a study of the national press, Jorge Martínez Ríos and his research team at the National University (UNAM) reported 41 occupations of land between January 1940 and October 1972. During this period, there were two big upsurges in land seizures. One took place in 1958, with eight occupations in the north-east of the country alone. Another wave began in 1972, with nine occupations, mainly in the center and the north.

Although there was a decided sharpening of peasant struggles in 1943 and 1944 when Rubén Jaramillo took up arms, there were only two great waves of peasant resistance during the post-Cardenist epoch. Beginning in 1958, the first wave included the occupations at Michapa and El Guarín in 1960 and 1961, continued on to the formation of the Independent Peasant Central (CCI) in 1963, and culminated in the struggle of the small-dairymen of Puebla in 1963 and 1964. The second wave, described by Martínez Ríos, was much more powerful than he realized and lasted until 1976.

Number 18 of the journal *Punto Crítico* reports 25 occupations between April and October 1972 and 21 occupations between January and July 1973. Officially, the "heroic" army threw out the "invaders" on only 28 occasions, but the truth is that it did this in the majority of the occupations, aided by the Federal Police and the landlords' gunmen. In 1972, occupations were reported in 17 of Mexico's 32 states; in 1973, in 12 states. In Guanajuato, professionals and businesspeople declared that up to 12 May 1972, there were 46 occupations. In Tlaxcala, where "there are more acres per bull than a peasant owns," there were in June 1973 some 27 "land invasions."

Invasions in Lieu of Land Reform

What chain of events led to these invasions? The story is a complicated one. When President Cárdenas transformed Calles' National Revolutionary Party (PNR) into the Party of the Mexican Revolution (PRM) in 1938, control of the peasant movements passed from the top down.[1] Even though the peasants were being swept up in the net of corporatist control, under Cárdenas there was political participation by the peasants and much freedom of action. Alemán tightened the net of corporatist control by reforming Article 27 of the Constitution to give landlords a way to protect themselves by obtaining injunctions from the courts. Independent action by the peasants became "illegal," and from that moment we hear of "invasions" to get lands back through force – invasions carried out through popular mobilizations by people tired of waiting for the famous Mexican Revolution to give them justice. All of these actions were similar in demanding the land reform promised by the Constitution, the end of the great landed estates, of the red tape strangling the courts and the agrarian department, of the corruption rampant among officials, of army repression, of threats by local gunmen.[2]

Among other factors, one must add the population explosion and the proletarianization of the peasantry. A famous case is that of La Chontalpa, Tabasco, in which six communal farms (*ejidos*) worked for the Commercial Bank and an intermediary multinational corporation: Nestlé. These peasants-cum-proletarians lost control of production when technicians working for the bank and the company took command.[3]

Land-grabbing by already rich landowners accentuated the despair of peasants who had been waiting half a century for land reform and redistribution. Deprived of their lands, they had to survive as penny vendors and shoeshine "boys," by taking seasonal work as bricklayers during building booms in the cities, and in other less respectable jobs. These "street people" were among the forgotten victims of the revolution made in their name.

Let us pursue this theme through some examples.[4] To get around the agrarian law, the great landlords used name-lenders, as did the North American Jenkins in Atencingo, Puebla, when he brought thousands of acres under his control. In Durango the widow of

Carother and in San Luis Potosí the two owners Malcom Niven and Robert Blagg pulled together 180,000 acres at the ex-hacienda of Micos near the town of Valles. On 18 June 1973, the occupation of these lands by the Campamento "Land and Freedom" was repressed. The landlords also used the names of their children to cover their illegal fusion of plots into great estates, as did Raúl González in Tlaxcala when he swept 6,600 acres under the control of his hacienda at Piedras Negras. In the same state, Luis Barroso held 27,600 acres at the Mimiahuapan hacienda.

In Guaymas, Sonora, the widow of President Obregón, with her certificate of "exceptionalism," held 15,000 acres. How much did the agrarian law allow her to hold? 400 acres: that is the limit of "small property," and it is probably too much. Obregón's huge estate was partially cut down in July 1971 when land was redistributed to 117 peasant families. But another political family, that of Calles, also had a large share of the booty picked up during that President's term of office. In San Luis Potosí, the PRI politician Gonzalo N. Santos was not lagging behind in the race for riches. In Morelos, the state made famous by Zapata, the ex-governors and real estate developers Estrada Cajigal and Rivera Crespo made themselves infamous, as did the banker Legorreta. In Puebla, the former mayor's aide Angela Azcárraga also enjoyed large holdings in land. In Sonora it is said that the landlords reign. In Veracruz, Jorge Roura Malpica got help from the PRI government in defending his possessions. At Poza Rica, the landlord Jorge Legorreta defended his little spread of 5,000 acres with hired gunmen: on 12 June 1973, "invaders" were driven off with bullets. In Chihuahua, the Ibarra family held 36,000 acres as the 1960s opened, but the peasants gave up hope of getting any until the guerrilla war of Arturo Gámiz exploded over the sierra. In the same state, the Terrazas family, famous for its huge holdings since the days of the dictator Díaz, along with landlord neighbors like ex-Congressman Mariano Valenzuela, also had a share in land-grabbing.

All these neo-landlords, rich men, and politicians had deliberately taken advantage of the injunction procedure against presidential resolutions. As the well-known student of peasant struggles, Francisco Julião, has pointed out, the peasants are legalists who believe in the law, and professional lawyers are only too eager to offer their services for a few centavos to help them struggle through the courts – in vain!

Julião's *Escucha campesino* (1971), consisting of his letters and talks to peasants on how to respond to the landlords' aggressions, appeared in Spanish translation on the eve of a new wave of land invasions beginning in the early 1970s, sparked in part by poor students with recollections of the 1968 student massacre. A political exile from the military dictatorship in Brazil in the 1960s, Julião had acquired hemispheric recognition for his organization of the Peasant Leagues in north-eastern Brazil. In the mid-1970s his advice was being sought on how to defend the land invasions by urban squatters in the *campamento* "La Lagunilla" in the *barrancas* of Cuernavaca.

A 1936 decree granted the inhabitants of San Antón, a poor and overpopulated suburb of Cuernavaca, approximately 720 hectares for their "Ejido San Antón." But the *ejidatarios* who began cultivating it were induced by the rising price of land to rent and then to sell their parcels. As a result, the descendants of the original beneficiaries of the Agrarian Reform found themselves without land and a roof they could call their own.

In 1975, a group of disinherited youth from this poor suburb resolved to recover the fields they considered their own. On 29 February 1976, in response to the local government's refusal to grant them land, some 350 families occupied the area. In a short time, no less than 2,000 people waited patiently for legal recognition of their *campamento*. Meanwhile, the disinherited youth armed themselves in the event of a showdown.

What advice did Julião offer? "Organize for peaceful land take-overs, but also prepare for the expected violent repression." The thorny problem was how to mobilize peasants in armed self-defense. Julião: "First, with the Bible's injunction of an eye for an eye, a tooth for a tooth; second, with appeals to the 1917 Constitution or fundamental law of the land; third, with songs of protest."[5]

The Rubén Jaramillo and Other Settlements

In the huge wave of land occupations, the most important were the people's settlement of Francisco Villa in the capital of Chihuahua (about which, more later) and the settlement Rubén Jaramillo four miles west of the old Mexico–Acapulco road near Temixco in Morelos. How did the Jaramillo settlement begin? On 31 March 1973, six families began the occupation of lands making up the 134-acre development project Villa de las Flores belonging to the state. On 5 April, hundreds of families took possession of 100,000 square meters, and by 20 May, the number of families had reached 2,000, after dividing up the land into lots measuring 200–400 square meters. This proletarian settlement was penetrated and manipulated by government organizations; when that tactic failed, the settlement was assaulted by the army. It had a socialist program and a struggle committee with various branches, but it did not achieve the hoped-for success in putting down roots and winning support from other popular organizations. It was also too near the federal capital for the government's comfort. The government could not allow a "bad example," and repression fell upon the settlement.[6]

Another *campamento* was the "Land and Freedom" colony in San Luis Potosí. It appeared on 18 June 1973 when lands were taken back from the Don Tomás estate embracing 180,000 acres. The peasants had been struggling for 35 years against this hacienda. It was made up of the ex-hacienda Micos in the town of Valles, along with development projects such as Oklahoma City, Colonia Mexico, Micos Ranch. This *campamento* too was repressed.[7]

In Mexico City's environs, 35 families raised the banner of "Land to the Tiller" and occupied 700 acres in Iztacalco during 1959. Between May and August 1975 was born the *campamento* "October 2," a squatters' settlement repressed many times. It had 5,000 families that repeatedly stood together against the government's efforts to make it disappear. The vast Mexico City slum area called Netzahualcóyotl, today containing almost six million people, is a complicated case. The government has often split the area into smaller divisions, following the old divide-and-rule maxim.[8]

During the last year of President Echeverría's reign, there were occupations in Sinaloa and Sonora. In Sonora on 20 October 1975, the peasants at Valle del Yaqui occupied 200 acres, property of the great landowner Miguel Dengel registered in the name of his nine-year-old son. The struggle against this landlord had already lasted 20 years.

These movements did not follow any pattern. Sometimes the peasants occupied communal lands (*ejidos*); at other times they seized the large illegal estates; occasionally they occupied state lands. The "invasions" occurred both in the environs of cities and in remote country areas. One common feature is that they were invariably carried out by poor people, and often enough they had waited decades for the Mexican Revolution to reach them. The population explosion barely accounts for the events, since it overlooks the multitude of cases in which the peasants had been waiting 40 years for the land granted to them in the 1930s, long before there was any demographic problem.

The occupation movements were spontaneous and disorganized, but they were of tremendous importance. They produced many cadres who joined the independent peasant leagues and the opposition parties, thus orienting the swirling masses and channeling their energy toward political action. They came out of the people; they did not take up a paternalistic attitude. Their leaders avoided sectarian fanaticism and authoritarian methods. The spontaneous struggle of the rural masses produced cadres schooled in libertarianism.

Various peasant organizations have taken part in the land occupations. The National Peasant Confederation (CNC), the central government organization, has itself given rise to a few, while co-opting others. The Mexican Agrarian Council (CAM) and the General Union of Mexican Workers and Peasants (UGOCM), founded by Jacinto López, have sparked many land seizures. Naturally, independent peasant organizations have many occupations to their credit: the Independent Popular Union (UPI) in Durango and the Agrarian Particular Committee (CPA) at Xonaca in Puebla are examples of the smaller organizations at work. The most important of these independent movements was the Independent Peasant Central (CCI) led by Ramón Danzós Palomino.

The Independent Peasant Central

The CCI appeared in answer to the first wave of land occupations and the seizures led by Jaramillo at El Guarín and Michapa Plains. But in 1964 the CCI split when its general secretary, Danzós Palomino, a PCM stalwart since 1936, stood as a presidential candidate for the leftist People's Electoral Front. Half of its membership continued under his leadership in the "democratic CCI," consisting mostly of agricultural laborers, landless peasants, and petitioners for land to the government's agrarian reform agencies. The "splitters," whose leaders had been expelled by the CCI's Executive Committee, then moved closer to the PRI and, in doing so, were rewarded by government subsidies denied to the "independent CCI."[9]

Near the end of 1961, the Organizing Commission of the CCI, containing Jaramillo and Genaro Vázquez, was formed; at a regional level, one of the organizers was Lucio Cabañas. The CCI was founded on 6 January 1963 with approximately one million members. Its first National Congress took place in January 1965. In the same year, it joined the International Association of Agricultural Workers' Unions (UISTABP), which represented more than 34 million members.[10]

In 1964, the CNC peasants and the small milk producers in Puebla urged the CCI to take the initiative against Puebla businessmen and the state governor General Antonio Nava Castillo, who were trying to force them to sell their milk to a pasteurizer owned by the state so as to bring millions in profit to the governor and his allies. The CCI called a protest meeting for 13 October 1964; 8,000 people turned out. The national security police, the federal police, and the state police also appeared, and there was a savage repression of the peasants.

The University of Puebla was drawn into the fray. It declared a general strike in solidarity with the peasants; 50,000 people participated. The students seized vehicles used by the government for political repression and set them afire. The government made the student actions an excuse for more force, and the army occupied Puebla. A little later, Governor Nava Castillo "resigned," and his successor repealed the milk pasteurization decree.[11]

In July 1967 the "democratic CCI," backed by the Communist Party, convened its second National Congress. Although weakened numerically, its adoption of a new program contributed to radicalizing it. Its new five-point program called for:

- An integral agrarian reform with voluntary collectivization.
- The organization of agricultural workers in independent trade unions.
- A workers' and peasants' united front.
- Freedom for political prisoners.
- Solidarity with the people's struggles in Cuba and Vietnam.

Although there is no mention of land takeovers in the program, within a short time the mounting repression of independent actions by the CCI, including torture, imprisonment, and assassination of its militants, impelled the peasants to begin land occupations in sheer desperation.[12]

The expropriations began in response to the repression of the agrarian march from Puebla and Tlaxcala toward Mexico City on 10 April 1972. This march, organized by the CCI, was stopped twice, the second time at Llano Grande on the highway leading from Puebla to Mexico City. President Echeverría was playing the role of a "new Cárdenas," or trying at least to sound like one, and he ordered General Leopoldo Garduño del Campo to use 600 soldiers to load the demonstrators on military trucks and whisk them away to a "dialogue" with the President. The aim of the march was not to end up chatting with the President but to honor the memory of Emiliano Zapata and to hold a mass meeting in front of the agrarian offices in Mexico City. The meeting was shelved because of open threats of repression.[13]

In May 1973, the CCI called a national session of the Central Council of its Executive Committee. It decided to proclaim a national week of struggle for the land from 20 to 26 July. The response was overwhelming. As a result of this initiative by the "democratic" or "independent" CCI, more than 70 occupations of great landed estates occurred, most of them led by CCI militants. These actions had a multiplier effect. Pressured by the landowners, Echeverría announced during the Annual Convention of the National Cattlemen's Association (CNG) at the end of 1973 that he would permit no more "invasions." Everything would have to be done legally and calmly in order to defend "small property."[14]

Chihuahua's Francisco Villa Settlement

A popular experience that stands out for the lessons it offers is the proletarian settlement "Francisco Villa" in Chihuahua. It was able to resist many repressive blows and has given birth to organizational innovations that reach beyond regional and state boundaries, among them popular assemblies, popular defense committees, neighborhood committees, and popular courts. All these were worked out through iron organizational discipline in worker–peasant alliances with student participation.

The history of the "Francisco Villa" settlement dates from 17 June

1968 when the poor in Chihuahua City without a decent place to live began a mobilization on the outskirts of the town.[15] They occupied vacant lands and later fertile fields belonging to the old landlord Luis Terrazas. Before the 1910 Revolution, he had owned the state! The landless masses seized a piece of his "Quinta de las Carolinas." This first land invasion was followed by others. Thus the settlement "Francisco Villa" was founded three years after the death of Arturo Gámiz, one year after the guerrilla war of Oscar González, and in the same year as the popular student movement. By 1980, the settlement had at least 25,000 inhabitants.

The militancy prevailing among the downtrodden people who founded the settlement was born of a decade of struggle. The years between 1960 and 1964 saw the mobilizations of the UGOCM. The assassinations of the guerrillas who attacked the Madera Barracks caused widespread revulsion. The repression of the popular student movement at Tlatelolco by Díaz Ordaz created real hatred for that president. The electoral farce that put Echeverría in office and the rise in the cost of living during his term further discredited the government while fueling the Chihuahuan resistance.

The beginnings of the Popular Defense Committee (CDP) can be traced to the Popular Solidarity Front of 1969, formed to fight against the treachery of the union bureaucracy in the Pepsi Cola Company of Chihuahua. The Authentic Labor Front (FAT), Christian in ideology, led this struggle for people's democracy. The Popular Solidarity Front broke up because of the proselytizing carried on by various parties including the PCM and because of bureaucratic manipulation. The Front had united organizations of workers, students, and political parties.

Chihuahua's Committee Against Electoral Farce won the support of most of the students; it gave them experience in spreading propaganda on a broad scale. It brought off a gigantic meeting against Presidents Díaz Ordaz and Luis Echeverría. The Committee for Struggle Against the High Cost of Living grouped together many independent and popular forces to work against the rising price of sugar and the sales taxes. Its tactics? Denunciation of price hikes and colorful protest actions. A broad front emerged which helped to politicize the masses, but it eventually split into a popular–student wing and a petty-bourgeois wing. The members gained valuable experience in organizing popular resistance.

Near the end of 1971, Manuel Valles Muela and his friends in the Railwaymen's Union Movement (MSF) seized the local branch of this sold-out union and held it. They wanted to get the union back under the control of the rank and file. Expecting repression of their direct action, they established relations with the "Francisco Villa" settlement, the Chihuahua Steelworkers' Union, the Electrical Workers' Union of the Mexican Republic (STERM), the Student Council, and the teachers in Section Eight. They planned to sign a pact of alliance by April 1972; their main aim was to remove the co-opted union bureaucracy.

Origins and Tactics of the First Popular Defense Committee

While discussions were in progress, a new guerrilla band appeared – the Armed Commandos of Chihuahua.[16] On 15 January 1972, a group of three commandos assaulted three banks in the state capital: the Mexican Commercial Bank, the National Bank of Mexico, and the Commercial Bank. The three attacks were carried out simultaneously. In the first and second, the guerrillas got away cleanly, but some fell in the third, thus helping to give rise to the Popular Defense Committee (CDP). This triple action, known as Operation Madera, aimed to promote peaceful resistance in the course of funding the armed struggle.

How did the third attack go? At 9.30 a.m., the guerrillas surveyed the bank branch from a distance. Its windows were large and circular, giving a clear view to the guards and the army guarding the bank. The commandos argued about whether to proceed with the attack, for the risks were great. The decision was to attack. A number of people were killed in the action: Pablo Martínez, Avelina Gallegos, and Oscar Montes fell; a woman trying to walk out of the bank was slain in the exchange of shots; the police killed by mistake a student passing the bank on foot; and a soldier shot and wounded in the back the manager of a nearby laundry. Ramiro Díaz Avalos, the commandos' driver, fled with the rest of the guerrillas. He was a student at the Vocational School Number Five, belonging to the National Polytechnical Institute. Avelina Gallegos, killed in action, was a fifth-year law student at the University of Chihuahua.

A reward of 200,000 pesos was offered for information leading to the arrest of the fugitives. Soldiers from the fifth military zone and federal police agents launched a manhunt. Then Rosendo Muñoz Colomo, a commando who had just joined the guerrillas, sought protection from his lawyer, who betrayed him to the police. Rosendo was arrested on 16 January. He was forced to talk, and Marco Antonio Pizarro and Marco Antonio Razcón were also arrested. Although Francisco Pizarro, Mario Olguín, Mario Terrazas, and Ramiro Díaz Avalos remained at large, police murdered in cold blood on the same day the engineer Diego Lucero Martínez, a graduate of the Autonomous University of Chihuahua, ex-president of its Student Society and founder or the Armed Commandos of Chihuahua.

On 17 January, District Attorney Antonio Quesada Fornelli announced that Diego Lucero had died resisting arrest. The facts are otherwise. Adolfo Anchondo Salazar had loaned his house to Diego as a hideout. Adolfo saw Diego twice after the police had arrested the guerrilla; Diego was being carried around in a patrol car. Adolfo concluded that the police had murdered him. As word spread, the law students at the Autonomous University of Chihuahua met in a permanent assembly. They left the assembly en masse to march to the governor demanding an investigation. Governor Oscar Flores appointed an investigating commission, which quickly exposed the lies of the DA and the police.

The people were agitated. In December 1971 the STERM had already tried to organize Coordinating Committees of Popular Action (CCAP) against the union bureaucracies in order to recover a contract lost in October. In general, the people were struggling against the top-down control wielded by the PRI, and efforts were made to fight off this control wherever there was a show of popular solidarity. The Chihuahua Steelworkers' Union and the students had tried without success to channel this popular energy against the government. Finally, the armed struggle coupled with police brutality brought about the long-awaited Popular Assembly.

The "Francisco Villa" settlement and the Student Coordinating Committee called for a Popular Assembly to meet in the central plaza on 19 January. There the people voted a unanimous "No!" to the question whether it was a crime against society for the "expropriators" to rob banks. Then the Popular Assembly set forth its demands: removal and prosecution of the District Attorney and the chief of police. On 26 January, the Popular Assembly met again in front of the state capitol building, 15,000 strong. The people marched to the governor's house. They called on him to address the crowd and to listen to its demand that the authorities responsible for the murder be prosecuted.

The Popular Defense Committee (CDP), the directing organ of the Popular Assembly, brought together representatives from the following groups: the Student Society of the University of Chihuahua; the Technological Institute of the Normal School; Section Eight of the Revolutionary Teachers' Movement; the STERM; the Chihuahua Steelworkers; the MSF; the "Francisco Villa" settlement; the Chihuahua University Union; and the Authentic Labor Front (FAT). The committee embraced the interests of students, workers, and "squatters" in defense of civil rights. It arose from a conjuncture in which people confronted the government. It was for the poor; its main aim was "expropriation of the bourgeoisie." It had no permanent leaders. Commissions were formed to discuss every matter that concerned the assembly. When they reached a decision, the Popular Assembly voted on it. As a general rule, any initiative by an individual leader in the name of the assembly without its authorization was rejected. In order to coordinate work and make decisions, the commissions continually returned to the Popular Assembly for consultation.

Subsequent events accelerated and reinforced the popular resistance. On 20 January 1972, the police hanged the guerrilla Ramiro Díaz; his body showed hemorrhage through the mouth. The next day, "Gaspar" was taken from the police station to the town of General Trías, given a running start of 500 meters, and then brought down while "attempting to escape." He had been arrested along with Héctor Lucero Hernández, brother of the dead engineer, Diego Lucero. Héctor had named the place where the loot was hidden. On 24 January 1972, the people returned to their struggle in the streets. Four days later, the Archbishop of Chihuahua declared his solidarity with the struggle, an unusual act that came too late. Taking advantage of the correlation of forces, the university went on strike, demanding a democratic student council, more scholarships, and more buildings for classes.

On 14 February 1972, the governor, pressured by the popular mobilization directed by the CDP, accepted the supposed resignation of the District Attorney but not that of the Police Inspector, and the investigating commission with popular participation was dissolved. The governor, in order to wash his hands of the affair of the DA, submitted the case to an "Academy of Penal Sciences," composed mainly of members of the state government and his judicial yes-men. With this maneuver, the authorities made fools of the people by reinstating the criminal officials in their posts.

Immediately the CDP mobilized, closing ranks with the students on strike and counter-attacking with the formation of neighborhood committees. These spread information, politicized the people, and gathered support for the demonstrations, which soon brought 20,000 into the streets. The CDP kept up the struggle with the old tactics of mass mobilization and new ways of contacting organizations not belonging to it. Finally, it won from the governor the legalization of its lands with title deeds to them.

The government tried to divide the settlement with an urban development program in 1974, which involved provocations, evictions, bribes, and intimidation, but the committee fought it off. The authorities targeted the settlements of "Francisco Villa" and "Emiliano Zapata" because "squatters" supplied the most militant and numerous forces encouraging the Chihuahuan people to take part in the mass mobilizations.

The force of the CDP lay in its ability to mobilize different sectors of the people and in its capacity for negotiation facing the Mexican state, from which it wrested its demands by force. On 30 September 1976, it had an interview with President Echeverría within its own liberated territory in the "Francisco Villa" settlement. The President was obliged to enter without bodyguards. In the *campamento*, he had to listen to reproaches from two directors of the CDP because of repression and government co-option of union leaders.

The CDP was an alternative form of organization that grew and benefited workers, peasants, and other sectors of the popular classes. It was an imposing challenge to the bourgeoisie and the bureaucratic state. Altogether, twenty organizations made up the CDP in Chihuahua: the "Francisco Villa" settlement of Chihuahua; División del Norte in Saúz; Dr Pablo Gómez; Arroyo de la Cantera; Emiliano Zapata; Sections 5 and 31 of the MSF and the Stevedores' Union; Revolutionary Union Action of the SNTE; Civic Union; Villa Juárez;

NCP El Saúz; Revolutionary Peasant Forces Central; Ciénega de Ortíz Ejidos; Guadalupe Victoria; Francisco Villa in Aldama; Peasant Groups of Las Animas and La Concepción; and various student groups.

An Invigorating Example

In order to demand land and credit, Popular Defense Committees popped up like mushrooms in Ciudad Anáhuac, Jiménez, Delicias, Parral, Flores Magón, and Camargo. In Ciudad Juárez, a CDP sprang up against generalized corruption; it made alliances with teachers, students, squatters, workers, and drivers who demanded lower bus fares. The Committee also rallied the taxi drivers against their exploiters. It organized struggles against landlords and real-estate speculators.

The example set by the CDP in Ciudad Chihuahua spread not only to other cities throughout the state, but also to Durango, Puebla, Oaxaca, Chiapas, and other states, with local variations. Their principal targets consisted of those who held political power in the PRI-controlled federal and state governments and government co-opted union bureaucracies – the so-called enemies of the people, including big financiers and foreign investors wielding economic power thanks to the PRI government and the system of presidential despotism. Their principal tactics consisted of protest meetings, popular fronts, land seizures, and workers' and student strikes – clear examples of the power of mobilized masses.

Notes

1. Luis Javier Garrido, *El partido de la revolución institucionalizada: La formación del nuevo estado en México (1928–1945)* (Mexico City: Siglo XXI, 1982), pp. 245, 247.
2. "Concluye la etapa de acción contra el poder del latifundismo," *Excélsior* (4 December 1946), in Gerardo Davila and Manlio Tirado (eds), *Como México no hay dos: Porfirismo – Revolución – Neoporfirismo* (Mexico City: Nuestro Tiempo, 1971), p. 97; and in the same work, "Transcendental proyecto de reformas al artículo 27 constitucional," *Tiempo* (13 December 1946), pp. 97–8; and "Bassols insiste en su impugnación del nuevo artículo 27", *Excélsior* (11 December 1946), pp. 98–9.
3. Carlos Bonilla Machorro, *Caña amarga: Ingenio San Cristóbal* (Mexico City: Publicidad Editora, 1975), p. 281.
4. For this review of peasant land invasions, see *Punto Crítico*, vol. 2, no. 18 (June–July 1973): 24–32.

5. Hodges' interview with Francisco Julião at his home in Cuernavaca, Morelos, 17 December 1977. See his letters and talks to peasants in Francisco Julião, *Escucha campesino* (Mexico City: Extemporáneos, 1971), pp. 130, 135, 183–7.

6. Elena Poniatowska, *Fuerte es el silencio* (Mexico City: Era, 1980), pp. 197–8, 238, 256, 267.

7. "San Luis Potosí: Campamento Tierra y Libertad," *Punto Crítico*, vol. 2, no. 18 (June–July 1973), pp. 33–5.

8. At the Escuela Nacional de Educación Profesional (ENEP–Aragón) in Netzahualcóyotl, Donald Hodges was a visiting professor from March to August 1982. Hodges taught a course on rural sociology in Mexico from which some of the data in this chapter is taken. See his "El marco conceptual marxista en la sociología agraria" (with Ross Gandy), *Códice* (Mexico City: January–March 1985).

9. Ilán Semo, "El ocaso de los mitos (1958–1968)," in Ilán Semo and Américo Saldívar, *México, un pueblo en la historia*, 4 vols., ed. Enrique Semo (Mexico City: Universidad Autónoma de Puebla and Editorial Nueva Imágen,1982), vol. 4, pp. 88–90; and Ramón Danzós Palomino, *Desde la cárcel de Atlixco: vida y lucha de un dirigente campesino* (Mexico City: Fondo de Cultura Popular, 1974), pp. 153–4.

10. Américo Saldívar, "Una década de crisis y luchas (1969–1978)," in Semo and Saldívar, *México, un pueblo*, pp. 221–2; and Angeles Ortiz Mendoza, "La CCI: historia de una lucha (antecedentes de la CIOAC)," *Estudios Políticos*, vol. 4, no. 15 (July–September 1978): 120–2. Following the 1964 split in the CCI, Danzós Palomino continued as the head of the "authentic CCI," later renamed the Central Independiente de Obreros Agrícolas y Campesinos (CIOAC).

11. Danzós Palomino, *Desde la cárcel de Atlixco*, pp. 108–18.

12. Ilán Semo, "El ocaso de los mitos," in Semo and Saldívar, *México, un pueblo*, p. 91; and Danzós Palomino, *Desde la cárcel de Atlixco*, pp. 157–60.

13. Danzós Palomino, *Desde la cárcel de Atlixco*, pp. 128–9.

14. Ibid., pp. 130–1, 135.

15. For the following extended account of the Chihuahua resistance, see Victor Orozco, "Las luchas populares en Chihuahua," *Cuadernos Políticos*, no. 9 (July–September 1976), pp. 49–66; "Reportaje: en Chihuahua se organiza la resistencia cívica," *Punto Crítico*, vol. 1, no. 5 (May 1972), pp. 27–30; and "Chihuahua 1972: una experiencia de lucha popular," *Punto Crítico*, vol. 1, no. 8 (August 1972), pp. 6–15.

16. On the Armed Commandos of Chihuahua, see "El comando armado de Chihuahua rompe el silencio," *Punto Crítico*, vol. 1, no. 6 (June 1972), pp. 25–31.

14 Galvanizing the Indigenous People of Chiapas

In a journalistic blitz, César Romero Jacobo published the first full-scale book on the 1994 new year's uprising, on the armed background and political significance of the Zapatista Army of National Liberation (EZLN), only two months after the event. Remarkably, he was among the first to note that the EZLN was the brainchild of a little-known guerrilla group, the Armed Forces of National Liberation (FALN), also referred to in the press as the Armed Forces of Liberation (FAL) and the National Liberation Forces (FLN). Its sole armed action was in February 1974, ending in defeat by the army in Ocozingo, Chiapas, although it also had bases in Nuevo León and the state of México. It was under the command of the "disappeared politician" César (Fernando) Yáñez and was supported by the Emiliano Zapata Revolutionary Brigade (BREZ), a faction of the 23 September Communist League that had adopted a reformist line and had shifted its political–military operations from Torreón, Coahuila, to the state of Chiapas.[1]

On a visit to Mexico City in October 1995 in search of political support for the EZLN, Commander Yáñez (pseudonym Germán) was detained by the authorities for the illegal possession of arms. An impressive figure both physically and intellectually, he was quickly released on the grounds that imprisonment might wreck the chances of the peace dialogue that had begun in April. On receiving his liberty, he defended the peace process because political conditions in Mexico were no longer the same as they had been when he belonged to the FLN between 1968 and 1978. (That Yáñez was the commander of the EZLN accounts for the title of sub-commander used by Marcos.) However, while acknowledging that he had spent the last decade in the

Lacandon jungle, he denied having any personal connection with the EZLN.[2]

Insurgency Destined to Grow

Romero's account of Subcomandante Marcos' political strategy acknowledges the role of the post-Guevarist reassessment of urban and rural guerrilla warfare in Donald Hodges and Abraham Guillén's *Revaloración de la guerrilla urbana*.[3] Published in Mexico in 1977 and distributed by the Mexican Workers' Party (PMT), this work defends the thesis that armed actions have no future unless they are demonstrably linked and subordinated to popular movements. Precisely that has been the saving grace of the EZLN.

"We are faced with a new revolution in the name of effective suffrage," Romero hypothesizes, "understood as the antechamber to people's power." That is a far cry from the guerrilla movements of the 1960s and 1970s, aimed at the seizure of power by a politico-military vanguard operating under its own steam. The EZLN's strategy of armed reformism follows the guidelines of Abraham Guillén's strategy of the people in arms adopted during the Spanish Civil War. Its modus operandi is "to combine the idea of a prolonged people's war *a la Vietnam* with tactics that would have a political rather than military impact and that have as their goal the struggle 'for democracy, if necessary with bullets.'"[4]

In defense of this sanguine assessment, Romero cites the widely respected Mexican political scientist and political commentator Jorge G. Castañeda, according to whom the EZLN is a guerrilla movement condemned to grow instead of disappear, provided it cleaves to its present line. "The EZLN's objective is not to seize power or to defeat the government militarily, but rather to be the 'people's armed fist' that imposes with machine guns what intellectuals and political leaders, civic movements, intermediaries and intransigents cannot achieve by themselves alone."[5]

That the EZLN was unique in the annals of Latin American guerrilla struggles was testified to by Marcos himself in a communiqué to the press on 6 January 1994.

> To obtain the arms [we needed], we never resorted to robbing, kidnapping, or extortion. Furthermore, we maintained ourselves

with the resources provided by honest and humble people throughout Mexico. It is due to the fact that we never resorted to banditry to obtain resources that the State's repressive apparatus never detected our actions during ten years of serious and careful preparations.

There we have in substance Abraham Guillén's neo-anarchist strategy that accounts for the EZLN's uniqueness.

Rather than a recycled Marxist guerrilla movement, the EZLN is a people's movement. Thanks to Marcos, it is now a people with a voice. The indigenous peoples of Chiapas are Mexicans to exploit, says Marcos, but they cannot have an opinion when it comes to national politics. "The country wants Chiapan petroleum, Chiapan electric energy, Chiapan primary materials, the Chiapan workforce, ultimately, Chiapan blood, but it does not want Chiapan indigenous people's opinion on running the country."[6]

The Mexican army is an internal police force carefully dispersed throughout the 31 states of the federation. Military presence is always heavy in the southern, Indian, state of Chiapas. On 31 December 1993, the soldiers there celebrated the incoming year with rivers of tequila; and exactly at midnight, as they toasted the new year, the Free Trade Agreement with the United States went into effect.

The sun rose over the mountains of Chiapas on New Year's Day to warm the soldiers sleeping off the effects of the cactus juice. Hundreds of armed guerrillas came out of the jungle and drove the hung-over soldiers away from the central highland towns. This uprising of the indigenous peoples of Mexico electrified the world. Their leader was a mysterious guerrilla who called himself Subcomandante Marcos.

Subcomandante Marcos

Who was this hooded man? For a year after the uprising, his charismatic eyes peered at the media through the disguise of a ski mask, but the government finally identified him as Rafael Sebastián Guillén Vicente. In 1957, Rafael was born into the large family of a Tampico businessman who owned a chain of furniture stores. The bourgeois father admired communism while finding it utopian, and he surrounded his children with books and poetry. In high school, Rafael studied under the Jesuits, became an excellent orator and poet, did his social service in Tampico's poor neighborhoods, and from 1977 to 1981 studied philosophy at the National University in Mexico City, winning the coveted Gabino Barreda Prize as the best student of his class. His Marxist thesis on "Althusser and Education" received Honorable Mention.

During the 1970s, Marxism had more influence in Mexican universities than elsewhere in Latin America (except for Cuba), and the student movement sparked by the massacre of peaceful demonstrators at Tlatelolco was peaking. Such was Rafael's generational formation. When a strike of the professors broke out at the National University, he drew posters and wrote pamphlets for his teachers' use. While still a student, he gave classes on graphic design in the Autonomous University of Xochimilco. For several years, he continued as a professor there until 1984, urging his students to study design in the context of "the modes of production" and to analyse its social role. Then he vanished into the Lacandon jungle in the south to join a guerrilla group of the FLN.[7]

Chiapas is the richest state in Mexico, yet the indigenous inhabitants are the poorest. The rich own the land and export chocolate, avocados, mangos, bananas, coffee, beef, and precious woods while the Indians need corn patches, schools, doctors, and jobs. Chiapas is one of the treasures of the western hemisphere, containing biodiversity, minerals, uranium, oil, gas, and hydroelectric power transmitted to the rest of Mexico. But inside Chiapas, most of the indigenous peoples lack electricity.

When the Indians carry out peaceful land seizures they are met with private armies of the rich, who kill them. In Chiapas, the life of a chicken is worth more than that of an Indian. During the wave of revolutionary activity by intellectuals and students throughout Mexico in the 1970s, groups of Maoists, Trotskyists, Guevarists, and Leninists pullulated in Chiapas, each carving a niche for itself in the remote state in order to put into practice its political theory. Chiapas became a political–religious laboratory for utopians. The progressive Catholic Church led by the "Red Bishop," Samuel Ruiz García, was the most important force of all.

In 1969, students from Monterrey who admired the Cuban Revolution founded the FLN, and in 1983 the FLN set up a guerrilla band in the Lacandon jungle. It was to this revolutionary *foco* that Rafael Guillén came in 1984. The *foco*, calling itself the Zapatista Army of National Liberation (EZLN), was deep in the jungle, wandering about among jaguars and parrots. Rafael learned to fire a rifle, find water, hike and hunt, and eat what was available. He took the name Marcos, won respect by enduring the hardships of a guerrilla, and became a *subcomandante*. The isolated group had no support from the indigenous communities and had to supply itself with food and medicine. It was a classic Guevarist *foco*.[8]

When in 1985 the socialist guerrillas contacted nearby communities, they found a warm reception. The catechists trained by liberation theologian Bishop Ruiz in the Diocese of San Cristóbal de las Casas had been working among the Indians, teaching them that Jesus was a friend of the poor and an enemy of the rich, that the gospel meant salvation in this world by organizing to fight economic and cultural oppression, and that everyone had a God-given right to land and freedom. The Church believed that reforms were not only necessary but inevitable. The Tojolabale and Chole peoples accepted this progressive doctrine and began to organize for change.[9]

The Indigenous Peoples' Road to Revolution

Marcos' group arrived to push for much more than reform – it urged revolution. Why did traditional Indian peasants lend an ear to urban, white, intellectual revolutionaries?

The peasant struggles of Latin America pass through three stages: legal protest, civil disobedience, and armed struggle.[10] The movement of Emiliano Zapata provides a classic example. In 1909, Zapata sued the landowner robbing corn patches from his village and got no justice, so in 1910 he passed on to peaceful takeovers of the stolen lands until in 1911 he graduated to guerrilla warfare. In that year, he proclaimed his *Plan de Ayala* as the goal of his guerrilla strategy: the stolen lands would be returned to the villages, one third of the great landed estates would pass to remaining landless peasants – with landowner compensation – and, finally, any *hacendado* who resisted the moderate reform would be subject to complete expropriation. The legalistic and conservative peasants merely wanted their property back and a few corn patches for those still landless, but every *hacendado* resisted to the death both obedience to law and moderate reform. So the ruling class provoked a total social revolution – Zapata expropriated them all![11]

For decades, the cattle barons and the agrocapitalists pushed the indigenous peoples of Chiapas from fertile lands; the Indians spent what little money they had in legal actions brought to the authorities – in vain. Peaceful land takeovers ended in violent repression. For decades, the ruling class carried on a reign of terror against the Indian villages. Amnesty International repeatedly denounced the assassinations, disappearances, torture, beatings, and jailings of indigenous leaders opposed to the systematic oppression. In 1972, President Luis Echeverría's government published the decree of the Lacandon Community, stripping 26 villages of Tzeltal and Cholo peasants of their lands and handing them over to logging companies.[12] Without lands, the subsistence peasants were doomed to extinction; resistance was a matter of life and death. In Chiapas, the ruling class and the PRI dictatorship have been working for a revolution.

According to the ruling authorities and their "police theory of history," revolutions are made by a handful of conspirators who trick the foolish masses into an uprising. But social scientists of all persuasions agree that revolutions are generated by political and economic conditions and that the individual leader is a substitutable variable – if Marcos had been killed, perhaps someone else would have led the uprising on 1 January 1994.

Much of the progressive Church work in Chiapas aimed at convincing the Indians that it was not God's will for them to be poor and that they could organize to improve their living conditions. In Las Cañadas (the valleys of the Lacandón jungle), Marcos and his guerrillas found Catholic Indians organizing themselves in what would become the reformist Rural Association of Collective Interest (ARIC). Here and there in Chiapas, Marist priests were helping the Indians with small development projects that collectivized work and resources.

In 1984 and 1985, Marcos and his guerrillas visited the indigenous communities, vaccinated the people and offered them classes on Mexican history. Speaking patiently through translators, they talked of Father Morelos' guerrilla struggle for independence from Spain and of Lucio Cabañas' recent insurgency in the state of Guerrero; they talked of Cuba's struggle against capitalist imperialism. The Indians listened quietly with inscrutable faces. The guerrillas argued that a reformist struggle through ARIC was not enough and that only a revolution could change the local misery.

The peasants of Las Cañadas decided to take both the peaceful path and the revolutionary road at the same time. They did not want to put all their eggs in one basket. If they hit the government with an armed insurrection, then it might be willing to negotiate their demands. Families of Tzeltales, Tzotziles, Tojolabales, and Choles sent their young men to the mountains for guerrilla training. In 1986, the Zapatista Army of National Liberation grew rapidly, gaining hundreds of new recruits. The villages began to organize and coordinate activity on a regional level. By 1987, peasants joining up decided to remain in their towns, receive military instruction, and become a permanent militia.[13]

During the 1980s, liberationist Bishop Samuel Ruiz in San Cristóbal sympathized with socialism and looked upon the rising Zapatista movement with beaming eyes, but when Marcos told his young guerrilla men and women not to have children because their revolutionary activity would not allow time to raise them, and when he began distributing birth control pills, the Catholic Father's eyes turned peevish. By 1988, the Zapatista Army had expanded into a thousand combatants backed by the whole region, and the Bishop no longer saw Marcos as an ally but rather as a competitor. He began to reassert Church power over the Indians, and the Zapatistas experienced some desertions. In 1989, the collapse of bureaucratic socialism in the East warned the Bishop that Marcos' radical road might be a mistake. By 1990, distance was growing between Las Cañadas and San Cristóbal, but no real rupture had occurred.

On 12 October 1992, when all the Americas were celebrating the quincentenary of Columbus' arrival in the New World, thousands of Zapatistas in disguise marched into the old colonial town of San Cristóbal de las Casas armed with bows and arrows, and pulled down the statue of Diego de Mazariegos, the conquistador who had founded the city.[14]

In secret, the Zapatista communities voted to rise in revolution. Marcos had ordered his supporters to avoid cultivating poppies and marijuana in order not to attract repression by the army and also for moral reasons; likewise, he had avoided kidnapping the rich for ransom money. But lack of finances meant that his movement was badly armed. The Indian guerrillas had sold some cattle to buy hunting rifles and carbines; a few of the white commanders had obtained Uzis and AK–47s.

The January 1994 Uprising

The uprising that took over seven highland towns in Chiapas on 1 January 1994 combined the reformist tendency and the revolutionary tendency of Mexico's popular resistance. On the reformist hand, the small indigenous peasants, whose consciousness had been raised by the diocesan priests, finally lost patience after years of begging the government for land, credits, and decent prices for their products; they voted for an uprising because they felt they had nothing to lose, and they hoped that shooting at the government would make it listen to their demands. They were not interested in overthrowing a President in faraway Mexico City. On the revolutionary hand, the socialist intellectuals believed in Che Guevara's theory that a spark thrown into the powder box of a nation's hunger, disease, unemployment, and repression could trigger a revolutionary explosion of the people against a repressive regime. Although Marcos and his revolutionary elite had passed beyond Guevara's *foquista* model of isolated guerrilla bands shooting at the government – they had built a base among the Indians before opening fire – they hoped that the Chiapas uprising would detonate a mass insurrection of the nation. Their ultimate aim was the capture of government.[15]

The first communiqués of the EZLN made clear that the leaders were thinking with the revolutionary concepts of the 1970s: a politico-military organization would seize power and set up a proletarian dictatorship that would collectivize the land.[16] But Mexico was not ready for revolution. Most Mexicans live in cities, and innumerable surveys showed they rejected violence in the struggle to solve social problems. The majority hoped for peaceful reforms and for a democratic transition from the PRI dictatorship to representative democracy. Most of the left accepted the struggle for democracy as the top priority.

When 2,000 badly armed Tzeltales, Tzotziles, Tojolabales, and Choles, led by a handful of intellectuals with utopian aims, declared war on the Mexican state and its 140,000 troops on 1 January 1994, the nation rubbed its eyes in disbelief. Perhaps a third of the Mexicans sympathized with the terrible plight of the Mayas in Chiapas, while the rest looked upon the Indian guerrilla attack with racist hostility; but in urban Mexico, only the tiny revolutionary left was listening to Marcos' call to arms. Had the sub-commander thrown his revolutionary torch into a void? For years, Marcos had carried Miguel de Cervantes' *Don Quixote* in his knapsack, and he seemed indeed to be imitating the great dreamer. But he was not tilting at windmills: the Mexican military giant was real.

The army counter-attacked and drove the guerrillas out of the highland towns. In the Battle of Ocosingo, it was clear that Marcos lacked firepower. His Indians were armed mostly with hunting rifles and machetes; only a few had automatic weapons. The army advanced, the guerrillas retreated. Would there be a massacre of the indigenous people?

The cunning President Carlos Salinas, master of social communication, had convinced much of opinion in Europe and the US that Mexico's free-market reforms had modernized the country and had readied it for membership in the community of industrialized nations; an important part of this fiction was the new image of "free elections" and "parliamentary democracy" that the PRI dictatorship was cultivating for foreign consumption. Knowledgeable journalists suspected that Salinas was hoodwinking international opinion and resented his success based on duplicity. So hundreds of media people from all over the world and from Mexico City flew to Chiapas to take pictures of the coming massacre. On the internet, the news of Chiapas woke up the bored world left. After Cuba in the 1960s, Chile in the 1970s, and Nicaragua in the 1980s, here was a revolution to worship and to defend in the 1990s. In Frankfurt, Rome, and New York the left also boarded planes for Chiapas. As the cameras arrived, what would Salinas do? Drown in blood a downtrodden minority roaring for democracy while he was trying to create an image of a democratic Mexico? *The First Declaration from the Lacandón Jungle* made ten demands: for roofs, land, work, education, housing, health, peace, justice, freedom, and democracy.[17]

There is a long tradition in Mexican politics of parleying with threatening dissidents to find out how big a bone they hope to gnaw. After twelve days of mowing down Indians, Salinas ordered the army to cease fire so that he could parley. Manuel Camacho, who had resigned as Secretary of Foreign Relations, was sent by Salinas as his representative to negotiate with Marcos.

Don Quixote had brought the raging giant to a stop, and all the world goggled. Little did Salinas suspect that the government representatives were heading toward San Cristóbal to meet a myth-maker more cunning than he.

Marcos as Myth-Maker

In the center of San Cristóbal on the first day of the insurrection, Marcos began building his myth. The city was crowded with tourists. They gathered around the masked Marcos covered with a black poncho, with an Uzi hanging from his shoulder. He told journalists that the ski masks were to conceal the identities of the revolutionaries and also to protect those among them who were handsome. People laughed. The Zapatista Army aimed to bring down the government, he explained, and the uprising was the answer of the indigenous people to the Free Trade Agreement. "We have orders to march on to Mexico City." This was not a show for tourists, he urged; it was a real revolution. "Glory to God, glory to the owner of our earth, the Savior," sang Indians, and here and there could be heard strains of "The Internationale."[18]

The next day, Marcos withdrew his forces from San Cristóbal and fled from the advancing Mexican army. But soldiers roared into Ocosingo, a town of 13,000, and cut the occupying guerrillas to pieces with modern weapons. After the massacre at Ocosingo, it was clear that the badly armed Zapatistas were no match for the advancing military.

What saved the Zapatistas were the media and the political moment that trapped the PRI government. There were world headlines, TV news about an impending genocide in Chiapas, a massacre of the Mayas. And there was the emerging myth of Marcos that served to personalize the Indian struggle. He was the new Che Guevara with charismatic eyes, the new Emiliano Zapata with cartridge belts crossed over his chest in the classic style of the Mexican Revolution, the new *comandante* with a Mao cap and a pipe. And the myth was catapulted on a planetary scale by the internet. All of these factors brought image-conscious President Salinas to a quick decision. He ordered a ceasefire.

Marcos did not create his myth alone. It was the result of converging social forces: a despairing rebellion of the wretched of the earth, a movement of the radical Church for the poor, a media blitz of the world left, a fear among the political class in an election year. History created the role, but Marcos jumped into it and played his part to the hilt – with inventive skill.

Most revolutionaries have no sense of humor; they write mainly for the constituencies that support them, and they spout doctrinal formulas that bore the public. Marcos is that rare revolutionary combining a tragic sense of life with a jolly sense of humor, with an eye for the dramatic, writing for a broad public. Even the most envious of Mexico City's literary intellectuals admit that the man has talent.

From 21 February to 2 March, the first peace negotiations between the guerrillas and the government were held in the Cathedral of San Cristóbal.[19] (It has a small box at the door placed by Bishop Samuel Ruiz asking his parishioners for suggestions on how he can better serve the people.) No other government in the world would have agreed to sit down and parley with masked men. But the PRI in Mexico was a master of co-optation and manipulation.

The talks dragged on for months. World headlines appeared along with thousands of articles, television news stories, videos, books in several languages, internet news and web pages devoted to the EZLN, songs, posters, reviews, and calendars. Voices in support of the EZLN were both audible and numerous, especially in Europe and the Americas. The Mexican national daily *La Jornada* became the *subcomandante*'s mouthpiece, dutifully publishing his brilliant communiqués and articles – Marcos became a world-historical figure.

The government made its peace proposal and seemed to accept some of Marcos' demands. The EZLN then carried out a national consultation of groups of peasants, Indians, workers, teachers, housewives, children, students, and intellectuals. He claimed to have received 65,000 opinions, 98 per cent of them voting to reject the government proposal. So on 12 June 1994, the EZLN issued *The Second Declaration of the Lacandon Jungle* in which Marcos proclaimed a unilateral extension of the ceasefire, called for a peaceful transition to genuine democracy, and demanded that a National Democratic Convention meet in a Zapatista town to write a new

Constitution for Mexico. He continually threatened to renew hostilities while calling for peace, and so continued to combine the revolutionary and the reformist tendencies in his discourse.[20]

For months, the great showman set the stage for the Congress of Aguascalientes, thus imitating the Congress held by Pancho Villa and Emiliano Zapata at the height of the Mexican Revolution in October 1914. The Lacandon jungle buzzed with activity. Six hundred men built a 240-feet high by 150-feet wide stadium by cutting down hundreds of trees and laying logs on a hillside. They built twenty houses, cooking grills, latrines, and a library. Cables were laid to bring electricity from nearby Guadalupe Tepeyac. There was sound equipment with 11 microphones, and a giant tarpauline to keep off tropical rain. On 8 August, the left arrived from all over Mexico: neighborhood leaders, political scientists, peasant chiefs, a few union representatives, academics, resurrected Marxists, journalists from around the world, students, feminists, organizations defending the vote, lesbians and gays, writers, PRD activists and sympathizers and leftist sectarians of all sorts. There they debated and manifestoed. The EZLN paraded in front of them, dressed in shabby uniforms and ski masks. Marcos addressed the meeting with his clever eloquence: "Shall I remove my mask?" No, no! The myth must live on![21]

On 1 January 1995, the EZLN published the *Third Declaration of the Lacandon Jungle*, continuing the synthesis of revolutionary and reformist tendencies. This declaration invited civil society to create a Movement for National Liberation (MLN) to install a new government.[22] Civil society – the popular sectors in Mexico – would create the MLN that would somehow replace the government with a new one.

President Ernesto Zedillo had taken office. In January 1995, he proclaimed to the nation that he would never attack the EZLN, but would always be sitting by the telephone in the National Palace waiting for Marcos to call. The dispute with the indigenous people would be settled by negotiation. The President promised, "I will never attack first."[23]

But when Daniel Morales, a traitor who had been with Marcos in the original guerrilla *foco*, told the government who the mystery man was, Zedillo had second thoughts. Chiapas is one of the treasures of the hemisphere, and analysts at Chase Manhattan Bank openly demanded that the Mexican government extend sovereignty over all its territory or suffer lack of investment.[24] On 9 February, Zedillo's war tanks attacked and seized Zapatista positions in the Lacandon jungle, including their general headquarters in Guadalupe Tepeyac. It was announced on television that Marcos was Rafael Sebastián Guillén Vicente.

Marcos narrowly escaped capture and simply denied that he had ever heard of "that guy they call Guillén." The myth lived on. How to demystify Marcos? The government claimed he was a homosexual. He thanked the government for the lie, saying that brigades of leftist women had been formed to rehabilitate him.[25]

Peace Negotiations and Accords

On 22 April 1995, negotiations between the Mexican government and the EZLN were renewed at San Andrés Larráinzar, Chiapas. On 27 August, more than a million people took part in a consultation called by the Zapatistas. The majority showed itself in favor of turning the EZLN into a political force. On 1 January 1996, the *Fourth Declaration of the Lacandon Jungle* called for the formation of a Zapatista National Liberation Front (FZLN) to act peacefully on the political plane.[26]

On 16 February 1996, negotiations between the government and the EZLN bore fruit in the Accords of San Andrés Larráinzar. In the presence of international observers, the two parties agreed that the rights of the indigenous peoples would be elevated to constitutional status, to include rights to their culture, languages, and traditions. They further agreed that the Indian communities would be given semi-autonomy. The Accords were legally binding on the signatories.[27] Months passed and the government steadfastly refused to implement the Accords. The international community of solidarity with the EZLN and the bewildered Mexican left were caught unawares. They had not anticipated such blatant faithlessness on the government's part.

Marcos was trying to build a new political project outside the legal parties by appealing to civil society. But neither the Movement for National Liberation proposed in January, nor the Zapatista National Liberation Front, formed a year later were able to get off the ground, in spite of dozens of civil committees which took up Zapatista demands for direct democracy, social justice, and a new Constitution. Marcos got more response abroad. In Europe, left-wing intellectuals and youth followed his efforts with increasing zeal. From 27 July to 3 August 1996, people came from everywhere to the "Intercontinental Meeting for Humanity and Against Neoliberalism" at La Realidad in Zapatista territory.

In any event, Marcos refused to disarm and continued his efforts to mobilize support from the rest of Mexico. A thousand Zapatista Indians came to the capital in September 1997 to take part in a huge meeting. From the 13th to the 16th, they attended as observers the founding congress of the FZLN. Marcos, the promoter of this new organization, announced that the EZLN would not join it until the war in the south of the country was over. He kept up the posture of armed struggle without firing a shot while he demanded that Mexico travel the peaceful road to democracy.

Paramilitary Death Squads at Work

On 22 December 1997, a government-sponsored death squad mowed down 45 Tzotzil Indian women and children praying in a church at Acteal, a community thirty miles from San Cristóbal. The murdered Indians were sympathizers of the EZLN. This act of terror horrified the world and opened a new phase in the effort to eliminate the Zapatistas: low-intensity warfare. During 1998 and 1999, paramilitary forces of Indians trained and armed by the Mexican army murdered Zapatista sympathizers. Clearly enough, the government had decided to carry out the sort of repression used in El Salvador in the 1980s against the Marxist-Leninist guerrillas and their civilian supporters. But times had changed. The Cold War hysteria of the 1980s was history, and Marcos did not resemble the communist bogeyman. A shout of protest went up all over the world.

Marcos is a revolutionary, yet not even the US State Department classifies him as a "terrorist." From "somewhere in the Lacandon Jungle," as his communiqués put it, he continues to hypnotize the myriad ranks of the world left and to attract dozens of revolutionary currents crackling in the Mexican underground. How has this communist magician cast his spell?

Marcos' Strategy: Learning to Obey

His success has come from combining the reformist and revolutionary tendencies of the popular resistance. The 23 September League and the Democratic Tendency of the Electrical Workers epitomized the two poles of the popular resistance: the armed struggle transformed into a virtual end in itself, and the peaceful struggle for democracy likewise transformed from a means into an end. To have any chance of success, the resistance had to bring the two tendencies together and make them work in tandem. The peasant land invasions and the popular committees of self-defense represented a first step in that direction, following which the indigenous movement in Chiapas represented the fulfillment – the simultaneous and combined, instead of sequential and uncoordinated, application of revolutionary violence and reformist tactics within the framework of Marcos' myth-making.

In the panorama of the Mexican resistance, Marcos stands in a position intermediate to moderates and extremists, to both the partisans of peaceful reform and those of guerrilla warfare. He also succeeded in bringing them together, in forging a united front against the PRI dictatorship. He poked fun at himself and his critics in a communiqué in which he played the role of prosecutor at his own trial:

The Communists accuse him of being an anarchist: guilty.
The anarchists accuse him of being a Marxist: guilty.
The reformists accuse him of being an *ultra*: guilty.
The *ultras* accuse him of being a reformist: guilty.[28]

Che Guevara is Marcos' paragon of the ideal revolutionary. But which of Che's Janus-faces? The Che who parachuted into Bolivia at the head of a foreign invasion but failed to win a following among Bolivia's indigenous peoples while still alive, or the Che later idolized by Bolivia's illiterate peasants as the Christ of the Andes? Che the inveterate warrior, or Che in the role of the suffering servant? Régis Debray, the French intellectual taken prisoner in Bolivia for having participated in Che's guerrilla group, visited Marcos in the Lacandon *selva* and found the answer. In an interview afterward, he noted that Marcos' strategy was not only more realistic than Che's, but also more peaceful, that is, adapted to the Indians' way of life.[29] Unlike Che, Marcos was not leading a struggle to seize state power, but to minister to the Indians' daily needs and to bring their miserable plight to the government's and the world's attention.

"Che is closer to us than many people think. He is still around and alive thirty years on from his death," Marcos told a reporter in August 1997. "One way or another, all rebel movements in Latin America are the heirs to Che's rebellion." But unlike Che, who insisted on leading the Bolivian Indians, Marcos and the EZLN have learned the advantages of "leading by obeying."[30]

Che's handling of the Indian question alienated those he hoped to serve. Ramiro Reynaga, a Quechua Indian recruit, spent two years in Cuba undergoing political indoctrination and military training preparatory to joining Che's Bolivian campaign. But after returning to La Paz, he announced that "he was tired of it all and was giving up his career as a professional revolutionary." Fed up with the white man's ways, he adopted the name "Tawantinsuyu" – Quechua for the "four quarters" of the Inca world of his ancestors, with Cuzco instead of La Paz as the capital.[31]

Reynaga subsequently showed up in Cuernavaca, Mexico, where he spent his days behind closed doors writing a history of the Andean countries from the perspective of their Indian inhabitants – some 500 pages in small script. Concerned with five centuries of colonial oppression by the European invaders who "discovered" the New World, it is a story of repeated rebellions by the indigenous peoples, whom Che in his revolutionary impatience had been unable to mobilize. But where Che failed, Marcos succeeded by adapting to the Indians' way of life and by learning to obey.

Marcos arrived in Chiapas in 1983 as a full-fledged Marxist-Leninist, not as the anarchist he subsequently became. What brought about the change? As he recalled to a group of visiting young anarchists in May 1994: when the guerrillas offered political leadership and military training to the Indians, a choice had to be made between two ways of making decisions. On the one hand, "there was the initial proposal of the EZLN: a completely undemocratic and authoritarian proposal [by a political–military vanguard]." On the other hand, "there was the indigenous tradition that before the Conquest was a way of life, and that after the Conquest became their only way of surviving ... making decisions in common about problems that affect the entire community." It soon became evident that if the guerrillas did anything without consulting the Indians, they would lose their support. The guerrillas capitulated. Since nothing could be decided until every *compañero* had been consulted, strategic decisions came to be made democratically from below instead of autocratically from above.[32]

Thus Marcos and the EZLN began to live out the fictional roles made famous by Juan Méndez and his Indian *muchachos* in the fifth and sixth volumes of B. Traven's jungle novels, *The Rebellion of the Hanged* (1936) and *General from the Jungle* (1939). "'¡Tierra y Libertad!*' With this war cry an army of Indians marched out of the jungle in the south of the Republic, in order to overthrow the dictator and secure land and freedom for themselves." So opens *General from the Jungle*, although half a century later the dictator was no longer Porfirio Díaz but the PRI's presidential despot Carlos Salinas. As in Traven's novel, a half-crazy little army of Mayan peasants unknown to the rest of the world moved out of Mexico's southern rainforest under the leadership of an enigmatic commander and a professor, only this time merged in a single person. As if the 1910 revolution had never happened, the demands were the same: Land and Liberty![33]

What did the Zapatista *grito* mean to Marcos' own crazy little army? Little more than a cry for human dignity. As in Marcos' communiqué of 15 March 1994: "Shadows of tender fury, our path will clothe those who have nothing!" But only by rising up against those who live in the government palaces and the houses of the lords of the land and big business. As long as they "silence and murder our brothers, how can we ask our collective heart if it is time for peace to enter, hand in hand with dignity … over a road paved with the death of our dignity?"[34] The Chiapas Indians wanted only a little dignity to continue living in their one-room shacks on dirt floors, but with enough arable land to feed their families. Again they had shouted "¡Basta!" as in Traven's novels.

In a preview of the 1994 Chiapas uprising in Traven's *Rebellion of the Hanged*, the Indians in Chiapas' mahogany camps declared for land and liberty. "That, and nothing else, was their program." There would be no compromise regarding the end. But how were they to win? Said the Professor: "The strongest lion is helpless in the face of ten thousand ants, who can force him to abandon his prey. We are the ants, and the owners are the lions."[35]

The Mayans, said Marcos in his communiqué of 31 January 1994, had inherited a tradition of resistance along with other Mexicans with memories of the Conquest. "When our ancestors were surrounded on the outskirts of Grijalva and the Spanish troops demanded their political and spiritual submission, rather than betray themselves they threw themselves into the river [and drowned]." As heirs to the struggle of our Chiapan grandparents, "we have no choice but to honor this lesson in dignity.... The undignified and disrespectful peace in which we live continues to be, for us, an undeclared war of the powerful against our people." Thus the only alternative to an undignified peace is a dignified war.[36]

As Traven's jungle novels sum up the people's dilemma, they fight to win, but they actually lose. "Listen well, now," says the Professor. "Even if we lose this battle, even if we go down to the last man under the bullets of the federal soldiers and the rural police, even if not one of us should obtain land and liberty, we would have triumphed." That is because "to live as free men, even if only for a few months, is worth more than living a hundred years in slavery." When we die, we will have fallen not as exploited peons, but as free men who resisted oppression not just for ourselves, but also "for the liberty of all the peasants and workers, of all honest women and men!"[37]

Winning according to a Philistine's cost–benefit method of book-keeping ceases to be the sole criterion of success in politics and war: "True revolutions are not those which have as their only object the raising of salaries, the division of goods, or the winning of such and such privileges." To understand popular insurgency, one has to understand the motives that drive people to take up arms. We have seen that self-defense is one motive. Indignation at oppression is another. "The sincere revolutionary never thinks of the personal benefit rebellion may bring him," says the Professor. "He wants only to overthrow the social system under which he suffers and sees others suffer. And to destroy it and see the realization of the ideas he considers just, he will sacrifice himself and die."[38]

Like the Professor, Marcos is concerned less with a winning strategy than with a dignified one. "To live, we die," says Marcos, die in order to live in a dignified way.[39]

Notes

1. César Romero Jacobo, *Los Altos de Chiapas: La voz de las armas* (Mexico City: Planeta, 1994), pp. 140–1.
2. "Líder zapatista a favor de continuar el diálogo," *Diario de las Américas* (29 October 1995), published in Miami.
3. Romero, *Los Altos de Chiapas*, p. 138, on Donald Hodges and Abraham Guillén's *Revaloración de la guerrilla urbana* (Mexico City: El Caballito, 1977).
4. Romero, *Los Altos de Chiapas*, pp. 193, 194.
5. Castañeda cited in ibid., pp. 193–4. For a similar assessment of the EZLN as having combined a revolutionary with a reformist strategy, see Marc Cooper, *Starting From Chiapas: The Zapatistas Fire the Shot Heard Around the World* (Westfield, NJ: Open Magazine Pamphlet Series, 1994), pp. 2–3, 4–5.
6. Zapatista Communiqués on 6 January and 4 February 1994 in the appendices to Cooper, *Starting From Chiapas*, pp. 16, 23. On Guillén's neo-anarchism, see Donald Hodges, "Introduction: The Social and Political Philosophy of Abraham Guillén" in Donald C. Hodges, ed., *The Philosophy of the Urban Guerrilla: The Revolutionary Writings of Abraham Guillén* (New York: William Morrow, 1973), pp. 1–55. For an understanding of Marcos, we have relied on the interviews with him contained in the video, "Chiapas, la otra guerra", by Canal 6 de Julio, Medellín 33, Col. Roma, Mexico City, by video journalists with access to the underground. It contains interviews with guerrillas and also commentary by one of Mexico's leading historians, Lorenzo Meyer.
7. Andrés Oppenheimer, *Bordering on Chaos: Guerrillas, Stockbrokers, Politicians, and Mexico's Road to Prosperity* (New York: Little, Brown, 1996), pp. 235–63.
8. Bertrand de la Grange and Maite Rico, *Marcos, la genial impostura* (Mexico City: Aguilar, 1998), pp. 145–7, 172–6.
9. Ibid., pp. 155–6.
10. Gerrit Huizer, *El potencial revolucionario del campesino en América Latina* (Mexico City: Siglo XXI, 1976), pp. 293–313.
11. *Plan de Ayala* in Ismael Colmenares, ed., *Cien Años de Lucha de Clases en México* (1876–1976), vol. 1 (Mexico City: Quinto Sol, 1982), pp. 333–7; John Womack, *Emiliano Zapata*, trans. Frederic Illouz (Paris: Maspero, 1976), pp. 87–92, 103–4, 169–70.
12. De la Grange and Rico, *Marcos*, 149.
13. Ibid., pp. 177, 186.
14. Hermann Bellinghausen, "EZLN: 15 años," *La Jornada*, Mexico City, November 18, 1998.
15. *Nepantla*, Mexico City, 1991, no. 34: 3.
16. *EZLN: Documentos y comunicados*, Vol. 1 (Mexico City: Era, 1998). Primera Declaración de la Selva Lacandona, pp. 33–5; El Despertador Mexicano, pp. 36–48.
17. Ibid.
18. De la Grange and Rico, *Marcos*, pp. 298, 304, 293–306.
19. On the EZLN's 34 demands at the negotiating table, see its Communiqué of 1 March 1994 in *Shadows of Tender Fury: The Letters of Subcomandante Marcos and the Zapatista Army of National Liberation*, trans. Frank Bardacke, Leslie López, and the Watsonville, California, Human Rights Committee (New York: Monthly Review, 1995), pp. 155–62.
20. *EZLN: Documentos*, vol. 1, pp. 256–78.
21. Carlos Monsivais, "Crónica de una Convención (que no fue tanto) y de un acon-

tecimiento muy significativo," *Proceso*, 15 August 1994; Subcomandante Marcos, "Here is your flag, compañeros!" in *Shadows of Tender Fury*, pp. 241–51.

22. *EZLN: Documentos*, vol. 2, pp. 187–93.
23. On national television.
24. Oppenheimer, *Bordering on Chaos*, p. 244.
25. Marta Durán de Huerta, ed., *Yo, Marcos* (Mexico City: Milenio, 1994), pp. 19–20.
26. *EZLN: Documentos*, vol. 3, pp. 79–89.
27. Luis Hernández Navarro and Ramón Vera Herra (compiladores), *Acuerdos de San Andrés* (Mexico City: Era, 1998).
28. *La Jornada*, 5 May 1995.
29. Bill Weinberg, *Homage to Chiapas: The New Indigenous Struggles in Mexico* (London: Verso, 2000), pp. 160.
30. Ibid., pp. 189, 190; Marcos cited.
31. See Daniel James, *Che Guevara: A Biography* (New York: Stein & Day, 1969), pp. 289–90.
32. Weinberg, *Homage to Chiapas*, p. 197; Marcos cited.
33. B. Traven, *The Rebellion of the Hanged* (New York: Hill and Wang, 1952), pp. 210–16, 233–4; and *General from the Jungle*, trans. Desmond Vesey (New York: Hill and wang, n.d.), p. 1.
34. *Shadows of Tender Fury*, p. 174.
35. Traven, *The Rebellion of the Hanged*, p. 231.
36. *Shadows of Tender Fury*, pp. 103–4.
37. Traven, *The Rebellion of the Hanged*, p. 233.
38. Ibid., pp. 239, 246.
39. *Shadows of Tender Fury*, p. 138.

15 ✸ Core Parties of the Resistance

The core parties of the resistance produced its principal cadres. Almost without exception they were Marxist-Leninist, if not communist, in ideology. The one exception was a revolutionary nationalist party that appeared in 1974 and merged in 1987 with a coalition of former parties led by the dissolved Communist Party (PCM). Although each was committed to socialism, the means of arriving there were varied. The parties' assessments of the Mexican Revolution also differed. In 1985, there were as many as five core parties registered electorally and with representatives from each in the federal Chamber of Deputies.

In 1989, a sixth party of the resistance appeared – the Democratic Revolutionary Party (PRD) – by far the largest and most consequential. Although embracing several of the core parties that dissolved in the course of joining the bandwagon, it was not itself a core party. The core parties representing the principal cadres of the resistance subscribed to a maximum as well as a minimum program: their minimum program called for a democratic revolution in opposition to presidential despotism and the PRI monopoly of political power; their maximum program called for a socialist revolution. The PRD's maximum program was the minimum program of the core parties. The umbrella party was little more than a re-edition of President Lázaro Cárdenas' Party of the Mexican Revolution (PRM). Its presidential candidate was Lázaro's son Cuauhtémoc Cárdenas.

The Moscow-Directed Communist Party

The principal leaders of the resistance came out of the PCM. What explains this phenomenon? It can be explained by the mood of rebelliousness within the Party in reaction to the worst case of servility to foreign interests in the history of the international communist movement. It was precisely to the PCM that the Third International assigned the sordid task of preparing the assassination of Trotsky, Stalin's arch-enemy in exile in Mexico. But the Party's descent into the lower depths also accounts for its later energetic efforts to mend its ways and to rehabilitate itself. It accounts both for the independent currents generated within the Party and for the independence of character exhibited by its leaders and organizers. To a considerable degree, the effectiveness or lack thereof of a political party depends on the character, the personal strengths and weaknesses, of its leaders. This is especially evident in the case of the PCM.

The assassination of Trotsky was not a task designed to improve the image of the PCM. A sad result of the efforts to assassinate Trotsky was that the Party's membership dropped from 30,000 in 1939 to 13,000 in 1943, precisely during the critical years of the Second World War when the Soviet Union was at the peak of its popularity and the Communist Party in the United States rose from 30,000 to over 100,000 members. Its membership continued to plummet, partly owing to the Cold War, until it struck bottom in 1960 where it lay in almost total ruin with only 3,000 members.

Campa and Laborde not only denied the urgency of killing Trotsky, they also insisted that such a deed could have only unhappy results for the Mexican communists. Above all, they feared that Trotsky would be turned into a martyr, a specter that would haunt the Party and damage its reputation everywhere. Over this question the PCM suffered a serious split. Campa, Laborde, and the best cadres found themselves at loggerheads with the Third International.[1] Thus the patriotic and independent wing of the Party, the honorable wing, was expelled in 1940 for refusing to bow to a directive of the Soviet government.

Complying with this directive, the Mexican muralist David Siqueiros, at the head of a band of Party faithful, assaulted and machine-gunned Trotsky's house in the first attempt on his life in March 1940. When this effort failed, the Soviet government commissioned an agent of the GPU to finish him off. Ramon Mercader (Jacques Mornard), who killed Trotsky, was admitted into Trotsky's house owing to documents furnished by the GPU testifying to Mercader's Trotskyist background. After his capture by the police, he consistently denied any connection with the GPU, maintaining that he had killed Trotsky for having discredited the Trotskyist movement by using it for purely private purposes in a vain personal vendetta with Stalin.[2]

These were not the only versions of the events. To our informant, a close friend of Mercader who periodically visited him in prison, the alleged assassin confessed to changing his mind about killing Trotsky and to disobeying Moscow's orders when he realized that he could not safely escape Trotsky's bodyguards. So he tried instead to damage Trotsky politically by stealing documents linking Trotsky to representatives of the Nazi and Nipponese governments.[3]

In the search for incriminating evidence in Trotsky's files and while attempting to pry open a locked drawer in Trotsky's desk, he was surprised and violently attacked. In the ensuing struggle, he defended himself with an alpine climber's pick hanging on the wall. Mercader's private testimony contradicted the testimony he gave to the international press. Instead of a cold-blooded murder, we have a heated struggle in which Trotsky was the aggressor. After the event, he found himself covered with glory for having completed his mission where others had failed. But he did not complete it, according to his private account, in the way he led the Kremlin and the world to believe.[4]

The lamentable fact is that Trotsky died, and the responsibility for his death devolved upon the PCM. It was not until the re-entry of Campa and the majority of the Worker–Peasant Party of Mexico (POCM) into the Party in 1960 that the communists began the process of self-criticism culminating in the repudiation of the entire political line followed since 1937. Thus the level of degradation and servility that the Party had fallen to by 1940 finally led to remorse concerning this prostitution. In this way the PCM, in great measure thanks to Campa, recuperated its honesty and its independence, and reformed itself into one of the most astute parties in the Americas.

It was able to do so because of the rebellious mood and maverick quality of those cadres that from 1940 to 1960 acted outside the PCM. We have seen that this list includes Rubén and Porfirio Jaramillo, Mónico Rodríguez, Othón Salazar, Valentín Campa, Demetrio Vallejo, Ramón Danzós Palomino, Lucio Cabañas, and the founders of the 23 September Communist League, among others. Some returned to the Party and contributed to invigorating it thanks to their personal influence and independence of character.

The Estranged Communist Party and Popular Socialist Parties

The first and oldest party in Mexico was the Mexican Communist Party (PCM), dating from 1919, ten years before the founding of the official party of the revolution in 1929. But in 1950 a second Marxist-Leninist party surfaced, the POCM, consisting of members of the PCM expelled following a series of purges in 1940, 1943, and 1948. The 1940 and 1943 dissidents had come together in 1946 to form Unified Socialist Action, after which the 1948 dissidents established on the heels of their expulsion the Movement for the Revindication of the Communist Party. The two groups soon began collaborating toward the creation of a second communist party, whose core consisted of eight of the fifteen PCM cells in the federal district that rebelled against the expulsion decision of 1948.[5]

A third Marxist-Leninist party appeared in 1960, the Popular Socialist Party (PPS), founded by Vicente Lombardo Toledano. Although a leader of the government party's left wing during the 1930s and early and middle 1940s, and one of the country's top trade unionists, Lombardo had been edged out of positions of authority until he broke with the PRI in 1947 and founded his own Popular Party (PP) in 1948. A Marxist-Leninist in sheep's clothing, he decided to come out into the open in 1960 by transforming the PP into the PPS. Committed in its Declaration of Principles to "scientific socialism" and to the "philosophy of Marxism–Leninism," and in its Statutes to the "dialectical materialism of Marx and Engels enriched by Lenin," the PPS differed from the POCM in constituting the so-called satellite left allied to the official party and dependent on it financially. Although Lombardo became the presidential candidate of the PP in 1952, during the next three decades it invariably supported the PRI's candidates for the country's highest office.[6]

Why Three Marxism–Leninisms?

Although the POCM dissolved in 1960, the bulk of its members being reaccepted into the PCM under its new leadership and the rump having merged forces with the newly created PPS, there is still the problem of accounting for the existence of three Marxist-Leninist parties prior to the mergers. Three such parties suggests that there is more than one Marxism–Leninism. How can that be? The conventional answer is that, like Holy writ, both Marxism and Leninism are subject to different interpretations.

In his "Theses on the National and Colonial Questions," drafted in June 1920 for the Second Congress of the Communist International, Lenin sketched the strategy for Communist parties in backward states and nations, in which feudal or patriarchal and patriarchal–peasant relations predominate – Mexico being an example. While Communist parties should form temporary alliances with bourgeois-democratic and national liberation movements in those countries, they should also insist on their organizational independence.[7] The question for Mexico was whether organizational independence was compatible with subsidies from the ruling party. That would be a matter of interpretation.

But there was also the matter of substance. Were the POCM and the PPS vanguard parties of a single class, as in the case of the PCM? Or were they parties of a bloc of two or three classes, as in the case of the European Social Democratic parties? The POCM was admittedly a labor–peasant party. As for the PPS, its Statutes defined it as a party of the laboring class, peasants, and intellectuals of Mexico, a party that included independent lawyers, accountants, physicians, and other professionals.[8]

The PCM was at least nominally Communist, if not always so in substance. The other two were counterfeits in both name and substance. The POCM was a party of two classes even though labor seems to have been hegemonic. The fact that it split in the course of dissolving in 1960 suggests that it was a halfway station en route to the PCM or the PPS.[9]

At most, the POCM and the PPS were Marxist parties with a Leninist veneer. In practice, if not in principle, they were parties shaped in the mold of the American Popular Revolutionary Alliance (APRA), formed in Mexico City in May 1924 by the Peruvian revolutionary and political exile Victor Raúl Haya de la Torre. Initially affiliated with the Communist International, its 1926 program favored a Marxist-type party based on manual and intellectual workers. But by

1928, Haya had so enlarged his popular alliance within a single party that it also included peasants and other middle sectors besides intellectual workers. As Haya explained in a major speech on 23 August 1931, following his return to Peru, APRA was a party of proletarians, peasants, and middle sectors including "small proprietors ... without state protection and technical support."[10]

Julio Antonio Mella, another political exile in Mexico and the founder of the Cuban Communist Party, was responsible for the first major critique of Haya's American Popular Revolutionary Alliance. Since the party was also known as the Alianza Revolucionaria Popular Americana (ARPA) – Spanish for "harp" – Mella satirized it as political music designed to eliminate class discord in favor of class harmony or conciliation. As Lenin noted in "The Tax in Kind" (April 1921), the main enemy of the proletariat under conditions of backwardness is precisely "small commodity production" in which the "petty-bourgeois element predominates."[11] So his criticism applies to the PPS and to a lesser extent to the POCM.

There was another matter of substance concerning which the three parties initially agreed but which would later divide them. In "The Tax in Kind," Lenin depicted the system of state capitalism as an ally of the proletariat in its struggle for socialism. In a revolutionary-democratic state such as the one under the quasi-socialist Kerensky, "state-monopoly capitalism inevitably and unavoidably implies a step ... toward socialism."[12] Since Mexico under the official parties of the Revolution (PNR–PRM–PRI) was in a situation comparable to that of Russia between February and October 1917, it followed that the Mexican state was an ally of the left in the struggle against private capitalism and petty commodity production. By an ally was meant a political force for united action against a common enemy.

How did the three Marxist-Leninist parties differ in relation to the ruling party in the struggle against presidential despotism? After becoming an ally of the official party under Cárdenas, the PCM's policy of "Unity at All Cost" during the Second World War – a policy based on a bloc of four classes including the bourgeoisie and petty bourgeoisie – signified a rupture with Leninism. It did not abandon this policy until the party's change of leadership and direction beginning with its 13th Congress in 1960. In practice, this policy meant following the lead of the ruling party, the policy followed by the

PPS. During the 1950s, therefore, the POCM was the only Marxist-Leninist party that hewed to a Leninist strategy of independence in fact as well as form.[13]

The PCM's leftward turn at its 13th Congress emerged as a result of its reassessment of the official party of the revolution from a bourgeois-democratic to a bourgeois-despotic party. This reassessment accounts for the PCM's increasing preoccupation with democracy as a condition of building socialism in Mexico, and for the party's heightened opposition to the subsidies and tax concessions granted to the multinationals when public funds were desperately needed to develop the nationalized sector. Even before the spate of privatizations in the 1980s and 1990s, the country's system of public enterprises was eroding because of the effective "denationalization of the productive apparatus." That is how matters stood for the PCM, whereas the PPS treated the official party as an ally rather than an enemy.[14]

Strategy for a "New Revolution"

While Lombardo continued to be the principal voice on the left in defense of the Mexican Revolution, the PCM gradually came to the conclusion that a "new revolution" was necessary not with, but against the system of presidential despotism. At its 14th Congress in 1963, it defined the "new revolution" not as socialist, but as a "democratic revolution of national liberation." It would be revolutionary in removing the reactionary sectors from power and in overcoming the principal obstacle to the country's development: domination by foreign capital. Going beyond a bourgeois–democratic revolution, it would target the rule of monopoly capital and the "state power that maintains the structure of dependency on imperialism." As the "first stage of a revolutionary process in which the second stage is the socialist transformation of society," it would rely on a bloc of four classes – labor, peasantry, petty bourgeoisie, and the national bourgeoisie disposed to confront imperialism. But its strategy would also include "armed struggle ... should the reactionary forces resort to repression and violence against the revolutionary aspirations of the masses."[15]

In the report of the Party's secretary to the plenum of the central committee held in December 1970, Arnoldo Martínez Verdugo recalled that, beginning with the 13th Congress in 1960, the PCM

214

began to sense the need for and inevitability of a "new revolution in contrast to all the reformist tendencies within and without the government that maintain the idea of the continuity and development of the Mexican Revolution." But it was not until the 15th Congress in 1967 that the PCM realized that the cycle of bourgeois-democratic revolutions had ended in Mexico with the Cardenist structural reforms between 1935 and 1939, and that afterwards, democratic tasks could be realized only by a socialist revolution.[16]

In his 1970 report to the Party's central committee, Martínez Verdugo added that the PCM "has come to the conclusion that work in the heart of most of the unions should be carried on with secret methods." Wherever this approach had been applied, he noted, the party's cadres had obtained results, widening their influence. The repressive situation in the country along with the brutal dictatorship of the union bureaucracy left no alternative. It needs recalling that in April 1965 the government tried to make the PCM illegal, publicly declaring that it had discovered a communist plot to carry out an armed uprising. The government attacked the Party's offices and those of the People's Electoral Front (FEP) of the CCI and arrested 70 leaders. In this way, repression limited the chance for open action by the Party and made clear the need for cover.[17]

In the same report, Martínez recalled that the 13th Congress had characterized the new revolution as democratic, a national liberation struggle focused on "the contradiction between the Mexican people and imperialism." This focus gave the national bourgeoisie a certain role in the revolution. Later, it was recognized that "not only the big bourgeoisie but also the whole bourgeois class has taken up a hostile attitude to the revolution." So the Party rejected the Report of the 14th Congress in 1963 and adopted a new political line. Since the 1940s, the Mexican bourgeoisie had united to fight the popular resistance. Thus in 1967 the 15th Congress decided for a new bloc of non-bourgeois forces.[18]

For the PCM, the fundamental enemy was redefined as the system of state monopoly capitalism. Beginning with the 1970s, a new stage had appeared in the development of Mexican capitalism: the organic connection between the monopolies, mostly foreign, and the state apparatus. This change meant the monopolization of the economy by foreign corporations with the organizing participation of the state, the sweeping aside of small and medium native production by the monopolies' productive apparatus with direct intervention by PRI bureaucrats in the government. Imperialism, identified by Lenin as the highest stage of capitalism, was no longer simply monopoly capitalism but rather state monopoly capitalism.

The PCM's 16th Congress in 1973 embodied this redefinition of imperialism in its "New Program for a New Revolution." For the first time in the party's history, the PCM rejected the thesis of a "bourgeoisie that may be considered national," a national bourgeoisie disposed to resist imperialism. For what had formerly been a democratic and national bourgeoisie had become a despotic one serving foreign interests. That signified a rupture with the Lombardist strategy of a bloc of four classes in favor of a new bloc of labor, peasantry, and middle and marginalized sectors in the big cities, including students. Also new was the PCM's resolution to embark on a policy of electoral abstention while interpreting the new wave of labor insurgency as foreshadowing the likely intervention of the US in the event of radical change – and armed struggle as the people's response.[19]

The Janus Faces of Electoral Reform

In 1977, there came another turnabout at the PCM's 18th Congress. In view of the political reforms and the prospect of becoming an electorally registered party, it opted to become a mass political party instead of a party of cadres. In union with other forces of the left, it began preparations for transforming itself into a party geared to winning votes.[20]

But the reforms were a trap. While recognizing that the government's democratic opening had come in response to popular pressures, the PCM missed the government's intention of strengthening the left in order to sap the growing strength of the bourgeois and restorationist National Action Party (PAN). With the PCM outlawed as the major opposition to presidential despotism, popular discontent began expressing itself in electoral support for the bourgeois party. In 1946, only 70,000 or so voted for the PAN's presidential candidate, but in 1970 the figure was 2 million. The PAN got only 3 per cent of the presidential vote in 1946; in 1970 it got 14 per cent.[21] Although in 1976 the PAN could not run a presidential candidate because it suffered a split between its older conservative leadership and new-line Christian

Democrats who tried to take over the Party, it made the PRI take stock of mounting opposition at the polls.

It seems that the PRI learned a lesson from its scrutiny of the electoral statistics since 1946. The popular response to the repressive regimes of Presidents Alemán and Ruiz Cortines was to increase votes for the PAN. Between 1946 and 1958, the vote for the PAN's presidential candidate increased tenfold. Only in response to the thaw under President López Mateos was the PAN's challenge to the PRI's political monopoly momentarily contained. But in 1970, incoming President Echeverría had to face a new upsurge of the PAN in response to the brutal repression under his predecessor Díaz Ordaz. Between 1958 and 1964, for example, the votes for the PAN's candidate increased by only 300,000 votes whereas between 1964 and 1970 the increase amounted to a million votes.[22] Echeverría reacted to this writing on the wall by initiating a so-called democratic opening, including a project for political reform later implemented by President López Portillo, one purpose of which was to fragment the opposition to presidential despotism by legalizing the PCM.

It was not the PCM that had compelled the PRI to undertake a change of political face and to modify its political line. It was the swelling movement of resistance to presidential despotism that was finding a political outlet through the PAN. But in the 1976 elections, the only opposition candidate, Valentín Campa, representing the then illegal Communist Party, got roughly 1.6 million votes, 10 per cent of the total.[23] Evidently, the PRI also had to take care that the PCM would not replace the PAN as a significant challenge to its rule.

The solution was simple: register every political party that obtained at least 100,000 registrants distributed in certain proportions throughout the various states and municipalities. The PRI even subsidized the development of a rival socialist party, the Socialist Workers' Party (PST), as a means of cutting into the communist vote. At the same time, a new political organization to the right of the PAN emerged – the Mexican Democratic Party (PDM), which was expected to weaken the PAN still further by splitting the conservative vote. In this way, through the proliferation or balkanization of political parties, the PRI under López Portillo was able to shore up its political monopoly. We may conclude that the underlying purpose of the reforms was "Divide and Rule!"[24]

The political crisis generated by the repression of the popular student movement on 2 October 1968 sharpened after the government repression on 10 June 1971. The belief spread that political and union democracy would never come from the official party. The so-called democratic opening offered by Echeverría's administration was taken as a concession to pressure from the masses rather than a reformist initiative by the government. Few people expected that there would really be a basic reform of the electoral system.

Faced with this correlation of social forces, the independent revolutionary groups had to choose between the following options: to enter one of the important parties of the Old Left, either the PPS or the PCM; or to form a new party. Since the PCM was seen as dogmatic and authoritarian, more interested in gaining members than in developing mass organizations, it could not expect widespread support. But the PPS was equally suspect; it had the reputation of working too closely with the PRI government, having backed it during the critical moments of popular resistance in 1959, 1968, and 1971. It had lost all respect in the popular sectors and among the revolutionary intelligentsia. There remained one way to go: form a new party.[25]

Near the end of 1971, the decision was made to set up a National Committee of Investigation and Coordination (CNAC) to investigate the possibilities of organizing a new party and to project alternatives to the PPS and the PCM. But the members of the Committee could not reach agreement. One current, led by Heberto Castillo and Demetrio Vallejo, refused to adopt a program not worked out by the workers and peasants themselves. This current wanted to adopt the language of the Mexican people rather than the formulas of Marxism–Leninism. The other current, led by Rafael Aguilar Talamantes, a former militant in the Communist Youth who had come to share Galván's revolutionary nationalist brand of Marxism–Leninism, came out openly for a transition to socialism.[26]

In this way, two new parties arose from the CNAC. The revolutionary populist current of Castillo and Vallejo formed the Mexican Workers' Party (PMT). The Marxist and socialist current became the Socialist Workers' Party (PST). Both published newspapers that took the side of the new movement for worker and peasant insurgency.[27] The PMT published *Popular Insurgency*, aimed at the workers, peasants, and squatters with low political consciousness. The PST published *The Socialist Insurgent*, aimed at the popular masses with a high level of political development.

The Mexican Workers' Party

The PMT differed from the other revolutionary parties in not beginning with a detailed analysis of the present political and economic situation or with a program of solutions founded on such an analysis. The process should be the reverse: first, the minimum program and later the analysis of the political panorama and the radicalization of the programmatic ideas. Theory and program alike should follow from the popular–student movement and the method of raising the political consciousness of the majorities that belong to no political party. The fundamental lesson of the popular–student conflict of 1968 was that the program should be the work of the majority of the members and not only of the vanguard; it should spring from concrete demands that a large number of workers can accept. These were to include both "short-range demands and middle-range demands that, once they are won, bring success ... and demands that in turn lead to new modifications and more profound programmatic ideas."[28]

The PMT was committed neither to armed struggle nor to the legal and constitutional road. The choice would depend on how the popular resistance movement developed. Was the resistance a continuation of the Mexican Revolution, or was it a preparation for a new democratic and socialist revolution? The PMT's position was open here too. The party noted only that within the government and the ruling party, it was impossible to carry out reforms of any importance. The PMT was also silent about the formation of a new state and the methods of work within the unions in the face of government repression. None the less, it agreed with the PCM on vital points: acceptance of the strategy of a worker–peasant–student–intellectual alliance against the groups in power and the exploiting classes, excluding a front with the middle bourgeois or the so-called national bourgeoisie; and the characterization of the principal enemy as the native bourgeoisie and imperialism vis-à-vis the exploited and working masses.[29]

Although the PMT stood closer to the positions of the PCM than to those of the PST, there were also some outstanding differences. One of the errors of this party was its determination to recruit workers and peasants with a low political consciousness. Its basic fault was spontaneism. In preparing and educating the working masses for a revolution, it made concessions to their political backwardness. Besides this, the PMT's organizational principles were of the social democratic kind: it was an organization of members rather than militants, yet its organizational structure permitting appeal to a broad electorate was worthless, for it had chosen not to take part in electoral activity.

There was no need to build a new party because the PCM had already turned into a new party. It had dropped its position of compromising with sectors of the bourgeoisie and had taken up a line that proposed alliances with only the exploited classes and the marginalized middle sectors. Since 1960, it had come out against the Lombardism and Neo-Lombardism of the PPS; it stood for an intransigent but nonsectarian program. At the same time, it had become a party of youth. Because of what happened in 1968, it had managed completely to renovate its ranks. It had a new leadership, balanced between aging adults and young people. The rebel youth had driven the PCM down once-forbidden paths.

The Socialist Workers' Party

The PST differed from the PMT in establishing close relations with old cadres in the PPS and with reformist groups that left or were expelled from the PCM. One of these was the Movement for Socialist Unity and Action (MAUS), which embraced some old revolutionaries from the extinct POCM led by Valentín Campa during the 1950s. Communist Left Unity (UIC) was another group linked to the PST.[30] The UIC was directed by a small group of ex-communist leaders from the PCM. They were expelled from the PCM for forming a reformist faction during the discussions of the 16th Party Congress in October 1973.

Shortly after its formation, the PST suffered a split-off, the Movement for Socialist Organization (MOS). It arose from internal differences over participation in the 1976 elections. The majority wanted to collaborate with the government in the struggle against imperialism and the big bourgeoisie while the minority wanted to join the Socialist League (Trotskyist) in supporting the PCM's presidential candidate. Soon the MOS became the Revolutionary Socialist Party (PSR). As a Marxist-Leninist party, it was even closer to the PCM than to the original currents from which it had sprung (CNAC).[31] Its newspaper, once called *Mosco*, was changed to *Comrade*. It had only a small membership and, like the Revolutionary Workers' Party (PRT), emerged from the fusion of the Socialist League with other Trotskyist groupuscules.

The PST was a youthful and reinvigorated version of the PPS. As defined in its 1977 Statutes, the PST is "a political organization of the Mexican working class," a class understood to include "laborers, peasants, and intellectual workers" plus a fourth sector of *colonos* (urban and rural squatters). Its strategic line targeting the workers' two fundamental enemies – foreign imperialism and the native big bourgeoisie – was a "popular revolutionary alliance." Such was the party's alternative to the reactionary strategy of "National Unity" or class collaboration proposed by the reactionary bourgeoisie, a popular alliance so solid that "the government has no other remedy than to base itself on the people in order to govern."[32]

Was this a new strategy? It was nothing less than a scaled-down, Mexican adaptation of Haya's dream of an American popular revolutionary alliance.

Like the PPS, the PST defined its philosophy as "dialectical materialism" and its political principles as "scientific socialism" – in other words, Marxism–Leninism. There was nothing novel about that, or about its Lombardist thesis that the government was still in the hands of the PRI's "national revolutionary sector" and desperately in need of popular support in order to resist the pressures of imperialism and the big bourgeoisie. The PST's 1981 "Program of Action" accordingly denounced the thesis adopted by certain sectors of the left, that the government was the principal enemy. On the contrary, it considered the ruling party as its ally, that is, the "national revolutionary group presently hegemonic within the state apparatus."[33]

Although the PST had relations with ex-members of the PCM and even with the PCM itself through the PSR, it had more in common with the PPS. Like the PPS, it insisted on the possibility of a renewal of the PRI government from within. The PMT denied that such a renewal was possible. Although the PMT refused openly to favor Marxism or socialism, it was actually closer to the PCM than to the PPS.[34] Thus, the space between the PCM and the PPS was filled by two new parties:

the PMT to the right of the PCM, and to its right but to the left of the PPS, the PST.

The Revolutionary Workers' Party

Beginning with two Marxist-Leninist parties in 1960, by 1976 the number had doubled. Four ostensible Marxist-Leninist parties! Surely, that approaches a world record, at least for 1976. They were not only legal, but also acquired official registration after meeting the conditions required of a mass political party as distinct from a groupuscule. Besides the PCM and the PPS, the list included the Socialist Workers' Party (PST) and the Revolutionary Workers' Party (PRT), a Trotskyist umbrella organization formed a year after the PST in 1976 and politically to the left of the PCM.

How did the PRT differ from the other core parties of the resistance? "With regard to countries with a belated bourgeois development, especially the colonial and semi-colonial countries," wrote Trotsky in 1929, "the complete and genuine solution of their tasks of achieving *democracy* and *national liberation* is conceivable only through the dictatorship of the proletariat as the leader of the subjugated nation, above all of its peasant masses" [emphasis in original]. Since Mexico continued to be a semi-colony of the United States, socialism would not arrive there by legal and constitutional means through a long period of democracy as the PCM, PPS, and PST believed. Under such conditions democracy is possible, Trotsky maintained, only as a consequence of proletarian dictatorship, that is, a workers' state. That meant that there could be no people's democracy as an intermediate stage between state capitalism and socialism. In support of his thesis that revolutionaries should not rely on bourgeois democracy as a trampoline to socialism, Trotsky cited Lenin's April 1919 article, "The Third International and Its Place in History," underscoring Russia's leap across bourgeois democracy to Soviet, or proletarian democracy.[35]

The PRT relied especially on Trotsky's articles on the Mexican Revolution during his exile in that country beginning in January 1937. His "Workers' Administration in Nationalized Industry" (June 1938) depicts the Janus faces of the official party and government. Because foreign capital plays a decisive role in industrially backward countries at the native bourgeoisie's expense, the "government oscillates between foreign capital and domestic, between the weak national bourgeoisie and the comparatively powerful proletariat." This unique status confers on the government a Bonapartist character that raises it above the classes and enables it to govern "either by becoming an instrument of foreign capital and submitting the proletariat to the chains of a police dictatorship or by manipulating and making concessions to the proletariat with the possibility of becoming independent of foreign capital."[36]

Under Cárdenas, according to Trotsky, Mexico had come under the dominion of state capitalism. None the less, he considered it to be "a grave error to believe that the road to socialism passes not through a proletarian revolution, but through the nationalization by the bourgeois state of the various branches of industry and their transfer into the hands of the workers' organizations."[37]

Not even under Cárdenas, it followed, should Mexican workers rely on a policy of continued nationalizations to bring about their emancipation. That was the Achilles' heel of Lombardism, according to the PRT, not just of Vallejo's and Galván's revolutionary nationalism, but also of the counterfeit socialism of the PPS and the PST. As for the PCM, its call for a "new revolution" against Mexico's despotic bourgeoisie and system of presidential despotism amounted to only a brief interlude in a long record of servility to the Lombardist strategy of supporting the ruling party. While the PCM followed a mainly opportunist or reformist strategy of working within the limits of the 1917 Constitution, the PRT continued to plug for a proletarian revolution. That explains why the PPS denounced Trotskyism as a conspiratorial force on the left and as an expression of ultra-leftism.[38]

Yet even the PRT had its deserters. In 1988, Adolfo Gilly, at the head of a youth fraction, joined the Cardenista Front in the company of two of the party's federal deputies, Ricardo Pascal and Pedro Peñaloza; in 1993, the PRT's secretary general Edgar Sánchez led another fraction into the Front's successor, Cuauhtémoc Cárdenas' new Party of the Democratic Revolution (PRD). They did not want to remain isolated. Trotskyism has a long record of Machiavellian "entrism" into other parties, and here was another instance. Thus, Trotskyism became an identifiable political current within the PRD and still survived outside it, even after losing its national registration.

The Electoral Scoreboard

Would President Echeverría's democratic opening, political reform, and system of proportional representation make a difference? Including later modifications, the new Federal Electoral Law officially adopted on 5 January 1973 stipulated: first, that 300 representatives to the Chamber of Deputies be elected by majority vote and 100 representatives by a system of proportional representation; second, that the total vote required for a party to become registered be reduced from 2.5 to 1.5 per cent; third, that the number of party affiliates required for registration be reduced from 75,000 to 65,000 nationwide; fourth, that a party with 1.5 per cent of the vote be granted 5 seats in the Chamber of Deputies and an additional seat for each 0.5 per cent in excess of the minimum up to a maximum of 25 seats.[39] By the early 1990s, however, the 1.5 per cent minimum had been raised to 2 per cent with the result that the two parties of the satellite left, the PPS and the PST (Frente Cardenista–Partido Cardenista), lost their registration and disappeared from the political scene.

Among the contending parties of the resistance, the PCM's prospects appeared the brightest. But that was small consolation. The party had been decried as a party of intellectuals, and so it was. Its weekly newspaper *Oposición* was too theoretical, and its monthly magazine *Machete* too slick to be understood or appreciated by most workers and peasants. Its approach to the masses continued to be patronizing and didactic. It showed a lack of internal democracy, and it disciplined its rank and file by belittling harangues and moral censure. Despite police repression and unofficial terrorism from anti-Communist hit squads, the Party was not organized to defend its members. Because membership in the Party was often less of an asset than a liability, there was a high rate of desertion that had to be continually remedied by attracting and training new recruits.

The rapid turnover in membership boded ill for the Party, if not for the resistance as a whole. Figures are provided by Arturo Martínez Nateras, member of the Party's central committee from 1972 to 1978. In the preface to his *Punto y seguido: ¿Crisis en el PCM?*, he begins with the observation that the number of ex-communists active in the

Mexican resistance was "notably superior to that of the present members of the PCM." Martínez Nateras tells us that when he took charge of the Party's organizational apparatus in 1974, there were 1,500 registered communists, of whom only 800 were not delinquent in the payment of their Party dues. By his own account, the Party had just lost close to 5,000 militants during the turbulent years following the events of 10 June 1971, when the Communist Youth deserted *en masse* in favor of armed struggle.[40]

The fact that the number of its nominal registrants leaped from 1,500 in 1974 to over 100,000 at the close of the registration campaign in 1978 was hardly cause for rejoicing, for most of these "affiliates," as they were called, had already been lost to the Party from sheer neglect, while those who remained were mostly inactive and did not pay their dues. To provide data from the state of Morelos: the Rubén Jaramillo Brigade during the last two weeks of January 1978 recruited approximately 750 registrants in Cuernavaca alone. Yet two years later in January 1980, the Party could count the number of activists in that city on the fingers of two hands.[41]

There was little cause for optimism concerning the Party's prospects. During the congressional elections of 1979, the Party performed outstandingly, becoming the third most important electoral force in the country. On the basis of its performance, Communist leaders predicted that the Party would soon overshadow the PAN to become the second most influential party in congress. But that was not saying much. The PRI permitted the PCM to be legalized in order to divide the growing opposition represented by the PAN as well as to let off steam from the nation's political boiler.

The new system of proportional representation led to a grand march of the core parties of the resistance into the electoral arena. In 1979, for the fist time since 1946, the PCM officially participated in the congressional elections, obtaining 18 seats in the Chamber of Deputies. By 1986, the PMT and even the Trotskyist PRT had privileged sinecures in the Chamber along with the Marxist leaders of the loyal opposition or satellite left – the PPS and PST.

These parties had been sucked in by the government's subtle tactics to the point of becoming reformist electoral machines instead of revolutionary vanguards. There was surely no Leninist vanguard in the Chamber of Deputies, not to mention representatives of the armed resistance! Thus it would not be long before the PCM opted to dissolve in favor of a merger with four other parties on the left, it being the largest. Founded in 1981, the Unified Socialist Party of Mexico (PSUM) resembled a Eurocommunist party in rejecting the demand for a dictatorship of the proletariat and transforming itself from a vanguard of professional revolutionaries into a mass political party that anybody could join.

As the logic of electoralism came to dominate the thinking of Mexico's communists, the PSUM moved steadily toward a merger with the non-Marxist left, mainly the PMT. By 1987, three remaining parties of the independent left, with the notable exception of the PRT, joined the PSUM and the PMT in a new umbrella party – the Mexican Socialist Party (PMS). Yet it took only two years for it in turn to dissolve in a merger with the new center–left party proceeding from a split of the Cardenista current from the PRI – Cuauhtémoc Cárdenas' Democratic Revolutionary Party (PRD).

How did the newly registered parties perform? In the 1979 elections, the PCM polled twice the combined votes of the PPS and PST. With 5 per cent of the total vote compared to the PAN's 10.8 per cent, it became the third most important party in Mexico. However, in the 1982 elections, the PSUM polled only 3.84 per cent. The PPS barely passed the cutoff with 1.53 per cent; and the PRT found itself threatened with extinction with only 1.03 per cent. (The PMT did not become a registered party until 1985 when it passed with 1.5 per cent of voter support.) Together, the core parties of the resistance polled less than 8 per cent of the total.[42]

The Marxist-Leninist parties did better in the 1988 elections. Renamed the Party of the Cardenist Front of National Reconstruction (PFCRN), the PST increased its support to 10.51 per cent while the PPS led the pack with 10.53 per cent. The losers were the parties of the independent left. The new umbrella organization calling itself the Mexican Socialist Party (PMS) polled only 3.57 per cent, and the PRT lost its electoral registration when it polled a mere 0.42 per cent. None the less, the overall showing of the core parties of the resistance had mushroomed from 7.83 per cent in 1982 to some 25 per cent six years later.[43]

The political reform was welcomed by all the country's political parties with the single exception of the PAN. Yet the PAN turned out to be its principal beneficiary. The reform did not contribute, as intended, to shoring up the parties of the left as a counterweight to the PAN's growing number of supporters. Within a little more than a decade, it had spelled the death of the independent left, followed by that of the satellite left a few years later. The reform had boomeranged by bankrupting the entire new system of proportional representation. By the end of the century, there were no parties that qualified for the 100 reserved seats in the Chamber of Deputies, and in the elections of 2000, the only surviving counterforce to the PAN was the PRD – a center–left party committed not to socialism but to a second edition by Son Cárdenas of Father Cárdenas' Party of the Mexican Revolution.

Except for the official party, the 2000 elections focused on a single issue. How to end the official party's more than 70 years of uninterrupted rule? Absorption with this overriding issue led to a rash of desertions from the PRD, whose popularity had tumbled from being the second strongest party in the nation to a feeble third with the prospect of polling less than 20 per cent of the vote. Thus the resistance to presidential despotism and to the official party's stranglehold ended in support for the bourgeois and restorationist PAN.

The 2000 elections turned into a caricature of the resistance. Without any core parties to lead it, the resistance had degenerated into support for the forces on the political right. If the Mexican Revolution was dead, it was not because the resistance was alive and kicking. It too had passed into the waste-basket of history with nothing to show for itself. Had the entire resistance been in vain?

Without exception, the core parties of the resistance had subscribed to the philosophy of dialectical materialism as interpreted by Lenin and the Communist International. They poked fun not just at organized religion, but also at personal beliefs in a salvationist deity. They deceived themselves, for they were not really atheists, but true believers on a different wavelength. After all, what is Marxism–Leninism if not a secular religion "on earth as it is in heaven"? There was no salvation in sight for Mexico's toiling and exploited poor, especially after their leaders deserted them for the promise of government sinecures made possible by the reform.

Misguided Intentions

We must follow the story of how this logic of misguided intentions and unintended consequences not only operated, but also called into question more than half a century's struggle by the country's Marxist-Leninist vanguards.

The first casualty was the PCM, which nibbled at the bait tossed to it by the PRI government until it was irretrievably hooked. At its 19th Congress in 1981, the PCM voted by a narrow margin to trash its former goal of a dictatorship of the proletariat for the more modest one of "democratic workers' power." Next, it abandoned its former role as a revolutionary vanguard in relation to other left formations by dissolving itself in order to create a new umbrella party, the Unified Socialist Party of Mexico (PSUM), with other ex-Communist groupuscules on the left. The logic of electoralism promoted the change in substance as well as form. After heated discussions with the PMT that had instigated the change but refused to join the new party, the partly Eurocommunized PSUM retained only the Marxist ideology of scientific socialism and the traditional emblems, including the hammer and sickle.[44]

Resistance to the proposed dissolution of the PCM at its 19th Congress came from a group called the "renovators." Led by Enrique Semo, Joel Ortega, and Rodolfo Echeverría, and supported by the distinguished political scientist and political commentator Jorge G. Castañeda among other party dignitaries, the renovators criticized the party's leadership for having lost its bearings, for becoming a partner to ideological dispersion and conciliation, for steamrolling the party into a hybrid union with groupuscules representing other currents, and for sacrificing the party's historical task of organizing the masses for the vain pursuit of electoral seats in the Chamber of Deputies. Most of them refused to join the PSUM. In a political communiqué published in *Unomásuno* (23 February 1982), they explained why. Among its signatories were Ortega, Echeverría, Castañeda, and a score of others. Among the leading renovators, Semo was the sole exception.[45]

The decisive break with the PCM's past came with the scuttling of the PSUM and the founding of a second umbrella party in 1987, the Mexican Socialist Party (PMS). The PMT had no qualms about joining it because the traditional trappings of the Communist International had been finally abandoned. The new party included groupuscules committed to an ideology of revolutionary nationalism rather than Marxism–Leninism and prepared to enter into a dialogue with the emerging "Democratic Current" within the PRI. As a result of their influence, reinforced by that of the former PMT, the PMS abandoned some more of the traditional baggage of Marxism-Leninism, including democratic centralism within the Party, the critique of a mixed economy and foreign investment, and reliance on foreign socialist models of development.[46]

The PMS program adopted in November 1987 still talked of a "new revolution" for the "conquest of political power by the laboring class and the entire working people." But what did it mean? Its all-consuming immediate objective was not mass work among exploited workers and peasants, the confrontation of property owners in fields and factories, but the "displacement of the governing group that responds mainly to the interests of the big bourgeoisie ... and imperialism." Without this preliminary step, nothing might be accomplished toward the goal of a people's democracy.[47]

Instead of a state socialism managed by appointed bureaucrats, the program called for the establishment of a regime of "social property." This would include not only nationally owned enterprises managed by the workers, but also trade union, cooperative, *ejidal*, and communal forms of property and collective enterprise. Small and medium private enterprises up to a maximum of 50 employees would be respected in what amounted to a mixed economy, including family-owned and operated farms up to a maximum of 20 hectares.[48] In substance, it was a Mexican equivalent of the Yugoslav model based on workers' self-management.

This model had been foreshadowed by the PSUM's earlier convergence on Eurocommunism. In upholding small private and collective forms of ownership, it placed the PMS to the right instead of the left of the Lombardist PPS and PST. Thus, in a 12 April 1982 interview, Mariano Leyva, the PST's candidate for governor in the State of Morelos, criticized the PSUM for having abandoned a policy of state socialism. "The PSUM," he declared, "was pursuing a policy not just of Eurocommunism but one that promised to end in the adoption of Yugoslavia's system of self-management by workers' collectives as a form of cooperativism – a virtual betrayal of the Marxist tradition."[49]

The PMS's contribution to the new party would be "to leave behind [the revolutionary left's] doctrinairism, vanguardism, voluntarism, and sectarianism," thereby making possible its "advance toward a socialist project rooted in the national reality." In the drive to organize a movement of the masses, it proposed a new "strategy of alliance of all the forces capable of contributing to a democratic change, inclusive of [bourgeois] entrepreneurs, the PAN, the Church, and the army" – all for the sake of establishing a "government by turns."[50]

Henceforth, the PAN would become a potential ally rather than an enemy. Ironically, the PSUM's "Alliance for Change" became the leading motif of the PAN and its candidate, Vicente Fox, in his bid for the presidency in the year 2000. By then, Castañeda, the former PCM "renovator," was not only one of Fox's closest advisors, he was also slated to become Mexico's new foreign minister in the event of a PAN victory at the polls.

The new party's "Declaration of Principles" was not reassuring. There was no mention of a new revolution. The only contemplated changes amounted to reforms and the enforcement of the 1917 Constitution. The goal: a popular democracy made possible by displacing the big bourgeoisie and state bureaucrats from power. There was no mention of socialism. Although a party of the resistance, it was not one of the core parties. The core parties had always given the resistance a socialist content. The overthrow of presidential despotism and the PRI's political monopoly signified only the tip of the political iceberg. In addition to their minimum program of an effective people's democracy, the core parties had proposed to build a post-capitalist order. The PRD had no maximum program, only a minimum one.[51] After all, it had emerged as the "Democratic Current" within the PRI and was led by establishment rather than anti-establishment elites.

By the turn of the century, the core parties of the resistance had thrown in the towel. All that remained of their heroic defiance was a pseudo-resistance in the name of the Party of the Democratic Revolution.

Notes

1. On the PCM's 1940 Purging Commission and Extraordinary Congress aimed at rooting out slackers in the party's anti-Trotsky campaign, see Barry Carr, *Marxism and Communism in Twentieth-Century Mexico* (Lincoln: University of Nebraska Press, 1992), pp. 67–79; and Campa's personal account in Valentín Campa, *Mi testimonio: memorias de un comunista mexicano*, 3rd rev. ed. (Mexico City: Cultura Popular, 1985; orig. pub. 1978), pp. 159–66.
2. The standard account of the assassination is in the third volume of Isaac Deutscher's Trotsky trilogy, *The Prophet Outcast. Trotsky: 1929–1940* (New York: Vintage, 1965), pp. 483–508.
3. The assassin evidently believed the accusations against Trotsky levelled by Kamenev and Zinoviev at their trial in autumn 1936 and by Radek and Pyatakov at their trial in January 1937, during which prosecutor Vyshinsky charged Trotsky with having made a formal agreement with Hitler and the Mikado "in exchange for their aid in the struggle against Stalin." Ibid., pp. 333–4, 360.
4. Our informant, William Miller, Hollywood actor and double for Cary Grant, had distinguished himself as a political commissar in the International Brigades during the Spanish Civil War. Befriended by Siqueiros, who had risen to the rank of colonel, he was invited to come to Mexico after the war where he began a new life as a film maker.
5. Arnoldo Martínez Verdugo, *Partido Comunista Mexicano: trayectoria y perspectivas* (Mexico City: Cultura Popular, 1977), pp. 37–8, 51–2; and Carr, *Marxism and Communism*, pp. 149, 179.
6. Daniel Moreno, *Los partidos políticos del México contemporaneo*, 7th ed. (Mexico City: Costa-Amic, 1979), pp. 257, 260.
7. V.I. Lenin, "Theses on the National and Colonial Questions," Robert C. Tucker, ed., *The Lenin Anthology* (New York: Norton, 1975), pp. 623–4.
8. On the breakdown of the category of "intellectual workers" into lawyers, students, and assorted professional workers who are not exploited wage-earners and therefore do not belong to the proletariat, see Julio Antonio Mella, "¿Qué es el ARPA?" in *Documentos y artículos* (Havana: Instituto de Historia del Movimiento Comunista y la Revolución Socialista de Cuba, 1975), pp. 381–2.
9. Martínez Verdugo, *Partido Comunista Mexicano*, pp. 17, 21; and Partido Popular Socialista, "Estatutos," in Moreno, *Los partidos*, p. 260.
10. Víctor Raúl Haya de la Torre, *Política aprista*, 2nd ed. (Lima: Amauta, 1967), pp. 75–6; and Donald C. Hodges, *The Latin American Revolution: Politics and Strategy from Apro-Marxism to Guevarism* (New York: William Morrow, 1974), p. 129.
11. Mella, "¿Qué es el ARPA?" pp. 377–8; and V.I. Lenin, "The Tax in Kind," *Selected Works*, 3 vols. (New York: International Publishers, 1967), vol. 3, pp. 584, 585.
12. Lenin, "The Tax in Kind," vol. 3, pp. 585, 589.
13. Campa, *Mi testimonio*, pp. 233–7; and Carr, *Marxism and Communism*, pp. 179–80, 194–5, 219. On the PCM's "Lombardist ideology" from 1940 to 1960, see Lourdes Quintanilla Obregón, *Lombardismo y sindicatos en América Latina* (Mexico City: Fontamara, 1982), pp. 11–12, 15, 37–42.
14. Carr, *Marxism and Communism*, pp. 61–2, 150–1; and Manuel Aguilera Gómez, *La desnacionalización de la economía mexicana* (Mexico City: Fondo de Cultura Económica, 1975), pp. 85–120.
15. PCM, *Programa del Partido Comunista Mexicano* (Mexico City: Ediciones del Comité Central, 1966), pp. 43–6.

16. Martínez Verdugo, *Partido Comunista Mexicano*, pp. 55, 76–7.
17. Ibid., pp. 60–61, 110–12.
18. Ibid., pp. 77–80.
19. Gerardo Unzueta, *Nuevo Programa para la nueva revolución: Documentos del XVI Congreso del Partido Comunista Mexicano* (Mexico City: Cultura Popular, 1974), pp. 9–13, 25–6, 43, 45, 71–3, 88.
20. PCM, *El Partido Comunista frente a la crisis actual. XVIII Congreso Nacional* (Mexico City: Ediciones del Comité Central, 1977), pp. 45–7.
21. Donald Hodges and Ross Gandy, *Mexico 1910–1982: Reform or Revolution?* 2nd rev. ed. (London: Zed Press, 1983), p. 117.
22. Ibid. Founded in 1939, the PAN emerged as a right-wing challenge to Cárdenas' PRM and its "Declaration of Principles," notably to the PRM's "fundamental objective" of preparing the people for "a democracy of workers preliminary to a socialist regime." The PAN's startling growth may be explained in part by subsequent right-wing defections from the PRI. See Manlio Fabio Murillo Soberanis, *La reforma política mexicana y el sistema pluripartidista* (Mexico City: Diana, 1979), pp. 70–1, 85.
23. Campa, *Mi testimonio*, p. 310.
24. Murillo, *La reforma política mexicana*, pp. 191–2, 196–8, 210–11; and Octavio Rodríguez Araujo, *La reforma política y los partidos en México*, 5th ed. (Mexico City: Siglo XXI, 1982), pp. 49–50, 53–6.
25. Heberto Castillo and Francisco Paoli Bolio, *¿Por qué un Nuevo Partido?* (Mexico City: Posada, 1975), pp. 142–5.
26. Rodríguez Araujo, *La reforma política y los partidos, en México*, pp. 179–80, 181–2, 183.
27. Ibid., pp. 183, 187.
28. Castillo and Paoli Bolio, *¿Por qué un Nuevo Partido?* pp. 110, 113, 114.
29. Ibid., pp. 116–18.
30. Rodríguez Araujo, *La reforma política*, p. 185; and Murillo, *La reforma política mexicana*, p. 115.
31. Rodríguez Araujo, *La reforma política*, pp. 219–20, 221–2, 226–7.
32. For the PST's 1977 "Declaration of Principles," "Program of Action," and "Statutes," see Partido Socialista de los Trabajadores, *Nueve Documentos* (Mexico City: Cuarta Conferencia Nacional de Organización, 26–27 March 1977), pp. 3–10.
33. For the PST's 1981 "Declaration of Principles," "Statutes," and "Program of Action," see Partido Socialista de los Trabajadores, *Documentos Básicos* (Mexico City: Ediciones del Comité Central, 1981), pp. 7–9, 13, 32–6.
34. PST, *Nueve Documentos*, pp. 7–8; and Castillo and Paoli Bolio, *¿Por qué un Nuevo Partido?* pp. 116–19, 120–1, 137–9, 144.
35. Leon Trotsky, *The Permanent Revolution*, in *The Permanent Revolution* and *Results and Prospects* (New York: Pathfinder, 1969), pp. 240, 242, 276, 278; and "Program of the Communist International's Sixth Congress" (1928), in William Lutz and Harry Brent, ed., *On Revolution* (Cambridge, MA: Winthrop, 1971), p. 159.
36. Leon Trotsky, "La administración obrera en la industria nacionalizada," *Por los Estados Unidos Socialistas de América Latina* (Buenos Aires: Coyoacán, 1961), pp. 25–6.
37. Ibid., p. 26.
38. Rodríguez Araujo, *La reforma política y los partidos en México*, pp. 208–13.
39. Murillo, *La reforma política mexicana*, pp. 155, 158, 165, 192.

40. Arturo Martínez Nateras, *Punto y seguido. ¿Crisis en el PCM?* (Mexico City: Edición del autor, 1980), p. 151.
41. Interviews with members of the brigade at Hodges' home in Cuernavaca, 14 January 1978.
42. Carr, *Marxism and Communism*, p. 315 (Table 14).
43. Ibid.
44. Ibid., pp. 284, 291–3.
45. Rodríguez Araujo, *La reforma política y los partidos*, pp. 329–38, 349, 352.
46. Carr, *Marxism and Communism*, pp. 308–9.
47. Partido Mexicano Socialista, *Documentos fundamentales* (Mexico City: Consejo Nacional del PMS, 1988), p. 14.
48. Ibid., p. 18.
49. Hodges' interview with Mariano Leyva at PST headquarters in Cuernavaca, Morelos, 12 April 1982.
50. Partido Mexicano Socialista, *La situación nacional y la construcción del Partido de la Revolución Democrática* (Mexico City: Consejo Nacional del PMS, 1989), pp. 3, 9.
51. PRD, *Documentos Básicos del Partido de la Revolución Democrática: Declaración de Principios y Estatutos* (Mexico City: PRD, 1990), pp. 10, 12, 24.

16 ✹ Why the Resistance Failed

Superficially, the popular resistance might be said to have been successful in achieving its main objective – the end of presidential despotism. For the first time in 60 years, an election was held in which the official party might lose not only the election but also the count. But the loss was to the PAN, not to mention the rump of the PRI that had broken with the party in 1987 and was posing as the people's voice.

A democratic opening had indeed been achieved. But it was brought about by forces other than the popular resistance, and in any case it was not the opening the resistance had struggled and died for. In the 2000 elections, not a single Marxist-Leninist party was represented. Instead of an independent left, the only party that came close to representing popular interests was the center-left PRD, an opening not for a new revolution and a new constitution, but for the weasel Constitution of 1917.

Although the PRI had betrayed the national revolutionary and Cardenista current during the 1940s and thereafter, the revolution was kept going by the popular resistance. During the years in which the resistance was in an ascendant phase, the revolution of 1910–19 experienced renewal. But whenever repression gained the upper hand and the popular forces retreated, the revolution slipped into reverse gear. Consequently, when the final phase of the resistance petered out owing to the political reforms and the disarticulation of the independent left in favor of wagging the PRD's tail, the revolution too came to an end. Notwithstanding the indigenous uprising in Chiapas – and the virtual "last stand" of *subcomandante* Marcos – by the turn of the

234

millennium one could reasonably conclude: The Revolution is dead! Communists made up the vanguard of the resistance from its beginning. Communists played a decisive role in the strikes at the Zacatepec sugar mill in 1943, in the teachers' movement and the occupation of the Secretariat of Education in 1958, in the railway workers' strikes in 1958–59, in the land seizures at Llanos de Michapa and El Guarín in 1961–62, in the milkmen's strike followed by a general strike in Puebla in 1963–64, and in the rural guerrilla movement of 1964–74. The influence of the PCM was exercised both directly and indirectly through the cadres in these movements under its direction. The cases of Jaramillo, Salazar, Campa, Vallejo, Galván, and Cabañas are only the most notorious examples. The founders of the urban guerrillas also came from the ranks of the PCM.

Periodizing the Resistance

Although the first wave of popular insurgency from 1942 to 1953 was dominated by the Jaramillista movement, we have seen that its Zapatista cloth was dyed a Communist red. The Communists' turn to dominate the resistance came during the second great popular tide of 1958–68 led by Othón Salazar, Valentín Campa, and Demetrio Vallejo. And in the third flow of the tide from 1971 to 1978, they continued to shape an opposition in the form of urban guerrilla movements, the carrying through of land reform, the struggle against union bureaucracy, and the launching of Campa's presidential campaign as the only popular alternative to the PRI. Yet, by the end of the century, not just the PCM but also the other Marxist-Leninist vanguards had disappeared from the political scene. The resistance might survive in the Chiapas jungles and in the mountains of Guerrero, but its main force was evidently spent.

The popular movements of resistance to presidential despotism, from the peasant mobilizations under Rubén Jaramillo and the great strikes of the 1940s and 1950s to the guerrilla struggles and land invasions of the 1960s and 1970s, had a beginning, middle, and end that defied human control. Sometimes these movements reinforced each other, setting off a chain reaction. When that happened, the resistance surged forward, or, metaphorically, there was a flow of the revolutionary tide.[1] Such a wave of resistance outlasted the rise and

235

fall of the separate movements that helped to constitute it. The momentum was retained as long as one partial victory led to another with a steamroller effect on the courage to resist. Similarly, a major defeat of the popular forces encouraged the reactionary elements in the government to step up the repression while it discouraged the resistance and tended to drive it underground. Then, when repression was greatest and the political situation increasingly hopeless, the turn was made to armed struggle. One defeat then led to another, contributing to the petering out of the resistance movement and to an ebb of the revolutionary tide.

A resistance movement gains momentum in response to a popular outburst or explosion that sets the masses in motion. Such an explosion can detonate a tide of popular activity, and a surging tide can in turn swell to the point that a new explosion occurs. But not every explosion results in a popular surge because it may be contained by brutal repression. Popular outbursts may occur during either the descending or the ascending phase of a wave of resistance. So may corresponding acts of repression.

The resistance began as an answer to the abandonment of the left-wing and popular current of *Cardenismo* by the ruling party. Differing from the beginnings of the resistance movement, the later waves and explosions arose as an answer to long periods of repression under right-wing administrations. The resistance surged during an economic boom – the developmentalist stage from 1940 to 1960 – but it continued in response to the structural economic crisis of later years. Although the second tide began to flow during the developmentalist years, its ebb corresponds to the economic crisis the country had been passing through since 1960. Differing from the first two great waves, the third rose with the sharpening of the structural economic crisis during the 1970s. This crisis was accentuated by the governmental repression of October 1968 and June 1971.

Although the economy developed at a fairly rapid pace during the period from 1940 to 1960, the possibilities of the so-called developmentalist stage were exhausted. The rate of growth fell, and the economy entered a period of prolonged monetary instability (inflation–devaluation). The acceleration of the process of capital concentration and the increasing deterioration of small and medium businesses had aggravated inequalities in the development of the economy and in the distribution of income. They were causes of a greater impoverishment of the workers owing to the progressive growth of unemployment and underemployment. Besides the economic crisis, there was a growing political crisis in which the PRI government was losing its authority and effectiveness. The real content of the state's tutelary role had shown itself: the government had above all favored the interests of the multinational corporations and the financial oligarchy. The intensification of the popular resistance responded to the rising politico-economic crisis.

The resistance failed owing to a series of subjective as well as objective causes. We consider these below, starting with the subjective mistakes, in principle avoidable, before moving on to consider the objective conditions, by definition beyond human control.

Unrealizable Demands

Under the influence of the prevailing ideology of the Mexican Revolution, the masses increased their demands endlessly. Consequently, a revolutionary populist President like López Mateos or Echeverría reached a point beyond which he could make no more concessions – "¡No mas!" A repudiation of the "leftist" policy followed, which in turn led to more pressure from below until the government resorted to repression. A "democratic opening" is a way of reinforcing the system, so the doors cannot open too far. Democracy, yes – but not too much!

The strike of the railwaymen in 1959 demanded too much from the government, and it was ruthlessly crushed. The popular student movement of 1968 also demanded too much; it really wanted a whole new society. The strike of the electrical workers in the democratic tendency in July 1976 asked for more than the government could give, but after the repression there were concessions. The same pattern occurred in the case of Lucio Cabañas and his movement in Guerrero. Was the government weaker in 1976 than in 1959? Or was Echeverría's government using more subtle tactics? After throwing a bone-breaking blow at the electrical workers, he suddenly presented himself as their benefactor. After killing Lucio Cabañas, he threw sops to the peasants of Guerrero. Thus a revolutionary nationalist president may both encourage and undermine the people's belief in their own power.

237

A Defective Analysis of Social Forces

Second, the left's defective analysis of social forces led to its mistaken assessment of presidential despotism. The left's confusion of the ruling clique with a state bourgeoisie, and of the subordinate state bureaucracy with mere functionaries of the capitalist class, resulted from ineptness. With only the rudiments of Marxist theory under their belts, the popular sectors were not equipped to amend it under new and unforeseen conditions. Instead, they dogmatically pigeonholed Mexico's population into Marx's three great classes (landowners, capitalists, and proletarians or wage-earners) and three intermediate and transitional ones (petty bourgeois, self-employed artisans, and peasants.)

Consequently, they mistook their struggle against presidential despotism for a struggle to the death against capitalism, when Mexico was the only member of the Organization of American States to be on friendly terms with Fidel Castro and the Cuban Revolution. As in the case of the corresponding theoretical confusion of the Weatherman in the United States, they took on two enemies at once and fought a war on two different fronts without realizing it. They missed a great opportunity, that of counting on Bakunin's "fourth great class" of intellectual workers as at least a partial and temporary ally in a joint effort to contain the local bourgeoisie.[2]

Although the 1917 Constitution was ambivalent, its mere enforcement could have been a first step toward improving the conditions of Mexico's laboring and exploited masses. Evidently, the PRI government had to be pushed in that direction, but the big advantage of Mexico's national revolution was precisely the president's near-absolute powers. As Manuel López Gallo relates in his economic and political history of Mexico, it was only since 1940 that *el presidente* became "uncontainable," that the powerful framework of government, entwined with the sinews of bureaucracy, had developed an enormous political muscle, to become a force not merely independent of the private sector but sufficiently powerful to curb the pretensions of its members. A political reform leading to proportional representation would be a democratic opening mainly for the reactionary bourgeoisie. That is a lesson worth considering by the critics of Mexico's presidential despotism. In Mexico, the president is in a better position

238

than are the divided parties of the left to enact legislation in the interests of the popular classes.[3]

As the institutional embodiment of the revolution, the president is a dictator, but he is also a republican. Caesar too was a republican and a leader of the popular party, even in the course of overriding the constitution and controlling the outcome of elections. Just as his misfortune was to be betrayed by the aristocratic Brutus, so *el presidente*'s most dangerous enemies have come not from the popular resistance but from the political right – the treacherous plutocracy. Electoral democracy was not a major objective of the popular resistance. Trade-union democracy and people's democracy – government compliance with worker, peasant, and student demands – were the prime issues.

Like Caesar's dictatorship, presidential despotism may have been the lesser of two evils. As Vilfredo Pareto observed in his *Cours d'Economie Politique* (1897):

> The people of Tuscany were happier and less despoiled under the absolutist government of Peter Leopold than they are under the present constitutional government of Italy.... In Rome towards the end of the Republic, it was election which conferred power; but those chosen were so deplorable, and oppression was so great, that military despotism seemed to the vast majority of Romans a lesser evil. The situation had reached such a point that, in a sense, Caesar and Augustus were truly the benefactors of the subject class.[4]

Much the same might be said of the Mexican president under the system of presidential despotism.

A further consequence of the left's defective analysis of classes was its unrealistic conception of socialism. For the popular resistance, it signified not only public ownership, but also the end of corruption in public office and of *charrismo* among trade-union bureaucrats. Supposedly, socialism would do away with classes as well as class exploitation. That was asking too much of it, as if a privileged administrative–professional class were non-existent. A minimal instead of maximal definition of socialism might at least be reachable, not to mention socialism within the system of presidential despotism before the PRI found itself deserted by its left wing. So understood, socialism would abolish capitalist spoliation while leaving bureaucratic spoliation untouched. Even so, the popular sectors stood to benefit from it and from presidential despotism as the means thereto.

Strategical Incompetence

Third, the left's strategy of direct confrontation with the state as the main enemy was militarily disastrous as well as misconceived. Against the military power of the Mexican state, Cabañas' ambushes counted for little in the long run. As for the fate of Mexico's urban guerrillas, it was a repeat performance of the Weathermen in the United States. It was an ultra-leftist caricature of Guevarism at work, under conditions in which Che's theory of the guerrilla *foco* became inoperative because of the urban milieu.[5] A misconceived anarchist strategy that takes the state power as the exploited workers' principal enemy, it was headed for defeat from the start.

With the partial exception of the Revolutionary Action Movement (MAR), Mexico's guerrillas were unprepared militarily and were so lacking in organizational know-how that they were readily discovered or just as readily betrayed. Lenin had a name for such behavior unfit for professional revolutionaries – "primitivism" or "amateurishness." But he omitted from his indictment the Judas-like betrayal of one's comrades that makes of Mexico's guerrillas a special case. Once a guerrilla was captured, it was enough to threaten torture to make him squeal until virtually all were behind bars. As well-prepared militarily as were the comrades of the MAR – in Pyongyang, the training sessions began at 6 a.m. and ended at 11 p.m. daily for nine months – they were unprepared to die rather than to inform on their comrades.[6]

Although a shining example for the rest of Mexico's guerrillas, the "comrades of the MAR forgot the lessons of history and ignored the people's psychology." From the beginning, they bragged that their movement was born in the USSR, that they were trained in North Korea, and that their movement was initially financed by both governments. Such information should not be made public; that does not endear them to the people. The Cuban Revolution triumphed under purely nationalist auspices in the name of Jose Martí. Fidel concealed his Marxist sympathies and revealed them publicly only after his revolution had triumphed and in response to the CIA-backed invasion at the Bay of Pigs. Like the other ignorant and unthinking guerrillas, the

MAR tried to convert every mountain range in Mexico into a Sierra Maestra in the absence of a detailed analysis of the political circumstances. The objective and subjective conditions for launching a revolution in Mexico were neither the same nor even similar to those in Cuba. Consequently, "If Castro had confessed his sympathies for the USSR [at the beginning of his struggle], he would still be fighting or would already have died, as happened to Guevara in Bolivia and Allende in Chile."[7]

While in the countryside the guerrillas were successful in recruiting peasants, in the cities they were unsuccessful in recruiting workers. Made up mainly of students and ex-students, they rivaled one another in ultra-leftist proclamations and sectarianism to the point of considering rival guerrilla tendencies to be "the enemy within." They knew little or nothing about the organization and strategy of urban guerrillas in Argentina, Uruguay, and Brazil, nor had they read Abraham Guillén's classic writings on urban guerrilla warfare covering the experience and lessons of the southern cone. Only belatedly, in 1977, did Guillén's critique of these comparatively successful urban guerrillas become accessible to the Mexican public, thanks to López Gallo's publishing house El Caballito and to the distribution of the book by the PMT.[8]

Electoral Co-option

Fourth, the political significance of umbrella parties should be clear to any impartial observer. This was not the democratic opening the resistance wanted. The center–left party that swallowed the independent Marxist and Marxist-Leninist left was not a party of the working class in the sense of a bona fide labor party. It was not only the Mexican Revolution that was dead – the popular resistance had come to a dead end.

Following this transformation, the communist left in Mexico virtually disappeared. Not only were there no more communist parties, there were no more communists of any significance outside them either. As for the satellite socialist parties, the PPS failed the electoral test while the PST and its various name-changes also disappeared by the end of the century, leaving an empty hole in place of the quondam ideological fountainhead and springboard of the popular resistance going back to the 1940s.

The democratic current in the PRI, the nucleus of the center–left forces that found an outlet in the PRD, was all that remained as an organized popular opposition to the official party on a national level. It was not even committed to socialism – an effective democracy was all it demanded. As Cuauhtémoc never tired of repeating, his party's goal was simply to apply and enforce the 1917 Constitution. Although success in so doing signified an end to presidential despotism, it was only the minimum program of the resistance. The maximum program had always combined democracy with the left's demand for socialism – the twofold conditions of a worker's state en route to a republic of equals. In effect, the emergence of the democratic current as the main representative of the resistance, politically speaking, signified an end to the revolutionary aspirations of the popular sectors.

Paradoxically, the minimum program of the resistance contradicted its maximum program. Considering that in the elections of July 2000 the only viable alternative to the PRI's absolutism was the hitherto reactionary PAN, the traditional party of Mexico's bourgeoisie, what could the popular sectors expect from a democratic opening? As Bakunin noted, citing Pierre-Joseph Proudhon's reflections on the democratic opening during the 1848 revolution in France: "Universal suffrage is counter-revolution." One can judge by the events which followed: "The elections of 1848, in their great majority, were carried by priests, legitimists, partisans of monarchy, by the most reactionary elements of France."[9]

A democratic opening, to be sure, but for whom? Not for the popular classes, unless one stretches the word "popular" to include the cerebral salariat as distinct from wage-earners. At most, a democratic opening meant the end of the PRI's political monopoly, so that other sectors of privileged professionals, experts, technocrats, and bureaupreneurs might get their turn at ruling.

Instead of the Mexican future envisaged by the popular resistance and by its communist and socialist vanguards under the influence of Karl Marx, the forecasts of his mortal enemy Michael Bakunin have become the new reality. Instead of a victory of the popular classes, we have rule by a "fourth governing class." Following on the heels of "a priestly class, an aristocratic class, a bourgeois class ... finally, when all the other classes have exhausted themselves, the State then becomes the patrimony of the bureaucratic class."[10]

Cost–Benefit Miscalculations

Fifth, the PCM's sacrifices without anything to show for it was worthy only of saints. If only the masses benefit, by all means die on the barricades! A cost–benefit analysis would not undercut that kind of advice. But applied to Mexico, the popular resistance was not worth the sacrifices.

Consider the sequence of massacres to be laid at the door of presidential despotism, the crown of the PRI's repressive government. First, the massacre at the presidential palace on 23 September 1941, leaving 9 dead and 11 wounded. Second, the massacre of Genaro Vázquez' followers in Chilpancingo, Guerrero, on 30 December 1960 where 18 died and many more were wounded. Third, the massacre of his followers in Iguala, Guerrero, on 31 December 1961, with a death toll of 28. Fourth, the massacre at the schoolhouse in Atoyac, Guerrero, on 18 May 1967, where 7 died followed by 2 policemen killed in vengeance. Fifth, the massacre at the Plaza of Three Cultures in Mexico City on 2 October 1968, with an undetermined death count estimated at around 300 and twice that number wounded. Sixth, the massacre by ex-hawks in Mexico City on 10 June 1971, during which 30 died and hundreds were wounded. The list goes on.

Also to be weighed in the balance are the sacrifices made by the heroes of the resistance: Rubén Jaramillo, his wife and three sons taken by force from their home in Tlaquiltenango and systematically murdered by judicial police and army units among the ruins of Xochicalco, Morelos, in May 1962; or the cold-blooded assassination of Héctor Lucero, founder of the Armed Commandos of Chihuahua, in Ciudad Chihuahua in January 1972; or the mysterious circumstances surrounding the death of Genaro Vázquez a month later; or the successive deaths in combat of Arturo Gámiz, Lucio Cabañas, Carmelo Cortés, and Raúl Ramos Zavala, to mention some of the most prominent leaders of the armed resistance; or the long prison sentences of Valentín Campa and Demetrio Vallejo; or the personal travails and bitterness felt by Mónico Rodríguez and his close friend Edmundo Raya, former head of the Communist Youth of Mexico.

We can personally testify to this bitterness in the cases of Mónico and Edmundo. Our many sessions with Mónico ended nearly always in the same way: he would burst into tears and sob involuntarily from the painful recollections of his treatment not so much by the PRI government as by the Communist Party. He had dedicated his life to a cause for which his family had to suffer, not least his children, one of whom died prematurely for lack of medical care that the party failed to provide. As for Edmundo, in a face-to-face encounter with Campa at Mónico's *taller* in Chiconcuac, Morelos, in January 1978, he described in vivid detail how the PCM had repeatedly sold out the workers through surrendering its independence to popular, national, and democratic fronts with the middle classes and so-called progressive sectors of the bourgeoisie, not to mention its electoral pretensions that were good for nothing. And for all the years he had devoted to the party, he had nothing to show for it in his old age except a rented room in Chiconcuac without running water and without furniture except a bed and a place to hang his clothes.

We have no intention of belittling the sacrifices on behalf of exploited Mexican workers and peasants. But let the goal measure up to the sacrifices – they should not have been made for the sake of some measly reforms. Lives cannot be worth sacrificing when the goal is beyond reach. In words attributed to Mao Zedong by a Latin American comrade:

> The greatest talent in this work, comrade, is never to be associated with failure…. Never to attack the pillager of the treasury, if he is the owner of a great fortress. He might crush you and there is no use being a martyr…. The end remains the same; the means change according to our power … fight and lose. The blow of the dictator will always be on your head; he will torture you and yours. His police will crack your skull. And what's in it for you? Nothing, absolutely nothing! You will be alone – for no one cares to share blows. No human ambition is nourished on misfortune…. You are asking for heroes, not converts. And heroes are not recruited often. They are the divine exception! … The workers will be with you if you get something for them. They will abandon you if you do not, however lofty your principles.[11]

Because of its neoliberal policies, which might be fine for the economy but were disastrous for the popular sectors, the PRI failed to deliver the goods. From 71 per cent of the total vote in 1982, its showing at the polls collapsed to 51 per cent in 1994. But the PRI was not alone in deserting the popular cause. The core parties of the resistance were tempted by the "democratic opening" to dissolve and try their luck with a mass political party, Cárdenas' Democratic Revolutionary Party (PRD). As a result, they did worse in the year 2000, when the PRD polled only 19 per cent of the vote, than in 1988 when the core parties alone polled 25 per cent.

So the resistance turned into a dismal failure. In the early 1970s, the authors let their hopes get the better of their judgment. We frankly believed that the popular resistance would win and that Mexico by the year 2000 would become a socialist country along Eurocommunist lines. A mood of triumphalism prevailed owing in part to the US withdrawal from Vietnam, the victory of the Viet Cong, the Marxist takeovers of the former Portuguese colonies of Angola and Mozambique, and the development of the armed resistance in Mexico. All in vain, because we failed to pay due attention to the objective circumstances that prevented the popular resistance from reaching its goals.

Economic Realities

Sixth, governments in peripheral countries cannot meet the ever escalating demands of both the popular sectors and their own professional and administrative staffs, because they are simply too poor. The path of least resistance has been to take care of their own – those at the helm of the various government, state enterprise, educational, and trade union bureaucracies under government control. The insufficient tax base of the Mexican economy, the country's huge foreign debt, government subsidies and other concessions to foreign enterprises undermined the wherewithal to minister to popular needs.

States like Mexico on the periphery of the world economy cannot survive without insertion into the world market, which means bowing to the metropolitan centers making the big decisions. For the state to be powerful enough to stand up to foreign business, it must build an alliance with the popular classes against economic imperialism. But how far can the state go toward this alliance when it cannot even sustain the material life of its underlying population?

As a typical Third World country, Mexico faces a predicament. The state is strong facing the native proletariat and even the local bourgeoisie unassociated with the transnationals, but weak before the bourgeoisie associated with the transnationals. Since the national economic space is not the basis of the state, its political superstructure must answer to foreign interests.

To keep up the state apparatus, big financial transfusions are needed. A poor and backward country fails to generate this money from its own tax base: the powerful rich refuse to pay and the poor cannot. So the government seeks help abroad. The result is that the government falls into an abyss of debt, prints paper money, and regularly devalues the currency. The peripheral state must also finance its army, police, education, and propaganda. This means more trips to the implacable IMF and the banks following its lead. It cannot survive in the world economy without caving in to outside pressures. As it slides downhill, it picks up momentum toward the bottom, begging loans to pay the interest on astronomical debts. In the 1980s, of the 96 Third World countries making up two-thirds of the world's population, Mexico had the second largest debt. Here we have an explanation for the failure of the resistance to extract even the most basic concessions from the ruling party.

That is only part of the story. Hardly less important has been the changing correlation of class forces in Mexico. In 1940, at the end of the Cardenista "Workers' State" coinciding with the shift in government policy in favor of the national bourgeoisie, the social pact formalized in the 1917 Constitution was still intact. That is because the several parties to the pact – workers, peasants, bourgeoisie, and government professionals – were still roughly equal in influence, if not in income. The shift to technocratic policies in the 1980s and the dissolution of the core parties of the resistance had as their foundation an altogether new phenomenon: the transformation of the professional elite as overseer and arbiter of class conflict into a rival for the lion's share of the economic surplus and a social force ruling mainly in its own interests.

In the thinking of the Mexican left, the end of the revolution signified the triumph of neoliberalism, submission to the dictates of world capitalism, and the resurgence of Mexico's restorationist bourgeoisie. Because its thinking was still governed by Marx's categories applicable to nineteenth-century capitalism, it lacked an adequate understanding of the technical and corresponding organizational and occupational changes that were eroding Mexican capitalism in competition with the multinationals.

246

The failure of the resistance is to be explained in part by the changed role of professionals from a junior partner of Mexico's bourgeoisie into the economically dominant class. Mexico's professionals are no longer the economic underdog of former days. To improve their relative share vis-à-vis Mexico's propertied interests, they no longer need to rally Mexico's workers and peasants behind them with revolutionary rhetoric; they no longer need to act as umpire in the class struggle. The resistance thrived as long as workers, peasants, and poor students could count on professionals as their allies in the struggle against the bourgeoisie; it petered out when this arrangement ceased to benefit the newly thriving expertoisie.[12]

As a result of the increasing dependence of the economy on technical expertise, professionals no longer needed the PRI as a godfather and political trampoline to improve their economic fortunes. That also explains why professionals deserted the ruling party for political and not just economic reasons. By the year 2000, the PRD had also outlived its usefulness, which explains why it too was abandoned on the eve of the elections and after Fox's victory.

Jorge Castañeda's political career is testimony to this transformation. A professor at Mexico's National University, he began his political career as a militant in Mexico's Communist Party. When it dissolved, the bulk of the party's professional workers joined the PRD. But on the eve of the 2000 elections, he again deserted a sinking ship by switching to the PAN. After serving as a leading adviser to Fox, he was rewarded with the post of Foreign Minister in the new post-PRI and post-revolutionary cabinet. By then, the PAN too had changed colors from a mainly bourgeois party into a party representing also the rising fortunes of Mexico's professionals.

From Alemán's presidency through that of Díaz Ordaz, the Mexican left fretted over a potential bourgeois counter-revolution. It was taken for granted that imperialism signified a strengthening of capitalism under conditions of dependency. But dependence on international capital is not dependence on international capitalism. Increasingly, the multinationals have as their chief beneficiaries the millions of professionals who staff them. While dividends have become a constantly diminishing fraction of corporate earnings, interest on corporate bonds has failed to keep pace with executive and other professional salaries. Absentee ownership has so changed the character of international capital that it is no longer capitalist. Thus it was not just a bourgeois counter-revolution to which the PRI made concessions from 1946 to 1968, but also a post-bourgeois revolution in the making.

In Mexico, according to Jorge Carrión, writing in the early 1970s, the bourgeoisie was a dominant class dominated. To this depiction Alonso Aguilar added that the big and middle bourgeoisie together were dependent on the multinationals. Ironically, the so-called mixed enterprises – euphemistically referred to as Mexicanized because by law Mexicans must own a minimum of 51 per cent of the capital – "tend to be the most Americanized and, in general, the most *extran-jerizante* [foreign-like]."[13]

Although the Mexican plutocracy is a separate class, it is not a national bourgeoisie in the sense of being independent. The Monterrey group comes closest to constituting a national bourgeoisie because its enterprises almost without exception have a national origin and are funded exclusively by national capital. Yet this group of enterprises is the most Yankophile, the most anti-national sector of Mexico's capitalists, the most subordinated to the US economy, the most dominated not by private stockholders but by corporate elites.[14]

The growing power and influence of the Mexican bourgeoisie, its so-called takeover of the government, was at bottom a corporate coup, not a bourgeois one. The left, including comrades Carrión and Aguilar, failed to understand this. It was widely believed that there were only two options for Mexico: either a forward march to socialism in the sense of further expropriations and the precedence of the public over the private sector, or a bourgeois counter-revolution through successive privatizations. In fact, whether the public enterprises ended in the hands of multinationals, mixed enterprises, or Mexico's bourgeoisie, the outcome was the same: domination by professionals as the power behind the throne.

After the final spurt of nationalizations under Presidents Echeverría and Portillo, US-trained presidents applied neoliberal policies that ruined tens of thousands of small and middling Mexican capitalists: much of the national bourgeoisie could not compete with the invading transnational giants. That caused a big drop in capital income for Mexicans – the profit column in Mexico's statistics on national income tells the tearful tale. Profits sucked out by foreign companies do not appear in Mexico's gross national product.

Next, the high-tech companies that cornered Mexico's national bourgeoisie needed so much professional and technical expertise that the salaries of their Mexican employees ballooned. The graduates of the Monterrey Technological Institute's many branches no longer had to take jobs in the United States: daughter companies of US-based transnationals offered them positions in their native land. Not only did these transnational affiliates pay better salaries; they often paid better ordinary wages than native-owned industries. Along with the relative decline of capital income, there was a relative increase in both wages and professional salaries.

The resistance collapsed despite its momentary revival in the 1990s by the EZLN and the EPR. Once inaugurated as the new president, Fox promptly changed the operations and the image of the Mexican presidency. In place of presidential despotism, Mexico more nearly approximated the US system of presidential liberalism. Instead of the deadlock with the EZLN, the government withdrew troops from the disputed areas, returned to the negotiating table, and thereby overcame the protracted tensions with the indigenous peoples.

To conclude, the subjective and objective factors that undermined the resistance also undermined its *raison d'être*. There are still millions of Mexico's discontented, but they will henceforth have to target a different enemy, no longer the corrupt PRI and a threatening bourgeois counter-revolution, but the as yet unchallenged revolution of Mexico's professional elites.

Notes

1. On the role of revolutionary tides, advances and retreats, ebbs and flows of a popular resistance in the wake of a massacre that sets it off, see Lenin's "Lecture on the 1905 Revolution," in Robert C. Tucker, ed., *The Lenin Anthology* (New York: Norton, 1975), pp. 278–91.
2. Donald C. Hodges, "La guerra de guerrillas en los Estados Unidos," in Donald C. Hodges and Abraham Guillén, *Revaloración de la guerrilla urbana* (Mexico City: El Caballito, 1977), pp. 33–8.
3. Manuel López Gallo, *Economía y política en la historia de México* (Mexico City: El Caballito, 1967), pp. 578–85.
4. Vilfredo Pareto, *Cours d'Economie Politique* (1896), in idem, *Sociological Writings*, ed. S. E. Finer, trans. Derick Merfin (New York: Praeger, 1966), p. 118.
5. Hodges, "La guerra de guerrillas," pp. 22–9.
6. V.I. Lenin, "What Is To Be Done?" in Tucker, ed., *The Lenin Anthology*, pp. 60–2; and Camarada "Ernesto," *El guerrillero*, p. 185.
7. Camarada "Ernesto," *El guerrillero*, pp. 190, 191.

8. Abraham Guillén, "Lecciones de la guerrilla latinoamericana," in Hodges and Guillén, *Revaloración*, pp. 84–130.

9. Michael Bakunin, *The Political Philosophy of Bakunin: Scientific Anarchism*, ed. G.P. Maximoff (Glencoe, IL: Free Press, 1953), p. 214; from *The Knouto-Germanic Empire and the Social Revolution* (1870–71).

10. Michael Bakunin, "The International and Karl Marx" (1872), in ed. and trans. Sam Dolgoff, *Bakunin on Anarchy*, (New York: Knopf, 1972), pp. 294, 318–19.

11. Eudocio Ravines, *The Yenan Way* (New York: Scribner, 1951), pp. 151, 152, 157. Ravines is a liar who tells the truth. Mao supposedly gave him this advice at the Communist International's Seventh Congress in Moscow in August 1935, when Mao was in fact leading the 6,000-mile Long March from south-east China to Yenan in the north-west. Ravines was then the general secretary of the Peruvian Communist Party.

12. See *Estadísticas Históricas de México*, vol. 1, 4th ed. (Mexico City: Instituto Nacional de Estadísticas, Geografía e Informática, 1999), Tables 5.13 and 5.16.1 to 5.16.5; and, for an interpretation of similar data in the United States, Donald Hodges, *America's New Economic Order* (Aldershot, UK: Avebury, 1996), pp. 39–82, and idem, *Class Politics in the Information Age* (Urbana and Chicago: University of Illinois Press, 2000), pp. 99–122.

13. Jorge Carrión, "La burguesía nacionalista encadenada" and Alonso Aguilar M., "La oligarquía," in Jorge Carrión and Alonso Aguilar M., *La burguesía, la oligarquía, y el estado*, 2nd ed. (Mexico City: Nuestro Tiempo, 1974), pp. 31–8, 114–21.

14. Abraham Nuncio, *El Grupo Monterrey* (Mexico City: Nueva Imágen, 1982), pp. 41–53.

Appendix[1]
The Plan of Cerro Prieto, Township of Tlaquiltenango,
State of Morelos

TO THE PROGRESSIVE FORCES OF MEXICO:
Those who support and make up the REVOLUTIONARY NATIONAL JUNTA
with its seat in Cerro Prieto, Township of Tlaquiltenango, Morelos, in
the exercise of our class rights, make known to the citizens of this
country the following PLAN, based on the considerations that are
expressed herein:

FIRST: That the Mexican people, during their long revolutionary
journey from 1810 to our own day, have declared themselves
against tyranny.

SECOND: That the Constitution of 1917 legitimated the concern that
inspired the revolutionaries of the PLAN OF AYALA, among others,
who saw in it the fulfillment of their most cherished ideals.

THIRD: That this Constitution has been trampled on in recent years by
men in public office who have used their power to commit the crime
of high treason against the country, seeing that to maintain and
enrich themselves in the government they have had to resort to
violence that undermined the people's right to freely elect their
rulers.

FOURTH: That the local and federal authorities, fruit of the corrupted
political monopoly of the PRI, conspiring with the perverse leaders
of the trade unions and peasant associations, are again preparing to
make a mockery of democratic principles by imposing another
president of the republic during the next six years.

FIFTH: That all monopoly is anti-constitutional and anti-patriotic.
None the less, the milk, bread, flour, sugar, and electrical and

251

metallurgical industries – all of them – are monopolized and, if by some strange quirk anything remains, brutal exploitation has not left us even any pigsties. Because the UNION OF SCAVENGERS is controlled by a monopoly, poor Mexicans do not have a right even to garbage.

SIXTH: That these monopolies are, in addition to being anti-constitutional, organized by foreigners who are interested only in amassing wealth in order to export it to their own countries, and that the government, in order to even the score, has decreed the devaluation of our currency. In this way, Mexico has been converted into a supplier of raw materials and into a consumer of industrial goods, giving rise to want and inflation that become worse every day.

SEVENTH: That the government is not absolute. None the less, it behaves like a despot and totalitarian by imposing authorities, governors, deputies, senators, magistrates, etc., by increasing taxes to enrich itself and also to maintain a swarm of bureaucrats (parasites of money and of the public), sheltered by the Judicial Statute and Law of Immobility. It permits the exploitation of natural resources, as in the SAN RAFAEL AGREEMENT, but it does not allow the villages, even on their own properties, to cut down a single weed.

EIGHTH: That these proceedings take place with such ill will that, if we do not defend our rights, the government imposed on us now and in the future will go on treating the people as a real enemy. This government is a long way from protecting the people's rights precisely because it is not a government of the people.

NINTH: That the Revolution flouted in this way has created a new class of rich people who are at the same time generals, governors, deputies, senators, men of influence, householders, monopolists; these people, in connivance with foreign companies sheltered by the "Good Neighbor Policy," exploit the worker in the city and the countryside to the utmost degree.

TENTH: That these abuses in the public domain are only a small reflection of the bourgeois and capitalist regime that has Mexico in its clutches but ought to disappear.

ELEVENTH: That there are revolutionary chiefs in this country who are trying to make a new revolution, but whose program, if they have any, we ignore. Therefore, we have to proclaim the present one.

TWELFTH: That the distribution of land in individual parcels has contributed to the exploitation of man by man, has added to the traffic in hunger, has provoked disorganization, and has caused the failure in part of the national agrarian program, which has not achieved its goals. Consequently, these parcels must be reorganized in a collective form, putting an end to the "protected zones" whose owners are chiefs of operation, military commanders, governors, senators, former presidents of the republic, and gentlemen farmers, so that they may be turned over to the villages whose *ejidos* are too small.

THIRTEENTH: That agriculture is a decisive factor in the life of the people and must be stimulated with machinery, fertilizers, etc., produced inside the country, which requires according to this plan the immediate establishment of a heavy industry that can manufacture all the machines the people need – locomotives, trucks, buses, planes, sewing machines, typewriters, tractors – and all that currently comes to us from foreign markets and naturally results in our country in an economic bloodletting of millions upon millions of pesos that we greatly need to spend here. In order to achieve this objective, we shall proceed to the expropriation of the electrical industry.

FOURTEENTH: That the Constitution has not been observed for the following reasons: although Article 28 prohibits monopolies, Article 4 guarantees "free trade," so that a private merchant or purchasing agent for the government can appeal to it for protection, as do all monopolists and intermediaries; the same is true of the producers of alcoholic beverages, whose "industrial freedom" is inviolable. This leads to the conclusion that the first twenty-nine articles of the Constitution are only a dead letter, because in practice they have permitted the libertinism of the press, the clergy, the capitalist bourgeoisie, to the point of traffic in "justice," all to the disadvantage of the country and particularly of the peasantry, which in spite of everything that is said continues to live in the most frightful misery. Consequently, the Constitution should be immediately revised, so that it may become a practical law and not a bloody trick. For example, there should be a decree forbidding the production of alcoholic beverages, the result of which would be to end drunkenness and to free the country from all its dismal consequences.

FIFTEENTH: That the result of the so-called Revolution of 1910 is not, not anything like, the triumph of the social revolution – considering what we have seen from the preceding observations – so that there is a need to guide this new struggle to conquer public power and to establish a government of "genuine workers on the land and in the factories," a National Council of Workers that would be born from below, that would be the administrator of the public wealth, that would renew itself periodically, confiscating the riches and the stately homes acquired in the shadow of the Revolution in order to turn them over to the poor or to benevolent societies, while new population centers are established in healthful surroundings.

SIXTEENTH: That foreign trade has been and continues to be unfavorable to Mexico, which makes it imperative that our money should be revalued, that the sale abroad of basic necessities and raw materials should be suspended, and, if there are surpluses after all internal needs are met, that these should be sold or exchanged with the country that will pay most for them, which is to say that exchange should occur on the basis of reciprocity.

SEVENTEENTH: That the increase in the workers' wages has been illusory in practice and has even served as a pretext to raise the prices of basic necessities, bringing increased want so that the worker can never get along with what he earns and must always ask for a bigger increase in wages, hurting without intending to hurt the peasant on the *ejido* to the extent of betraying the peasant slogan "Land and Liberty." Consequently, this problem must be resolved immediately, so that the worker may see that the country's improvement does not rest on a nominal increase in wages but on the disappearance of entrepreneurs, monopolists, and intermediaries, big and small, who in their eagerness to become rich quickly, make the articles of prime necessity pass from hand to hand before reaching the consumer, exploiting step by step the worker whether on the farm or in the factory, which explains why the peasant's product turns on his own misery. This is to say that the Mexican Revolution was exclusively an agrarian one, and that it is necessary that this new revolution should extend its scope of action so that, just as the landed estates were turned over to the peasants, the factories shall be turned over to the workers – no matter what.

BECAUSE OF WHAT HAS BEEN SHOWN AND ESTABLISHED, IT SHOULD BE
RESOLVED AND IS RESOLVED:

FIRST: The disavowal of the present legislative, executive, and judicial
powers, both federal and local, with the exception of those identified with this plan.

SECOND: The REVOLUTIONARY NATIONAL JUNTA declares before the
nation and the entire world that it makes the PLAN OF AYALA its own
plan with the additions mentioned in the following points of resolution for not having been fulfilled in their totality. Taking into consideration that the people are heeded only when they take up arms,
it will struggle alongside them until it secures the victory of the
present plan.

THIRD: As an additional part of the PLAN OF AYALA, we make the clari-
fication that the lands, mountains, and waters that have been transferred or in the future shall be transferred to the villages will be
governed by the collective system in conformity with the regulation
that will be expedited for that purpose.

FOURTH: By virtue of the fact that the Mexican people are exploited
with respect to articles of prime necessity – sugar, bread, milk,
cloth, electricity, fertilizers, machinery, etc. – those industries will
be nationalized and administered by the workers themselves,
without losing sight of the need to establish a heavy industry for
manufacturing tractors, trucks, and all the machinery required for
the development and progress of a civilized people.

FIFTH: Once the revolution is victorious, the Junta of Revolutionary
Chiefs, assembled in a Constituent Congress, will map out the new
constitution of the republic according to this plan.

MEXICANS! Come join the ranks of the Revolutionary Movement of the
People! Do not respond with indifference to the anguished call of the
homeland! The afflicted native land expects each one of its sons to do
his duty! Be on time for the historic encounter with destiny!
"MEXICO FOR THE MEXICANS"
Cerro Prieto, Tlaquiltenango, Morelos, 28 November 19__.[2]
Signed: *Rubén Jaramillo*

Notes

1. Translated by Donald C. Hodges from the sole surviving mimeographed copy in the possession of Mónico Rodríguez and his son-in-law Renato Ravelo.
2. The date is missing. In anticipation of Jaramillo's second armed uprising in 1953, this adapted version of the original 1943 document appeared after the July elections in 1952, but before the new president Ruiz Cortines took office in December. The clues to dating the 1952 document are the references to the PRI's imposition of a new president "during the next six years" (Fourth Article); to other "revolutionary chiefs," the Henriquista generals on the eve of the 1952 presidential succession (Eleventh Article); and to the Revolutionary National Junta and the Junta of Revolutionary Chiefs, Jaramillo among them (Second and Fifth Resolutions).

❀ Bibliography

Aguilar Mora, Manuel, *El bonapartismo mexicano* (Mexico City: Juan Pablos, 1982).

—— *La crisis de la izquierda en México* (Mexico City: Juan Pablos, 1978).

Alonso, Antonio, *El movimiento ferrocarrilero en México 1958–1959* (Mexico City: Era, 1972).

Anguiano, Arturo, *El Estado y la política obrera del cardenismo* (Mexico City: Era, 1975).

Anon, *Rubén Jaramillo: Vida y luchas de un dirigente campesino (1900–1962)* (n.p., n.d.).

Araiza, Luis, *Historia del movimiento obrero mexicano*, 4 vols. (Mexico City: Cuauhtémoc, 1965).

Argüedas, Leda, "El movimiento de liberación nacional: una experiencia de la izquierda mexicana en los sesentas," *Revista Mexicana de Sociología* (Mexico City: January–March, 1977).

Avila Camacho y su ideología: ¡La Revolución en marcha! Gira electoral (Mexico City: Partido de la Revolución Mexicana, 1940).

Bakunin, Michael, *The Political Philosophy of Bakunin: Scientific Anarchism*, ed. G.P. Maximoff (Glencoe, IL: Free Press, 1953).

Baumann, Michael L., *B. Traven: An Introduction* (Albuquerque: University of New Mexico Press, 1976).

Bonilla Machorro, Carlos, *Caña amarga: Ingenio San Cristóbal* (Mexico Ciy: Publicidad Editora, 1975).

Campa, Valentín, *Mi testimonio: memorias de un comunista mexicano*, 3rd rev. ed. (Mexico City: Cultura Popular, 1985; orig. pub. 1978).

Cárdenas, Lázaro, *Ideario político* (Mexico City: Era, 1972).

Carr, Barry, *Marxism and Communism in Twentieth-Century Mexico* (Lincoln: University of Nebraska Press, 1992).

Carrión, Jorge and Alonso Aguilar M., *La burguesía, la oligarquía, y el estado*, 2nd ed. (Mexico City: Nuestro Tiempo, 1974).

Castañeda, Jorge, *Utopia Unarmed: The Latin American Left After the Cold War* (New York: Vintage, 1994).

Castillo, Heberto and Francisco Paoli Bolio, *¿Por qué un Nuevo Partido?* (Mexico City: Posada, 1975).

Colmenares, Ismael, ed., *Cien Años de Lucha de Clases en México* (1876– 1976), vol. 1 (Mexico City: Quinto Sol, 1982).

Condes Lara, Enrique, "Enseñanzas de la lucha electricista," *Socialismo*, no. 5 (Mexico City: Primer Trimestre, 1976).

Cooper, Marc, *Starting From Chiapas: The Zapatistas Fire the Shot Heard Around the World* (Westfield, NJ: Open Magazine Pamphlet Series, 1994).

Córdova, Arnaldo, *La política de masas del cardenismo* (Mexico City: Era, 1974).

Danzós Palomino, Ramón, *Desde la cárcel de Atlixco: vida y lucha de un dirigente campesino* (Mexico City: Fondo de Cultural Popular, 1974).

Dávila, Gerardo and Manlio Tirado, eds, *Como México no hay dos: Porfirismo – Revolución – Neoporfirismo* (Mexico City: Nuestro Tiempo, 1971).

De la Grange, Bertrand and Maite Rico, *Marcos, la genial impostura* (Mexico City: Aguilar, 1998).

De Mora, Juan Miguel, *Lucio Cabañas: su vida y su muerte* (Mexico City: Editores Asociados, 1974).

Deutscher, Isaac, *The Prophet Outcast. Trotsky: 1929–1940* (New York: Vintage, 1965).

Dolgoff, Sam, ed. and trans., *Bakunin on Anarchy*, (New York: Knopf, 1972).

Durán de Huerta, Marta, ed., *Yo, Marcos* (Mexico City: Milenio, 1994).

"Ernesto," *El Guerrillero* (Guadalajara: Graphos, 1974).

Estadísticas Históricas de México, vol. 1, 4th ed. (Mexico City: Instituto Nacional de Estadísticas, Geografía e Informática, 1999).

EZLN: Documentos y comunicados, Vol. 1 (Mexico City: Era, 1998).

Foweraker, Joe and Ann L. Craig, eds, *Popular Movements and Political Change in Mexico* (Boulder: Lynne Rienner, 1990).

Gallo, Manuel López, *Economía y Política en la Historia de México* (Mexico City: El Caballito, 1967).

Gandy, Ross, *Introducción a la sociología histórica marxista* (Mexico City: Era, 1978).

Garrido, Luis Javier, *El partido de la revolución institucionalizada: La formación del nuevo estado en México (1928–1945)* (Mexico City: Siglo XXI, 1982).

Gill, Mario, *Los Ferrocarrileros* (Mexico City: Extemporáneos, 1971).

Gilly, Adolfo, *La revolución interrumpida*, 4th ed. (Mexico City: El Caballito, 1974; orig. pub. 1971).

Godines Jr., Prudencio, *¡Que poca mad … era!* (Mexico City: n.p., 1968).

Gómez, Manuel Aguilera, *La desnacionalización de la economía mexicana* (Mexico City: Fondo de Cultura Económica, 1975).

Gómez, Pablo, *Los Gastos Secretos del Presidente* (Mexico City: Grijalbo, 1996).

Gómez-Tagle, Silvia, Marcelo Miquet Fleury, José Luis Reyna and Francisco Zapata, *Tres estudios sobre el movimiento obrero en México* (Mexico City: Colegio de México, 1976).

González Casanova, Pablo, *La Democracia en México* (Mexico City: Era, 1974).

Guevara, Ernesto "Che," "La Guerra de Guerrillas," *Obras 1957–1967*, 2 vols. (Havana: Casa de las Américas, 1970).

Haya de la Torre, Victor Raúl, *Política aprista*, 2nd ed. (Lima: Amauta, 1967).

Hernandez Navarro, Luis and Ramón Vera Herra (compiladores), *Acuerdos de San Andrés* (Mexico City: Era, 1998).

Hirales Morán, Gustavo, *La liga comunista 23 de septiembre: orígenes y naufragio* (Mexico City: Cultura Popular, 1977).

Hodges, Donald C., *The Legacy of Che Guevara: A Documentary Study* (London: Thames and Hudson, 1977).

—— ed., *The Philosophy of the Urban Guerrilla: The Revolutionary Writings of Abraham Guillén* (New York: William Morrow, 1973).

—— *The Latin American Revolution: Politics and Strategy from Apro-Marxism to Guevarism* (New York: William Morrow, 1974).

—— *America's New Economic Order* (Aldershot, UK: Avebury, 1996).

—— *Class Politics in the Information Age* (Urbana and Chicago: University of Illinois Press, 2000).

—— and Abraham Guillén, *Revaloración de la guerrilla urbana* (Mexico City: El Caballito, 1977).

—— and Ross Gandy, *Mexico 1910–1982: Reform or Revolution?* 2nd rev. ed. (London: Zed, 1983).

Huizer, Gerrit, *El potencial revolucionario del campesino en América Latina* (Mexico City: Siglo XXI, 1976).

Insurgencia obrera y nacionalismo revolucionario (Mexico City: El Caballito, 1973).

James, Daniel, *Che Guevara: A Biography* (New York: Stein & Day, 1969).

Jaramillo, Rubén, *Autobiografía*, and Froylán C. Manjarrez, *La matanza de Xochicalco*, 2nd ed. (Mexico City: Nuestro Tiempo, 1973).

Kenner, Martin and James Petras, eds, *Fidel Castro Speaks* (New York: Grove Press, 1969).

Kiejman, Claude and Jean Francis Held, *Mexico, le pain et les joux* (Paris: Du Seuil, 1969).

La CTM y la Confederación de Cámaras Industriales, *20 años de lucha* (Mexico City: Confederación Nacional de Industria de la Transformación, 1961).

Lerner de Sheinbaum, Bertha and Susana Ralsky de Cimet, *El poder de los presidentes: Alcances y perspectivas (1910–1973)* (Mexico City: Instituto Mexicano de Estudios Políticos, 1976).

López, Jaime, *10 años de guerrillas en México 1964–1974* (Mexico City: Posada, 1974).

Los Partidos Políticos en México (Mexico City: Fondo de Cultura Económica, 1978).

Loyo Brambila, Aurora, *El Movimiento Magisterial de 1958 en México* (Mexico City: Era, 1979).

Lutz, William and Harry Brent, ed., *On Revolution* (Cambridge, MA: Winthrop, 1971).

Macín, Raúl, *Jaramillo: un profeta olvidado* (Montevideo, Uruguay: Tierra Nueva, 1970).

Manjarrez, Froylán C., *see* Jaramillo.

Martínez Nateras, Arturo, *Punto y seguido. ¿Crisis en el PCM?* (Mexico City: Edición del autor, 1980).

Martínez Verdugo, Arnoldo, *Partido Comunista Mexicano: trayectoría y perspectivas* (Mexico City: Cultura Popular, 1977).

Marx, Karl, *The Poverty of Philosophy* (1847) in Karl Marx and Frederick Engels, *Collected Works*, 46 vols. (New York: International Publishers, 1975–1992).

Mayo, Baloy , *La guerrilla de Genaro y Lucio: Análisis y resultados* (Mexico City: Diógenes, 1980).

Medin, Tzvi, *Ideología y praxis política de Lázaro Cárdenas*, 2nd. ed. (Mexico City: Siglo XXI, 1974).

Medina Valdés, Gerardo, *Operación 10 de Junio* (Mexico City: Universo, 1972).

Mella, Julio Antonio, "¿Qué es el ARPA?" in *Documentos y artículos* (Havana: Instituto de Historia del Movimiento Comunista y la Revolución Socialista de Cuba, 1975).

Michels, Robert, *Political Parties: A Sociolgical Study of the Oligarchical Tendencies of Modern Democracy*, trans. Eden and Cedar Paul (Glencoe, IL: Free Press, 1958; orig. pub. 1915).

MLN, *Programa y llamamiento del Movimiento de Liberación Nacional* (Mexico City: MLN, 1961).

Monsiváis, Carlos and Antonio García de León, *EZLN: Documentos y Comunicados*, I, II, III (Mexico City: Era, 1997).

Moreno, Daniel, *Los partidos políticos del México contemporaneo*, 7th ed. (Mexico City: Costa-Amic, 1979).

Murillo Soberanis, Manlio Fabio, *La reforma política mexicana y el sistema pluri-partidista* (Mexico City: Diana, 1979).

Narváez, Rubén, *La sucesión presidencial: Teoría y práctica del tapadismo* (Mexico City: Instituto Mexicano de Sociología Política, 1981).

Natividad Rosales, José, *¿Quién es Lucio Cabañas? ¿Qué pasa con la guerrilla en México?* (Mexico City: Posada, 1976).

Nuncio, Abraham, *El Grupo Monterrey* (Mexico City: Nueva Imagen, 1982).

Oppenheimer, Andrés, *Bordering on Chaos: Guerrillas, Stockbrokers, Politicians, and Mexico's Road to Prosperity* (New York: Little, Brown, 1996).

Ortiz, Orlando , *Genaro Vázquez* (Mexico City: Diógenes, 1973).

Partido Mexicano Socialista, *Documentos fundamentales* (Mexico City: Consejo Nacional del PMS, 1988).

Partido Mexicano Socialista, *La situación nacional y la construcción del Partido de la Revolución Democrática* (Mexico City: Consejo Nacional del PMS, 1989).

Partido Socialista de los Trabajadores, *Documentos Básicos* (Mexico City: Ediciones del Comité Central, 1981).

PCM, *El Partido Comunista frente a la crisis actual. XVIII Congreso Nacional* (Mexico City: Ediciones del Comité Central, 1977).

Pellicer de Brody, Olga, *México y la revolución cubana* (Mexico City: El Colegio de México, 1972).

Pimentel Aguilar, Ramón, *El secuestro: ¿Lucha política o provocación?* (Mexico City: Posada, 1974).

Poniatowska, Elena, *La noche de Tlatelolco* (Mexico City: Era, 1978).

PRD, *Documentos Básicos del Partido de la Revolución Democrática: Declaración de Principios y Estatutos* (Mexico City: PRD, 1990).

Quiles Ponce, Enrique, *Henríquez y Cárdenas ¡Presentes! Hechos y realidades de la campaña henriquista* (Mexico City: Costa Amic, 1980).

Ramírez Gómez, Ramon, *El movimiento estudiantil de México*, 2 vols. (Mexico City: Era, 1969).

Ramírez Jacome, Gilberto and Emilio Salim Cabrera, *La Clase Política Mexicana* (Mexico City: Edamex, 1987).

Raskin, Jonah, *My Search for B. Traven* (New York: Methuen, 1980).

Ravelo, Renato, *Los jaramillistas* (Mexico City: Nuestro Tiempo, 1978).

Rodríguez Araujo, Octavio, *La reforma política y los partidos en México*, 5th ed. (Mexico City: Siglo XXI, 1982).

Romero Jacobo, César, *Los Altos de Chiapas: La voz de las armas* (Mexico City: Planeta, 1994).

Ronfeldt, David, *Atencingo: La política de la lucha agraria en un ejido mexicano* (Mexico City: Fondo de Cultura Económica, 1975).

Scherer García, Julio and Carlos Monsiváis, *Parte de Guerra: Tlatelolco 1968* (Mexico City: Nuevo Siglo Aguilar, 1999).

Schürer, Ernst and Philip Jenkins, eds, *B. Traven: Life and Work* (University Park: Pennsylvania State University, 1987).

Semo, Ilán and Américo Saldívar, *México, un pueblo en la historia*, 4 vols., ed. Enrique Semo (Mexico City: Universidad Autónoma de Puebla and Editorial Nueva Imagen, 1982).

Shadows of Tender Fury: The Letters of Subcomandante Marcos and the Zapatista Army of National Liberation, trans. Frank Bardacke, Leslie López, and the Watsonville, California, Human Rights Committee (New York: Monthly Review, 1995).

Shulgovski, Anatoli, *México en la encrucijada de su historia*, tr. Armando Martínez Verdugo (Mexico City: Cultura Popular, 1968).

Suárez, Luis, *Lucio Cabañas, el guerrillero sin esperanza* (Mexico City: Roca, 1976).

Traven, B., *The Rebellion of the Hanged* (New York: Hill and Wang, 1952).

Trotsky, Leon, "La administración obrera en la industria nacionalizada," *Por los Estados Unidos Socialistas de América Latina* (Buenos Aires: Coyoacán, 1961).

—— *The Permanent Revolution* and *Results and Prospects* (New York: Pathfinder, 1969).

Tucker, Robert C., ed., *The Lenin Anthology* (New York: Norton, 1975).

Unzueta, Gerardo, *Nuevo Programa para la nueva revolución: Documentos del XVI Congreso del Partido Comunista Mexicano* (Mexico City: Cultura Popular, 1974).

Weinberg, Bill, *Homage to Chiapas: The New Indigenous Struggles in Mexico* (London: Verso, 2000).

Wences Reza, Rosalio, *El movimiento estudiantil y los problemas nacionales* (Mexico City: Nuestro Tiempo, 1971).

Womack, John, *Emiliano Zapata*, trans. Frederic Illouz (Paris: Maspero, 1976).

Zermeño, Sergio, *México: Una democracia utópica* (Mexico City: Siglo XXI, 1978).

Zogbaum, Heidi, *B. Traven. A Vision of Mexico* (Wilmington, DE: Scholarly Resources, 1992).

⊛ Index

Federation of Unions of Workers at the Service
of the State (FSTSE), 58-9
Figueroa, Rubén, 123, 128
"Fish, the" (Sergio Ramíro Ramirez), 136, 139-
44
Flores Curiel, Rogelio, 144
Flores, Oscar, 183
Foweraker, Joe, 17
Fox, Vicente, 230, 247, 249
"Francisco Villa" settlement, 176, 180, 182-5
Franco, Francisco, 18
Free Union of Copra Associtions (ULAC), 111
Fuentes, Félix, 137

Gallardo, Juan, 120
Gallegos, Avelina, 182
Gallo, Manuel López, 80
Galván, Rafael, 157-8, 162-3, 164-70, 218, 223,
235
Gámiz, Arturo, 88-9, 91, 120, 147, 152, 175,
181, 143
García Barragán, General, 100
Garza Leal ('the elbow'), 140
Garza Sada, Eugenio, 153
"Gaspar", 184
General Union of Mexican Workers and
Peasants (UGOCM), 87-9, 140, 181
Gill, Mario, 74, 79
Gilly, Adolfo, 223
Gómez, Pablo, 91, 185
Gómez Souza, Fabricio, 147-8
Gómez Zepeda, Luis, 33-5
Golden Shirts, 157
González Casanova, Pablo, 103, 139
González, Hank, 144
González, Juan Manuel, 72
González, Oscar, 89, 181
González, Raúl, 175
Grenadiers, 94, 96, 142-3
Guadalajara Students Federation (FEG), 149
Guarro, Alfonso, 143
Guerreran Civic Association/Committee, 107-13
guerrillas, B. Traven on, 7-11; Che Guevara on,
147; costs to, 243; Guevarist, 113; Indian,
196; Jaramillo, 44-56; Lacandones, 146-8,
150-1; Madera, 107; Marxist-Leninist, 201;
mistakes, 241; peasant, 43, 115, 175; prolif-
eration, 130-1; rural, 235; September 23
Communist League, 121, 146-50, 188, 210;
socialist, 192; training, 121; unrealistic
demands, 125-7; urban, 146-55, 240
Guevara, Che, 25, 70, 89, 98, 135, 141, 147,
150, 195, 197, 202-3; Guevarism, 240-1
Guillén, Abraham, 189-90, 241
Guillén Vicente, Rafael Sebastián (see Marcos)

Harp Helú, Alfredo, 129
Hawks, 134-6, 140-3

Haya de la Torre, Victor Raúl, 212-13, 221
Henríquez Guzmán, Miguel, 47
Hernández, Florentino Jaime, 114
Hernández, Jesús Araujo, 109
Hirales Morán, Gustavo, 153-4
Hirschfeld Almada, Julio, 155
Hodges, Donald, 189
House of the World Worker, 2, 6

Independent Peasant Central (CCI), 85, 111,
118, 140, 173, 178-80, 215
Independent Popular Union, Durango (UPI),
178
Independent Union Front (FSI), 140
indigenous peoples/Indians, 11, 17, 129, 194,
204-5; Catholic, 193; land occupations,
191; peons, 5, 8; proletarian, 4; racism
towards, 196; rights, 200; way of life, 202-3
Industrial-Labor Pact, 32
Institutional Revolutionary Party (PRI), xvi-xvii,
1, 47, 58-9, 66, 79, 84-6, 89, 101, 104-5,
110, 113, 123, 128, 133, 137-8, 157, 159,
161, 166, 168-70, 175, 179, 183, 186, 195-
8, 202, 204, 208, 211, 213-18, 221, 225,
228-30, 234, 237-9, 242-4, 247-9
insurgency, causes of, 18, 23-6, 191-4
Insurgent Popular Assembly, 130
Intercontinental Meeting for Humanity and
Against Neoliberalism, 201
International Association of Agricultural
Workers Unions (UISTABP), 179
International Monetary Fund, 246

Japan, 136
Jara, Heberto, 83
Jaramillo, Porfirio, 55-6, 61, 210
Jaramillo, Raquel, 55
Jaramillo, Rubén, xi, xiii-xix, 8-9, 24, 30-1, 38-
51, 60-1, 71, 88, 91, 110, 113, 122, 115,
173, 176, 179, 210, 235, 243, 255; assassi-
nation, 52-5, 93
Jenkins, William, 55-6, 174
Jiménez Sarmiento, David, 146, 151, 153
Julião, Francisco, 175-6

Karl Marx Trade Union, 61
Kennedy, John F., 53
Kramer, Abe, 75

Labor Bank, 20
Laborde, Hernán, 71, 209
Lacandones, 25, 146-7, 150-1, 153
"Land and Freedom" colony, 177
land occupations, 8, 41, 51-2, 173-81, 191, 235
Latin American Conference on National
Sovereignty, 82
law, Mexican system, 16
'leaderism/caudillismo', 71

Latin American Studies from Zed Books

Zed Books publishes on international and Third World issues. In addition to our general lists on economics, development, the environment, gender and politics, we also publish area studies in the fields of African Studies, Asian and Pacific Studies, Latin American and Caribbean Studies, and Middle East Studies. Our Latin American titles include:

Frédérique Apffel-Marglin with PRATEC (eds.), *The Spirit of Regeneration: Andean Culture Confronting Western Notions of Development*

Gianpaolo Baiocchi, *Radicals in Power: The Workers' Party (PT) and Experiments in Urban Democracy in Brazil*

Susan Bassnett (ed.), *Knives and Angels: Women Writers in Latin America*

Cristovam Buarque, *The End of Economics? Ethics and the Disorder of Progress*

Jacques M. Chevalier and Daniel Buckles, *A Land Without Gods: Process Theory, Maldevelopment and the Mexican Nahuas*

Raff Carmen and Miguel Sobrado (eds.), *A Future for the Excluded: Job Creation and Income Generation by the Poor: Clodomir Santos de Morais and the Organization Workshop*

Catherine Davies (ed.), *A Place in the Sun? Women Writers in Twentieth Century Cuba*

J. Demmers, A. F. Jilberto and B. Hogenboom (eds.), *Miraculous Metamorphoses: The Neoliberalisation of Latin American Populism*

Gustavo Esteva and Madhu Suri Prakash, *Grassroots Post-Modernism: Remaking the Soil of Cultures*

Stefano Harney, *Nationalism and Identity: Culture and the Imagination in a Caribbean Diaspora*

Clare Hargreaves, *Snowfields: The War on Cocaine in the Andes*

Andrew Higginbottom, *The Colombia Nightmare: Neoliberal Crisis and Dispossession in a Paramilitary State*

Donald Hodges and Ross Gandy, *Mexico under Siege: Popular Resistance to Presidential Despotism*

Elizabeth Jelin (ed.), *Women and Social Change in Latin America*

Michael Kaufman and Alfonso Dilla (eds.), *Community Power and Grassroots Democracy: The Transformation of Social Life*

Kees Koonings and Dirk Kruijt (eds.), *Political Armies: The Military and Nation Building in the Age of Democracy*

Kees Koonings and Kirk Kruijt (eds.), *Societies of Fear: The Legacy of Civil War, Violence and Terror in Latin America*

Peter Mayo, *Gramsci, Freire and Adult Education: Possibilities for Transformative Action*

Rhoda E. Reddock, *Women, Labour and Politics in Trinidad and Tobago*

Teivo Teivainen, *Enter Economism, Exit Politics: Experts, Economic Policy and the Damage to Democracy*

Oscar Ugarteche, *The False Dilemma: Is Globalization the Only Choice?*

Bill Weinberg, *War on the Land: Ecology and Politics in Central America*

Gregory Wilpert, *Revolution and Counter-Revolution in Venezuela: The Fall and Rise of Hugo Chavez*

For full details of this list and Zed's other subject and general catalogues, please write to: The Marketing Department, Zed Books, 7 Cynthia Street, London N1 9JF, UK or email Sales@zedbooks.demon.co.uk

Visit our website at: http://www.zedbooks.demon.co.uk